THE FINAL INNINGS

THE FINAL INNINGS

THE CRICKETERS OF SUMMER 1939

CHRISTOPHER SANDFORD

Christopher Sandford is a regular contributor to newspapers and magazines on both sides of the Atlantic. He has written biographies of cricket legends Godfrey Evans, Tom Graveney and Imran Khan, as well as of Paul McCartney, Steve McQueen, Arthur Conan Doyle and Harry Houdini. *The Final Over* (The History Press, 2014), the predecessor to *The Final Innings*, was shortlisted for The Cricket Society and MCC Book of the Year Award.

Jacket illustrations: *Front:* British infantry at El Alamein (Alamy) / Derbyshire v Lancashire, 1939 (Mirrorpix). *Back:* Gunners of the Surrey & Sussex Yeomanry play an impromptu game of cricket in Italy. (public domain)

First published 2019
This paperback edition published 2020

The History Press
97 St George's Place
Cheltenham, GL50 3QB
www.thehistorypress.co.uk

British Library Cataloguing in Publication Data.
A catalogue record for this book is available from the British Library.

ISBN 978 0 7509 9469 9

Typesetting and origination by The History Press
Printed and bound in Great Britain by TJ Books Limited

To Jack Surendranath

'The cricket's gone; we only hear machines.'

David McCord

'I am all right, I have only been slightly hurt. *Saluti affettuosi.*'

*Hedley Verity's last recorded words before he died
from wounds received on the Italian front*

'Ohne Hast, aber ohne Rast' – ('Without haste, but without end.')

Adolf Hitler on cricket

CONTENTS

PREFACE

This book, first published to coincide with the eightieth anniversary of the outbreak of the Second World War, is a homage to the cricketers at all levels of the game who served their country. It is not a statistical record of each and every individual combatant player of the 1939 English season. Others, notably Nigel McCrery in his book *The Coming Storm*, have already performed that task admirably well. Nor is it a strictly chronological trawl of each of the 290 or so first-class matches played during that ill-fated summer, for that, too, has been done, chiefly in the pages of *Wisden*. No slight is intended on the name of any cricketer who might be missing, and anyone interested in reading more about the subject will find some suggestions in the bibliography at the back of the book. Every effort has nonetheless been made to portray the events exactly as they occurred, and to record as accurately as possible the stories of the men and women who lived them. I only wish I could blame someone listed below for the shortcomings of the text. They are mine alone.

By our standards, the English cricketers of 1939 were ill-paid and almost ludicrously badly treated by their clubs. But with a few rare exceptions, they were a remarkably convivial and high-spirited group. It's this same spirit that's hopefully celebrated in this book. Rather than loitering over the scores of each match, *The Final Innings* attempts to follow certain players and their families, both on and off the field, during that strange summer. It seeks to shed light on the daily lives of such individuals; to demonstrate what it meant to be an 'amateur' or a 'professional' eighty years ago; and to show again the arbitrary nature of war, where one man could fall and the one next to him come home and live to be 90.

Above all, I've tried to portray the individuals seen here as flesh-and-blood characters, not merely as statistics, and to show them in the context of how they reacted to the partly ludicrous, partly horrific events of the period from around March to September 1939. Cricket after all is a reflection of life, and by and large cricketers answered the crisis in exactly the same way as everyone else. The records show that they volunteered at broadly the same rate as other young men, and they died, too, in equal proportion. It is a very human story.

For archive material, input or advice I should thank, institutionally: Alibris, *America*, *The American Conservative*, Bookcase, Bookfinder, *Bright Lights*, the British Library, the British Museum, British Newspaper Archive, Cambridge University Library, *Chronicles*, CricInfo, Cricket Archive, Cricket Australia, the *Cricketer*, the Cricket Society, Cricket West Indies, Derbyshire CCC, Essex CCC, General Register Office, Hampshire CCC, Hampshire Record Office, *Hedgehog Review*, Hillingdon Libraries, the Imperial War Museum, Kent CCC, King's College Library London, Lancashire CCC, the MCC Library, Middlesex CCC, National Army Museum, *National Review*, *Navy News*, Northamptonshire CCC, the *Oldie*, the Peter Edwards Museum and Library, Public Record Office, Renton Public Library, *Russian Life*, St Martin's Press, Seaside Library Oregon, South Africa Cricket Association, the *Sunday Express*, Surrey CCC, Sussex CCC, Touchstone, UK National Archives, USA Cricket Association, University of Montana, University of Puget Sound, Vital Records, Wirral Archives Service, Worcestershire CCC, Yorkshire CCC.

Professionally: Wendy Adams, Dave Allen, Leann Alspaugh, Val Baker, Phil Barnes, Sue Black, Rob Boddie, Geoff Boycott, Jennifer Boyer, Phil Britt, Michael Cairns, Dan Chernow, Sophie Cooper, Robert Curphey, Paul Darlow, Cindy Da Silva, Alan Deane, Ted Dexter,

Michael Dorr, Lauren Dwyer, Mike Fargo, Jon Filby, Bill Furmedge, Jim Geller, Gethsemane Lutheran Church, Mayukh Ghosh, Tony Gill, Freddie Gray, Dominic Green, Ryan Grice, Tess Hines, The History Press, Robin B. James, David Jenkins, Neil Jenkinson, Adam Jones, Edith Keep, David Kelly, Imran Khan, Alex Legge, Barbara Levy, Cindy Link, Diana Lloyd, Barbara McLean, Christine McMorris, Robert Mann, Dave Mason, Jo Miller, Nicola Nye, Max Paley, Palgrave Macmillan, Jezz Palmer, David Pracy, Tim Reidy, Jim Repard, Tim Rice, Paul Richardson, Chris Ridler, William Roberts, David Robertson, Neil Robinson, Rebecca Romney, Jane Rosen, Malcolm Rowley, David Rymill, Sandy Cove Inn, Seattle CC, Paul Shelley, Don Short, Andrew Stuart, Charles Vann, Adele Warlow, Alan Weyer, Aaron Wolf, the late Tom Wolfe, David Wood, Andrew Yates, Tony Yeo.

Personally: Lisa Armstead, Rev. Maynard Atik, Pete Barnes, the late David Blake, Rocco Bowen, Robert and Hilary Bruce, Jon Burke, John Bush, Lincoln Callaghan, Don Carson, Common Ground, Alice Cooper, Tim Cox, Celia Culpan, the Davenport, Monty Dennison, Ted Dexter, Micky Dolenz, the Dowdall family, John and Barbara Dungee, the late Godfrey Evans, Malcolm Galfe, Garden Court Hotel, the late Gay Hussar, Jay Gilmartin, James Graham, the late Tom Graveney, Jeff and Rita Griffin, Grumbles, Steve and Jo Hackett, Masood Halim, Nigel Hancock, Hermino, Alastair Hignell, Charles Hillman, Alex Holmes, Hotel Vancouver, Jo Jacobius, Julian James, Peter Jia, Tom Johnston, Lincoln Kamell, Carol Lamb, Terry Lambert, Belinda Lawson, Eugene Lemcio, Todd Linse, the Lorimer family, Nick Lowe, Robert Dean Lurie, Les McBride, Heather and Mason McEachran, Charles McIntosh, the Macris, Lee Mattson, Jim Meyersahm, Sheila Mohn, the Morgans, Harry Mount, Colleen Murray, the late John Murray, the National Gallery, Greg Nowak, Chuck Ogmund, Phil Oppenheim, Valya Page, Peter Parfitt, Robin Parish, Jim Parks, Owen Paterson, Peter Perchard, Greg Phillips, the late Chris Pickrell, Roman Polanski, Robert and Jewell Prins, the Prins family, the late Bert Robinson, Ailsa Rushbrooke, Debbie Saks, Sam, the late Sefton Sandford, Sue Sandford, Peter Scaramanga, Seattle Prep., Pat Simmons, Dorothy Smith, Fred and

Cindy Smith, Debbie Standish, the Stanley family, the late Thaddeus Stuart, Jack Surendranath, Belinda and Ian Taylor, Thomas Toughill, Hugh Turbervill, the late Ben and Mary Tyvand, Diana Villar, Ross Viner, Lisbeth Vogl, Karin and Soleil Wieland, Debbie Wild, Andy Williamson, the Willis Fleming family, Mary Wilson, Heng and Lang Woon, Doris and Felicia Zhu, the Zombies.

My deepest thanks, as always, to Karen and Nicholas Sandford.

C.S.
2019

I

GOLDEN AGE

Captain Gerald de Lisle Hough arrived early at the St Lawrence Ground, Canterbury, on the Easter Monday of 10 April 1939 to begin reviving the place from its winter's sleep. Although just 44, the Kent secretary-manager looked a full decade older. Hough was dark and short, and habitually wore a long and dilapidated tweed jacket that emphasised his lack of height. Moreover, his small frame was wracked with arthritis, and he walked with what was called a 'cork-screwing' gait, propelled up and down by a thick wooden cane. 'Hough seemed to us a rather comic figure, straight out of Charles Dickens,' the 18-year-old Godfrey Evans, then Kent's reserve-team wicketkeeper, remembered. 'I'm afraid some of the younger guys did impersonations of him behind his back. My attitude was, "You are an old fogey and I'm a teenager full of sap. You'll spoil my fun if I let you, so here I go. Catch me if you can."'

For all that, Hough was a hardworking and efficient administrator whose physical infirmity was balanced by a number of professional skills. He was a fluent writer and, despite his frailty, a commanding figure in committee meetings with his deep baritone voice and unerring grasp of detail. Although Hough himself rarely mentioned it, he was also a bona fide war hero. Commissioned in September 1914 in the Royal West Kent Regiment, he had been severely wounded a year later at Loos, a battle that was then widely regarded as the epitome of horror in its failed assault under chlorine gas on a series of German-held slag heaps. After several months' convalescence, Hough had returned to the front in June 1916 and promptly been wounded a second time when a high-explosive shell landed close to his dugout at Vachelles in the killing fields around the river Somme. That had effectively brought an end to his war. Hough served a further two years in a reserve battalion stationed in the market town of Wendover in Buckinghamshire, where he was mentioned in dispatches for 'exceptional wardship', and resigned his commission only in September 1921, with the rank of captain.

Despite his injuries, Hough had also been a distinguished all-round cricketer who bowled off-spin and had a 'thumping power and crispness about his handling of the bat that gave every stroke character and frequently left cover-point wringing his hands'. Having hit 30 and 87, both times not out, in his first representative appearance for Lionel Robinson's XI in a match against the Australian Forces, it was sometimes suggested that Hough's name should be included by *Wisden* on the list of those who have scored a century on their first-class debut, an honour the almanack ultimately denied him. Curiously, Hough also took a wicket with his first delivery in county cricket, when he bowled his former army colleague Joseph Dixon for 6 when playing for Kent against Essex at Leyton in June 1919. A teammate reported that 'Gerry accepted the toast we drank to him that night with considerable enthusiasm.'

Twenty years later, Godfrey Evans and the other young hopefuls reporting to Canterbury had no idea that their seemingly decrepit club secretary had once been considered among the brightest all-round prospects of post-war cricket, and widely tipped to be a future England player. Instead, Hough had appeared in just a dozen more matches, privately conceding that his war wounds were proving 'tedious' during long days in the field, and that it would be unfair on his county colleagues for him to carry on. After scoring 11 and 0 in Kent's crushing defeat by Lancashire in July 1920, the 26-year-old quietly slipped into retirement. He spent much of the next decade teaching at Bradfield College in Berkshire. In later life, one hot-headed Bradfield student remembered that he had been invited to bowl in the nets one day and was still 'tearing in like the east wind even after the little chap had effortlessly carted me back over my head for about the twelfth time'.

Hough took over the secretary's position at Kent in August 1933, in the middle of what proved to be a golden period for the county, with players like Tich Freeman, Frank Woolley and Les Ames all at or close to the peak of their powers. Nothing could make good the hard financial realities of running even a successful English cricket club in the depths of a recession, however, and like other county officials Hough was forced to cut costs where he could. By 1939 a rising young star like Godfrey Evans was paid only a basic £130 a year, 'with third-class rail fare and a two-course meal allowance, *sans* drink' thrown in for away fixtures. 'By around early August each year the committee would be looking for names to chop from the next season's payroll,' he recalled.

Nonetheless, Hough was generally able to balance the books, and was remembered for one dressing-room speech that Evans paraphrased as 'like something Churchill gave the troops during the war – "Each one of you buggers should ask himself every day what he can do, how he can contribute to the final goal" – that kind of thing.' The Kent yearbook for 1939 reports that 'In spite of the weather and the international situation, attendances were up by 7,000.' In time Hough told his committee that the club's financial situation was 'not wholly deficient', and that a 'modest outlay on the regular employment of a masseur for the first time had proved a successful experiment'.

In fact, Hough was better positioned than many of his cash-strapped counterparts on cricket's county circuit, where even A.F. Davey, the secretary of metropolitan Surrey – a club that boasted the king as its patron – wrote that a balanced budget was beyond his reach in 1939 and 'at present only a distant dream'. Davey's committee had come to this conclusion long before he did. 'Without corrective action there is a looming risk of several first-class venues facing financial difficulties and even insolvency,' *The Times* wrote, in words that were to be echoed at regular intervals during the later twentieth century, when reviewing the English county scene as a whole.

At least in 1939 there was no conflict between the traditionalists who remain wedded to the three- or four-day championship format and those who crave an expanded Twenty20 competition and other cash-generating innovations, simply because the concept of limited-overs cricket barely existed eighty years ago. Even a tentative proposal that Rowland Ryder, the longstanding secretary of Warwickshire, put forward for two-day county matches to be played on a Saturday and a Monday came back with a one-word comment stamped across the paper: 'Rejected'.

It's worth dwelling a moment longer on English county cricket's straitened finances in 1939, if only to dispel the myth that a golden age still characterised by dashing, moustachioed amateurs and suitably defer-ential yeoman professionals, performing in front of packed, shirt-sleeved crowds debating between overs such hot issues as the lob-bowling controversy of the 1770s, or whether Lumpy Stevens would have been a match for Sydney Barnes, was necessarily one that might have been expected to survive after the war. Reviewing the 1939 season in *Wisden*, R.C. 'Crusoe' Robertson-Glasgow wrote: 'Three-day cricket, in peace, was scarcely maintaining the public interest except in matches between the few best, or the locally rivalrous teams, and how many will [now] pay even sixpence to watch cricket for three days between scratch or constantly varying elevens?' An anonymous correspondent wrote to the *Cricketer* with a damning comparison that December. 'The MCC will bring out its finest fizz to drink in the acclaim of another brilliant year at Lord's. To many others tending to the health of an English cricket club today it will be a case of counting every penny and praying for a possible resumption following the hostilities.'*

---

* The unnamed writer had a point: the MCC's auditors reported that same month that 100,933 spectators had each paid around 2s at the turnstiles over the four days of the England v Australia Lord's Test in 1938, and that after all expenses were met the club had made a net profit of £41,823-1s-1d (roughly £1.3 million today) during the year as a whole.

Of Derbyshire's season, *Wisden* reported: 'The wet summer hit the county hard financially. A testimonial fund for Worthington amounted to £720', or roughly £19,000 in today's money, to reward an England Test star then in his sixteenth consecutive year of service with the county. For their part, Gloucestershire enjoyed one of their more successful campaigns in 1939. 'Always ready to offer or accept a sporting challenge in the hope of providing an interesting finish, they set the fashion in the enterprising cricket which prevailed over most of the country,' it was reported. Yet when the officials at Bristol added up the final figures in September, they too were forced to admit: 'Considering the team's achievements, our matches were not well patronised.' It was the same story at Lancashire, 'where rain seemed to follow the team, causing 13 blank days', and tributes in the annual report to the 'grand work of our batsmen' were drowned out by statistics of spiralling costs, falling revenues and only 'fitfully successful' investments.

Gates were also a concern at Sussex, where the 36-year-old all-rounder Jim Parks, then in his thirteenth and final season at the club, 'failed to recapture his [past] glories, and this, besides the imminence of war, may have accounted for his benefit bringing him no more than £734-10-6, including collections and subscriptions.' Further on in the same report of the county's 1939 fortunes, a sad note concludes: 'The weather and the international situation, causing the match with the West Indies team to be cancelled, accounted for a loss on the year of £1,853.' 'It wasn't just me winding his career down,' Parks later reflected. 'Some of us thought the club's number was up, too.'

Even at county champions Yorkshire, *Wisden* wrote: 'After making the usual allowances and bonuses, the committee reported a profit on the season of £54' – about the amount the club would have needed to buy each one of its sixteen professional players a basic off-the-peg suit, had it wished to do so, with just enough left over for a modest team dinner.

Perhaps the one exception to the financial woes afflicting England's county cricket circuit came at Middlesex, a club in the enviable position of playing their home matches at a venue then unchallenged as the sport's global headquarters. Lord's was not immune from the effects of the build-up to war in 1939, with a barrage balloon already casting its dark shadow over the Mound Stand when play got underway in the championship match against Somerset on 23 August, the Long Room stripped of its treasures, and sandbags packed up at the gates. But it is the little rituals that most accurately represent the old spirit of the ground and its uniquely prosperous county tenant. The Lord's authorities were particularly concerned early that season not with civil defence, but with 'a project for replacing the present Bakery with one located in the disused Racket Court … This move will involve the loss of one Squash Court, but will increase the efficiency of the Refreshment Department.'

Reading the catalogue of gifts made to the Marylebone club at the time much of Europe was mobilising for war that summer is to evoke thoughts of P.G. Wodehouse. The list begins with a vote of thanks 'to Earl Grey for the photograph of a sculptured arm holding a ball dating from the time of the Ptolemies'. Gratitude was also expressed to 'Mr R.K. Mugliston for a belt buckle', and 'Sir Colin MacRae for a picture of I Zingari v The Army taken shortly after the relief of Bloemfontein in the South African War.' There were many 'heads and horns' of dead animals donated by the club's hunting element – possibly a majority of the 6,996 (then all-male) members, each paying around £15 a year in order to sit in the Lord's pavilion, wear the distinctive scarlet and gold colours, and enjoy other perks. On match days, meanwhile, the amateurs' dressing-room attendant continued to lay out the players' neatly pressed flannels at the start of play; continued to arrange symmetrically the freshly ironed morning newspapers on the polished side table, and to supply a steady succession of cups of tea and other refreshments served on a crested silver tray. The professional players were not so fortunate, and the 21-year-old Denis Compton later described his core working environment in 1939 as characterised by the 'pong of old socks and stale fag smoke'.

In the same week that Gerald Hough was airing out the musty back rooms in the Canterbury pavilion and writing elegiacally in his diary of 'a day of awakening blue, all varnish and high hopes', the Home Office sent out letters of instruction to 65,000 official 'enumerators' who would descend upon every household in England and Wales later in the summer to carry out what became the most comprehensive survey (as opposed to formal census) ever taken of the population. The data gathered offers an intriguing snapshot of a generally contented nation set in the context of the deteriorating European order of the late 1930s. To take the figure which made the greatest impression on contemporary public opinion: between January 1933 and January 1937, the total number of unemployed British males fell from 22.8 to 13.2 per cent of the available workforce, and by the beginning of 1939 the figure was 8.1 per cent. By Christmas of that year, with the nation now at war, what had been among the worst unemployment figures in Europe had been turned into a labour shortage.

The statistics also illustrate how Britons' working lives have changed since 1939 – especially for women, 9.3 million of whom were then described as carrying out 'unpaid domestic duties', with 588,000 more working as live-in or full-time household servants. It was also a relatively young society: the figures show that the average age for men was 33 and for women 34, compared to 39 and 40 in 2019. Out of the 41 million people surveyed, just 111 were aged 100 or more, less than 1 per cent of the total of 13,000 British centurions today.

Despite the apparent drudgery of many men's and more particularly women's lives, the historian Martin Pugh describes it as a 'feminine' era, with some modest innovations in areas like hemlines and hairstyles, and a wealth of popular magazines such as *Good Housekeeping* focusing on the virtues of home and hearth. The data reveals that 46.2 per cent of the population was married, and that 6.5 per cent had been widowed, but that just 0.1 per cent was divorced. Today 37 per cent of the total population is married, and the divorce rate hovers at around 45 per cent. In 1939 roughly one in twenty of British children was born out of wedlock, a tenth of the modern figure.

'Business as usual' was the motto reintroduced by many British retailers during the summer of 1939, echoing the slogan adopted under conditions of similar international disquiet twenty-five years earlier. The self-confidence of the phrase concealed a wide variety of individual household fortunes, with the 'finest fizz' available at some tables and a diet rich in commodities like bully beef, boiled potatoes and rice pudding, frequently with a cigarette chaser, at others. George Orwell described the age as one centred around 'tinned food, the *Picture Post* and the combustion engine'. The arts scene was similarly diverse: 1939 found Barbara Cartland already in full sail with her eighteenth novel, *The Bitter Winds of Love*, but it also saw the publication of James Joyce's *Finnegans Wake*. Roughly 20,000 British households had a television set before their manufacture ceased during the war. The international film industry was booming, with *Wuthering Heights*, *The Four Feathers*, *Goodbye, Mr. Chips*, *The Wizard of Oz* and *Gone With the Wind* among the new releases. It was also something of a golden age for music, high and low. Arnold Bax, Benjamin Britten and William Walton all debuted new concertos, while the song most frequently heard on Britain's 9 million household radio sets was the Leeds-born Michael Carr's 'South of the Border (Down Mexico Way)'.

In November 1939, a 38-year-old Iowa farmboy-turned-advertising executive named George Gallup and his young female assistant sailed for Britain, where over the next six weeks they enlisted a small team of regional helpers to knock on a total of 6,200 doors in London, Birmingham, Manchester, Glasgow and (rather curiously) the area around Mamble in Worcestershire, in order to ask residents about their attitudes to everything from the war to the advent of tinned tomato juice on British breakfast tables. One of Gallup's conclusions when publishing his poll in June 1940 was that 'the forces of conformity ... after the great rise in the unorthodox spiritual movement in the 1920s ... coupled with the natural anxieties of the German war, [had] led to a religious revival that appears to be both intense and pervasive.' Just over 65 per cent of adult Britons canvassed agreed that they drew 'significant comfort' from regular church attendance. Paradoxically, only 48 per cent of respondents admitted to believing in life after death, although this figure would rise as the nation's war losses mounted. Britons, Gallup wrote, were prone 'to a certain fatalism even in happier times' and 'often abide the ills of life more stoically than [their] American cousins'. His poll also confirmed that the 'physical, social and political milieu in the United Kingdom remains sharply status-conscious', and perhaps even more than the statistics it's reading some of the newspaper headlines of the day ('Butler Driven Mad by Jealousy'; 'Lady Lansdowne and Staff will Take a Shooting Lodge for August'; 'City of London Regiment Seeks Men: Upper- and Middle-Class Only Need Apply') that tells the tale.

Cricket itself was still conducted 'in a reverent atmosphere, much akin to a church', wrote the drama critic and composer Herbert Farjeon, author of the immortal song 'I've danced with a man, who's danced with a girl, who's danced with the Prince of Wales'. 'The chief difference is that most of those in attendance at Lord's would not seem to be faking it.' Alfred Hitchcock caught some of the intrinsic spirit of the game in his 1939 film *The Lady Vanishes*, which sees two impeccably upper-crust cricket buffs navigating their way home through the jack-booted officials and villainous spies of the Balkan nation of 'Bandrika' in order to watch the final overs of the Test at Old Trafford. It might not be a stretch to say that the director intended the characters to be symbolic of a peculiarly British obstinacy in the face of Nazi aggression. In any event the *New York Times* reviewer wrote appreciatively of the 'bumbling aristocratic image of the English national sport' depicted in the film. 'Its devotees may be stolid and even a bit slow-witted in their Edwardian languor, but they are also the sort of calm, phlegmatic types who will battle to their last breath to preserve the British way of life.'

The testimony of almost all those who played first-class cricket in 1939 revealingly hints at the impassable gulf that existed between the classes, both on and off the field. 'It was a feudal system,' Godfrey Evans recalled, adding that throughout his twenty-year career he had never quite shaken the feeling that he was playing the part of some 'useful servant' in a rich man's house. With the exception of some of the more progressive-minded county sides, the captain still led his fellow amateurs on to the field of play through a separate gate than that used by the horny-handed professionals, a distinction that extended to matters involving meals, hotels and transportation. Lionel Tennyson, Hampshire's superbly *ancien régime* leader for much of the interwar years – and still playing representative cricket as late as 1944 – remained fond to the very end of his tenure of communicating with his batsmen in the middle by way of a telegram. If something about the current scoring rate displeased him, for instance, Tennyson's practice was to summon a messenger boy to the captain's dressing room and dictate a wire that might read: 'Too slow. Run self out', or, alternatively: 'No more boundaries. Restrain urge at once.' The messenger would then take the slip to the nearest post office, where it would be transcribed into a cable and in turn brought back to the ground to be ceremonially presented in between overs to the offending player.

Of course, the Lionel Tennyson school was by no means the whole story. It's true that the underlying British class structure would come under steadily increasing pressure from within and without in the years either side of the Second World War, but it's also true that the basic master-servant composition of most first-class cricket teams survived up until the abolition of 'player' and 'gentleman' status in 1963, and thus long enough to see the advent of the Rolling Stones, the hydrogen bomb and the space age. Even today it's still mildly odd to read press reports about Len Hutton's batting or Godfrey Evans's wicketkeeping in 1939 set amongst all the advertisements for butlers, maids or chauffeurs ('Rolls Certificate and discreet service essential'), or the lingering accounts in *Wisden* of innumerable matches such as Beaumont v Oratory, somewhat below the first-class, or to note that the almanack devoted 105 closely typed pages specifically to public-school cricket that year, which is roughly ninety-eight more than it does today.

These were far from the only points of distinction between the English summer sport as it appeared in 1939 and as it does now. Things were generally more haphazard back then when it came to playing conditions and facilities, with a touch of the ramshackle about even the great Test match grounds. Not yet troubled by health and safety requirements, these were often little more than mown fields circled by a few rudimentary stands, some covered, some not, whose architects seemed to have had a poor idea of comfort. Neville Cardus remembered that when watching England play the West Indies at Lord's, 'the boundary was no more than the toes of those spectators lying on the grass'. Denis Compton added that at one point the professionals' dressing room at cricket's headquarters had been not so much in need of repair as in 'imminent danger of collapse', with 'splintered floors and a couple of rusty tin baths'. These were conditions of Babylonian luxury compared to those at lesser grounds. A Kent-based reporter named Hugh Sidey remarked of the old press box at Canterbury, far removed from today's media centre: 'You'd look up from scribbling something in your note-book and find some inky-faced kid in the crowd staring at you through the broken glass in the window, probably wondering if it was your story that had made him choke on his cornflakes the other morning.'

When Kent played on their out-ground at Maidstone, Godfrey Evans remembered, the side's main concern was to 'not vanish down one of the gaping potholes on the wicket'. The non-playing amenities were equally basic, with a pervasive smell of boiled cabbage and other, more noxious odours that 'wafted over from the direction of the khazis'. On the occasions when Northamptonshire staged first-class fixtures at the Town Ground in Rushden, with its notoriously jerry-built pavilion, the visiting side generally found it best to first put on their whites at their hotel or, failing that, to struggle into them behind a nearby tree. When, in July 1939, Somerset hosted Essex at the Rowdens Road Ground in Wells, the teams performed on what was essentially a roped-off corner of a large dog-walking park. It had few pretensions to elegance. *Wisden* wrote that the first first-class match to be played at the venue, when Worcestershire beat Somerset by an innings and 105 runs in July 1935, went ahead in 'novel conditions'. It added: 'There were no sight-screens, and the match details were broadcast from the scorers' box by means of a microphone and loudspeakers.'

Born in September 1914, the MCC, Free Foresters and sometime Hampshire batsman John Manners was able to tell an interviewer more than a century later, 'The uncovered wickets were often unplayable' in the 1930s, before adding that what might now be considered sharp practice barely raised an eyebrow then. 'At Hampshire we had a medium-pacer called Creese. The first thing he did when he came on to bowl was bend down and rub the ball in the dirt.' Manners, currently the oldest living first-class cricketer, went on to confirm a widely held view of pre-war cricket when he admitted, 'Some of us were pretty sluggish in the field back then. Even the younger ones stopped the ball with their foot sometimes. You don't see that now.' A variation on this theme was provided by the 49-year-old Lionel Tennyson when, standing in the outfield at Lord's on the first morning of an MCC match in July 1939, he languidly trapped a windswept newspaper under his boot, picked it up and read it. He said later that the racing page was 'altogether more engrossing' than the cricket.

For all that, a certain amount of change was afoot in English cricket during that last pre-war season. For one thing, there were more professional players about on the county circuit generally. The ratio varied widely from side to side, but broadly speaking the further north you went, the greater the preponderance of cricketers who were paid for their services. At Essex they had twelve professionals and ten amateurs on the books in May 1939, while in Yorkshire the split was sixteen to four. At the equivalent stage in 1914 the figures had been, respectively, nine to fifteen and fourteen to seven. In recent years several former public-school players, like Gloucestershire's Charles Barnett, had felt able to turn professional, while the incomparable Wally Hammond had explored the boundaries of the English social divide by enjoying a grammar school education before going on to be paid to play cricket for seventeen seasons, and ultimately to refine his status within the prevailing class structure by declaring himself an amateur at the age of 35, largely in order to satisfy the established MCC concept of the gentleman Test captain.

Among the game's more technical innovations, 1939 was the one and only season in which English cricket adopted the 8-ball over. The home Tests were each of three days' duration (Saturday, Monday and Tuesday), and the fielding side could request a new ball after every 200 runs scored.

On 28 March of that year, the Advisory Committee of the MCC met at Lord's to discuss the age-old problem of the proper balance between bat and ball. It concluded: 'All counties must instruct their groundsmen that the ideal wicket is one which makes the conditions equal as between batsmen and bowlers without being dangerous ... Under no circumstances should pitches be prepared so as to favour the bat unduly.' Perhaps as a result, scores were generally lower in 1939 than in 1938. Only six English players managed an aggregate of 2,000 first-class runs compared to 11 the previous season, with even Hammond falling from 3,011 runs at an average of 75.27 to the relatively paltry total of 2,479 runs at 63.56. Of the leading bowlers, Hedley Verity took 158 first-class wickets in 1938, Tom Goddard took 114 and Doug Wright took 110. In 1939 the figures were 191, 200 and 141 respectively.

It was thought that there was little official need to dwell on any particular concerns about unsportsmanlike conduct in 1939, although the MCC politely reminded umpires that they 'should not allow themselves to be unduly influenced by appeals from such of the field who were not in a position to form a judgement on the point appealed upon', or by 'tricks – such as throwing up the ball, on appealing for a catch at the wicket, without waiting for the decision, etc.' Due to unspecified 'ricochet incidents' in the 1938 season, the MCC now also added the curious edict: 'The umpire is not a boundary.'

Technology, too, was marching on. National radio broadcasting – in part made possible by the work of the brilliant but underfunded British physicist and disciple of the paranormal, Sir Oliver Lodge – had begun in June 1920 when the 59-year-old Australian soprano Dame Nellie Melba introduced a concert of recorded opera music, which she fitfully accompanied in a karaoke-like effect, followed by a poetry recital and the national anthem, beamed out from a disused army hut at Writtle in Essex. The newly launched BBC issued a total of 206,000 household radio licences, at 10s each, in 1923. By 1930 the figure had jumped to 3 million licences and stood at close to 10 million on the outbreak of war in 1939. The demand for radio sets rose even in the Depression years, when there was a dip in the sale of almost every other popular commodity. 'Never a passenger on the austerity bandwagon, the wireless has become a friendly voice in nearly every British sitting room,' wrote Lodge, who had become convinced that the radio also permitted the spirit world to communicate with the living one over the ether.

John Reith, the morally austere director general of the BBC from 1927 to 1938, seems not to have shared Lodge's faith in the occult potential of the new medium, but wrote not long before his departure from the corporation: 'There are clear benefits to a service offer[ing] education and uplifting entertainment, and in so doing acting as an inspiration to and encourager of healthful recreation' – the slightly bombastic mandate that had been translated during the late 1920s and early 1930s into the first live broadcasts to be made of English cricket.

Reith's principal instrument in carrying his vision out was an Eton-and Cambridge-educated brigadier general's son named Seymour Joly de Lotbiniere. Born in 1905, 'Lobby' had joined the BBC after a brief and unhappy stint in the law and rose to become director of outside broadcasting from 1935 to 1940. His preferred commentator in those early days of 'trial and no little error', as he put it, was a former club cricketer and Oxford rugby blue named Howard Marshall. Marshall's descriptive powers were perfect both for the game and its frequent interruptions. Instead of talking exclusively about the cricket, the *Athletic News* wrote, his commentary typically 'dwelled upon matters such as the number of passing birds, and the variety of interesting hats to be seen in the ladies' stand', clearly a harbinger of much of today's radio coverage. The poet Edmund Blunden wrote appreciatively: 'On the air, Mr Howard Marshall makes every ball bowled, every shifting of a fieldsman so fertile with meaning that any wireless set may make a subtle cricket student of anybody.'

In October 1938, the BBC commissioned a 31-year-old rugby and cricket writer named Ernest William Swanton to commentate on that winter's MCC tour of South Africa. Even in his early incarnation, Swanton was a somewhat imperious figure, whose deep, fruity voice and commanding style earned him the nickname 'Jim' as a humorous reference to 'Gentleman Jim, the Journalist'. He was not, it has to be said, an especially imaginative recorder of play in the style of Marshall, and he had no striking turn of phrase. But he was a sound, professional broadcaster nonetheless, who spoke lucidly and always with superb authority.

Swanton's winter engagement in South Africa represented only the most meagre financial outlay by the BBC. Arriving in Cape Town on 6 December 1938 and leaving again on 17 March 1939, he was paid £122 (roughly £3,200 today) for his services, a rate of about £1-4s per day, or just over £5 for each of the twenty-one first-class matches he covered. When the fifth and 'timeless' final Test at Durban developed into a ten-day marathon, and the Englishmen had to hurriedly revise their homeward travel plans as a result, the BBC sent Swanton a cable proposing that they pay him an extra £15 for his trouble. He accepted the offer.

As a result of all this, the first day of the Test at Johannesburg, which fell on Christmas Eve 1938, proved to be the first occasion when a live cricket broadcast was sent back to the UK. It was an inauspicious start. 'The commentary box held only one (no scorer),' Swanton recalled. 'I had not had time to get acclimatised to the 6,000-ft altitude, while on the field the action was minimal.'

As a whole, the match-day facilities both at home and abroad were not ones the modern commentator would envy. When broadcasting at the Oval, Swanton, generously padded even then, 'swayed up a narrow ladder into a rickety wooden cabin perched over the general direction of long-leg, from which half a dozen fielders, a batsman and an umpire were generally in view'. Howard Marshall added: 'Even attaining one's seat in those days required a stamina and agility normally associated with a Royal Marines obstacle course.'

Nonetheless, Swanton was on hand to join Marshall and their BBC colleague Michael Standing in the broadcasting box for the 1939 home Tests against the West Indies, the first to be covered ball by ball throughout the day, and which were also transmitted back to the Caribbean. There was some trepidation at the idea of providing six hours of uninterrupted live commentary for an audience of around 200,000 home listeners, let alone their fanatical overseas counterparts.

Swanton believed the initiative was the result of a rash promise 'made by a Governor of the BBC on a winter cruise of the West Indies ... When he came back to Broadcasting House there was some consternation at what he had let us in for.' The red-letter day duly came on 24 June 1939, when Swanton cleared his throat and announced drily that Bill Bowes would now come in to bowl the first ball of the first session of the match at Lord's, 'in the teeth of a brisk nor'easter', to the West Indies opener Rolph Grant. It was the gentle precursor to what became known eighteen years later as *Test Match Special*.

BBC Television had meanwhile provided occasional, rudimentary coverage of the Lord's and Oval Tests against Australia the previous summer, but only now matched the ambitions of its sound colleagues. *The Times* of 24 June lists: '11.30 a.m. cricket: Televised direct from Lord's, featuring commentary by Thomas Woodroffe', with a teatime segment billed as 'Percy Ponsonby Goes to the Test', followed by more 'televisual pictures until the close', which gave way to the news and an Edgar Wallace play called *Smoky Cell* before the airwaves shut down at 10.30 p.m.

Back in Canterbury, Gerald Hough, born in 1894, wrote a note to his committee wondering if they should invest the necessary 40 or 45 guineas in a new EKCO 'televisor set' for the members' lounge, but was worried about the possible effect this might have on 'one viewing the cricket at first hand, as opposed to through an inanimate box'. Hough was particularly concerned by the current BBC slogan, *You Can't Take Your Eyes From It*. 'Will we all someday soon be experiencing life this way, not conversing with one another, and never averting our gaze from the screen?' he asked, presciently.

2

CRICKET WITHOUT END

The fifteen players and three officials of the MCC touring party who assembled to catch their boat-train from London's Waterloo station on 21 October 1938, and who disembarked two weeks later at Cape Town, did so amid some little tension both in terms of cricket and the wider world. The side was led by Gloucestershire's Walter Hammond, a peerless batsman who was not so well cast for the man-management aspects of the job. 'Wally took on the captaincy with professional dedication,' his tour colleague Paul Gibb remembered. 'But he believed in letting you get on with it rather than offering you the benefit of his support or wisdom. We hardly saw him once stumps were drawn. I think "reticent" would be the word now, but at the time we thought him a gloomy sort of bugger.'

Hammond's biographer David Foot has suggested that he was suffering from what is known euphemistically as a 'social disease' contracted in the West Indies in 1925–26, and that this accounted for his mood swings later in life. There were strains, too, in Hammond's marriage to his long-suffering wife Dorothy, who saw photographs in the English press of her husband beaming down at a local beauty queen named Sybil Ness-Harvey at an official reception in Durban. 'But Dot, you know what it's like at these affairs,' Hammond protested in a letter home. 'I'm the captain now and have to mix.' Perhaps it was to further assuage her anxieties that he wrote: 'She's just another girl with a double-barrelled name out here.' But Mrs Hammond remained unmollified. Eight years later, having divorced Dorothy, Hammond married Sybil in a brief ceremony at Kingston Register Office, an event none of his Test or county cricket colleagues attended.

The lifestyles of one or two of the players who toured South Africa under Hammond's leadership perhaps also defied the MCC orthodoxy of the day. In particular, there was 22-year-old Bill Edrich of Middlesex, who was selected despite having scored only 67 runs at an average of 11 in four home Tests against Australia the previous summer. Apart from his form with the bat, Edrich also posed something of a challenge to the social decorum of the side. His drinking exploits were legendary, and he was judged even by Lionel Tennyson to have 'overdone the Bacchic rites' while playing in a side Tennyson led to India in the winter of 1937–38. Edrich was small and busy, with an upturned nose that gave him a vaguely feral air – 'like a randy mole' in one woman's later assessment. In time his England career would be rudely interrupted when he came back to the team hotel in the early hours of the morning of a Test match at Old Trafford and had to be helped to bed by the night porter, in the process waking the occupant of the next room, who happened to be the chairman of selectors.

Elsewhere in the South African tour party, there was 38-year-old Tom Goddard, a fine off-spinner for Gloucestershire in his day, who came almost to hate his county and Test captain. 'Don't like the way Wally behaves when his wife is away,' he remarked. The feud came to a head in 1947, when Hammond refused to play in Goddard's benefit match. Doug Wright of Kent had also had a modest time while bowling his leg-breaks against the 1938 Australians and had trouble with no balls due to his odd run-up. 'He waves his arms widely, and rocks on his legs like a small ship pitching and bobbing in a heavy sea,' one critic said of him. Standing 6ft 6in, the swarthily handsome Ken Farnes of Essex was another bowler who had been only fitfully successful the previous summer, and one who, despite having a 'glad animal action' and 'liking to thud the ball into the batsman's ribs', was widely suspected of being an intellectual. When sailing into Port Said on a previous MCC tour, Farnes wrote in his diary: 'We passed no other ship save the ship of the desert trotting through the sand. The sun fell. And the deep sunset red of the desert filled the western sky. Stars, with strange suddenness, bedewed the night.' Later he wrote: 'The sun came out and silvered the reef', but crossed out 'silvered' and inserted 'jewelled', evidently feeling that was the *mot juste*.

Hammond's tour also went ahead at a time of rising tension on the world stage. On 8 November 1938, the day on which MCC began their first match in South Africa, the British Home Secretary Samuel Hoare told the cabinet in Downing Street that his department was preparing an Air Raid Precautions Bill, and that ministers would need to discuss further the 'provision of blast-proof shelters in existing buildings'. That same week, Germany exploded in an orgy of state-sanctioned violence against its Jewish minority in the notorious pogrom of 9–10 November 1938, known, because of the shards of glass littering the pavements of Berlin and elsewhere, as Kristallnacht. Speaking two months later to an audience of army commanders in the Kroll opera house, Adolf Hitler restated his belief that Germany's future could only be secured by the appropriation of 'living space'. 'Be convinced, gentlemen,' he added, 'that when I think it possible, I will take action at once and never draw back from the most extreme measures.' In between playing cricket in Johannesburg in February 1939, Ken Farnes wrote in a letter back to a friend in Essex: 'A Napoleonic character, Herr Hitler' and asked: 'What will happen now?'

The eleventh MCC tour of South Africa nonetheless provided both agreeable cricket and a welcome relief from outside events, at least up until the moment of the fifth Test at Durban, which was to be played to a finish, whatever it took, if neither side then held more than a one-nil advantage in the series. This unique endurance test aside, *Wisden* judged it a 'highly successful visit by practically the full flower of England's cricketers, which gave a great fillip to the game in South Africa'. Three of the first four Tests were drawn, and England won the other one. Hammond scored 1,025 runs on the tour at an average of 60, and eight other batsmen besides him hit centuries. Four of the five major MCC wicket-takers were spinners. In the third Test at Durban, which England won, Eddie Paynter of Lancashire hit 243 in just over five hours. *Wisden* said: 'The game attracted big crowds, 12,000 people, who paid £1,200 – a ground record – watching play on the second day.'

The tourists moved around the southern continent by air-cooled train, with first-class seats for the amateurs, and travelled in some style as a whole, though Swanton later wrote in a serious libel: 'Many of the overnight accommodations were strictly of the Blackpool guesthouse variety.' The same commentator noted of South Africa in general:

> One encountered the black only in friends' houses where the servants, in retrospect, with their simplicity, humour and natural good manners seem[ed] not too unlike the West Indians one came later to know; in domestic surroundings, and at wayside stations where cheerful urchins offered delicious peaches for sale at the train windows as one relaxed in one's coupe.

The discrepancy in touring conditions as between then and now sometimes extended to the field of play. At Bulawayo in early February there was no 'grass of a uniform texture' in the middle, as promised, nor grass of any sort. The batsmen took guard on a threadbare matting wicket, and the outfield consisted of white sand sprinkled liberally over a crust of mud. A few days later, in Salisbury, the groundsman dried the pitch by the expedient of setting it on fire. In the innings victory over Orange Free State achieved on a 'malign trampoline' of a wicket in Bloemfontein, Norman Yardley of Yorkshire scored 182 and his county colleague Hedley Verity took 7-75 in the second innings, despite being hit for 42 runs in 3 overs by the Free State's number eleven, a local electrician appropriately named Sparks. A team of oxen laboriously dragged the heavy roller across the pitch at East London.

Socially, one could take the view that some of the Englishmen used the tour as an opportunity to boldly explore the limits of their wedding vows, and that this constituted a sorry lapse of personal morality as defined in the 1930s; or, conversely, that their behaviour was only the sort of thing that was bound to happen from time to time when red-blooded sportsmen are sent away from home for five months. As so often, Bill Edrich was the trailblazer in this particular area. Even under the captaincy of Lionel Tennyson, himself a noted swinger, Edrich had been discreetly warned to 'in future be more restrained in your cups'. It was good advice, but it apparently didn't work. Already married to the first of his five wives, Edrich appeared at the team hotel in Pretoria accompanied by a pneumatic young woman he introduced as 'Roxy – a masseuse' and whom the *Rand Daily Mail* described as the player's 'bosom friend' when she joined him at a civic function in the town. Swanton believed that this was 'not an entirely isolated fall from grace' on the Middlesex player's part. Earlier in the tour, Edrich had actually subjected himself to a strict routine of early nights and 'severely rationed drink and smoking' in a bid to recover his form with the bat, but found that this regimen only 'made me more nervous than before for the big occasion'.

By the time Edrich arrived at Durban for the climactic fifth Test he was emphatically off the wagon and only too happy to accept the pre-match hospitality of Harold 'Tuppy' Owen-Smith, the former Middlesex and South Africa all-rounder who lived in the city. 'They had to put Bill to bed early that morning,' Edrich's brother Eric later confided. 'He was still smiling when they shook him awake to go out to play in front of a full house.' Edrich managed only 1 run in the England first innings, but followed this with a knock of 219, made in seven and a quarter hours, in the second. During the afternoon interval, Flt Lt Albert Holmes, the moustachioed MCC manager, poured the not-out double centurion a glass of champagne with the words, 'I hear you train on the stuff.' Edrich downed a second glass as well but was then out in the first over after tea – if it could be called that – having both seen England to 447-3 and probably saved his own Test career in the process.

The moral latitude Edrich allowed himself in South Africa was matched by that of his captain Hammond, whose thick dark thatch of hair and twinkling eye was said to have been especially enticing to the tour's female spectators. Swanton recalled: 'Hugh Bartlett of Sussex was a magnificent player and very attractive chap. But at Bloemfontein he made the cardinal error of showing a good deal of interest in the girl Wally had his eyes on. An unwise thing to do.' Despite making a century in that particular match, Bartlett duly found himself out of favour when the England team was announced for the first Test soon afterwards: 'The first I knew of it was when I looked at the list pinned to the dressing room door and saw Bryan Valentine's name there instead of mine.'

Other players preferred a more elevated approach to their off-duty hours during the tour. Hedley Verity was said to have walked around each town on the team's itinerary dressed in a 'neat blue suit [and] what looked like a pair of dancing shoes', making many new friends wherever he went. The tall, sharp-eyed bowler, whom Swanton thought resembled an intelligent bird, received several offers of coaching appointments in the event he and his young family might wish to settle in South Africa. Verity's 22-year-old Yorkshire teammate Len Hutton had left his fiancée Dorothy behind in Pudsey but contented himself with a regimen of long-distance runs and early nights with a good book to solace the void. 'Anyone got a fag?' was the nearest Hutton ever came to a note of self-indulgence, a query quite often followed by 'Then I'll smoke one of my own.' For his part, Ken Farnes privately recorded five personal objectives for his time of South Africa, none of them specifically related to his bowling, but which included:

> To remain conscious of my inner, natural, more realised self instead of being overcome by successive and accumulated environments experienced on tour.

Elsewhere in his diary, Farnes admitted to feeling 'removed', 'dissociated' and 'disgruntled with myself', and aspiring to a 'subjugation of self' that would enable him to achieve 'the required metaphysical state'. His shining moment came early on in the tour when he took 7–38 to destroy the Western Province batting in the state match at Cape Town. 'Neither the South Africans nor I could quite believe it,' Farnes wrote.

The events that followed the England team's arrival for the limit-less Test at Durban beginning on Friday 3 March 1939 can be quickly summarised: The South African first innings of 530, made in supremely relaxed style, the first boundary coming only after nearly four hours of play; the crowds, big at first, growing smaller; the subsequently dimin-ished atmosphere, over which Farnes admitted, 'I should prefer to draw a veil … There was so much batting it would be tedious to mention details'; Verity's 766 deliveries in the Test; the final 'impossible' target of 696 to win; Edrich's hungover heroics; at lunch on the tenth day the tourists needing another 118 with 7 wickets in hand; the cussedness of heavy rain then falling just as the match seemed finally to be stag-gering to a close; the Englishmen declining the offer of a plane and instead hurrying for the night train to Cape Town in order to catch the mail steamer *Athlone Castle* home; Farnes's private remark that 'Even the Good Lord stopped on the seventh day and rested', and Hammond's public one that that 'I don't think timeless Tests are in the best interests of the game, and I sincerely hope that the last one has been played.' To date he has got his wish.*

The *Athlone Castle* herself, tricked out in purple livery in honour of the returning cricketers, her public rooms teeming with prospective brides of one sort of another, 'wasn't the worst place in the world to spend a damp fortnight in early spring', Swanton reflected. 'Bill Edrich was a lively young fellow at the time, and I daresay he added to his win-ter's score, as it were.' Early on in the voyage, Edrich decided to throw himself a 23rd birthday party, even though this was still at least a week early. He would remember forty years later:

There was a raging storm outside, I seem to recall, and the heating broke down in the ship's restaurant, but that didn't bother me at all. I drank toasts with the manager and toasts with the players, and somehow I

* The minutes of the Imperial Cricket Conference meeting at Lord's on 14 June 1939 read: 'Sir Pelham Warner stated that he had been asked by the South Africa Cricket Association to represent their dislike of Tests played without time limit, and that South Africa had submitted suggestions in this connection.'

35

managed to notice that the skipper had for company a well-upholstered young American lady who was wearing a low-cut frock and a diamond tiara and telling him how much she wanted him to bowl a maiden over. I think we'd earned our night out, because it wasn't as if any of us got rich from the tour. When everything was added up I put about 200 quid in the bank for my five months' work, so no wonder everyone enjoyed a bash when they could get one.

Edrich continued:

I had a great time. At least everyone told me I did. Somebody stuck a Red Indian headdress on my bonce and when I woke up that's all I was wearing. Luckily we were crossing the Equator later that day and we greeted it in fancy dress. Wally Hammond had a long black coat and a fat cigar in his mouth and he looked like a cross between a riverboat gambler and an undertaker. There were more toasts — toasts to King and Country, and the Empire, and the MCC, and then Kenny Farnes stood up and made one to world peace, and after that there was a bit of a lull in the room. He'd said something we all had on our minds.

Edrich always perked up at the prospect of a party, or for that matter the opportunity of overseas travel, and as he remembered it, 'One of the major advantages of touring was being able to just turn off the rest of the world for a few weeks.' The technology of the day helped reinforce this sense of isolation. 'Back then, neither the power of the BBC transmitters nor the efficiency of the *Athlone*'s broadcast equipment were adequate for really satisfactory results over any distance,' the ship's officer John Hodgson later wrote. 'However, as you approached the UK it was just possible to understand most of what the news reader was saying, and the majority of the passengers were able to follow the general trend of events.'

Just as the Englishmen had been settling in for the train journey to Cape Town following the final Test, Edrich had glanced out the window of his compartment and seen a newspaper vendor's stand on the platform with a headline announcing that German troops had entered

Czechoslovakia and that Hitler himself was now installed in the Royal Palace at Prague. Perhaps it was just as well that the tourists had then been able to pick up only fragmentary news reports for most of their homeward voyage. A day or two out into the Atlantic there had been a boat drill about what to do in the event of a capsize 'or other incident', however, and Edrich admitted that this for some reason gave him a 'queasy feeling inside – a sort of intrusion by the real world on our happy gang'. Just before the ship finally docked at Southampton early on 31 March, the first-class passenger lounge radio, now operating with total clarity, announced that the prime minister would be making a statement in the House of Commons later that afternoon, and that this would reportedly include a promise that in the event of an action which threatened Polish independence, His Majesty's Government would 'feel themselves bound to lend the Polish Government all support in their power'.

'And on that note,' said Edrich, 'we all trooped down the gangway and went off to play cricket for the summer.'

The folk memory of British domestic cricket in the inter-war years, at least at the level below the truly first class, was brilliantly captured in a comic novel entitled *England, Their England* written in 1933 by a melancholic Indian-born Scotsman named Archibald Macdonell. Macdonell, who had moved to London after being invalided out of the army suffering from wartime shell shock, perfected a style that combined out-and-out slapstick with a deep vein of affectionate bemusement at some of the foibles and affectations of his adopted home. The book's description of a 'typical' English cricket match is enlivened by a comic cast of characters ranging from the retired major to the village baker, all watched over by a row of beer-quaffing gaffers sitting on a rustic bench, and reaches its climax when, with the scores level, the blacksmith comes in to bat and hits his first ball straight up in the air. 'Up and up it went and then at the top it seemed to hang motionless, poised like a hawk, fighting as it were a heroic but forlorn battle against the chief invention of Sir Isaac Newton, and then it began its slow descent.' Macdonell manages to get in three pages of description during this interval, until at last the ball returns to earth and begins to ricochet liberally around between various bits of the fielding side's anatomies before being grabbed off the seat of the wicketkeeper's trousers, and the match is a tie. It's all a caricature, perhaps, but not one without a grain of truth in its depiction of the mingled charms and eccentricities of the national game.

Writing of the village and club cricket scene just before the outbreak of the Second World War, E. W. Swanton remembered a number of rich characters, such as 'Lord Ebbisham, father of the present peer, who as Sir Rowland Blades managed to combine the office of Lord Mayor of London with playing a lot of cricket.' Described as 'the best-dressed man in England', one E. Shirley Snell played his first match for the Incogniti club during the reign of Queen Victoria and his last one, at the age of 71, in 1953. Swanton also lingered fondly over the career of another staple of amateur cricket, 'Buns' Cartwright, a retired colonel of certain fixed social views, whose tenure in the Eton Ramblers XI bestrode the years between the world wars. 'Buns was seldom known to withhold any remark that came into his mind,' Swanton noted, adding that, while a lifelong bachelor, 'Buns was far from unappreciative of feminine company. A young cricketer once returned from a holiday in the South of France, saying: "Who do you think was there but old Buns. Yes, and Mrs Buns too. She was charming."'

Matching all these characters for sheer dedication to the game was a 'wonderfully dotty' London financier called Leslie Hindley. From early April to late September, the lugubrious-looking Hindley, invariably clad in a dark three-piece suit and a bowler hat, appeared to do nothing but drive about the country in his olive-green Chrysler convertible to watch cricket. Few fixtures at any level were immune from his attention. One day in 1939, Swanton recalls that Hindley saw the finishes of three games, at Leyton, Lord's and the Oval, and 'after the last one drove to Vincent Square in Westminster to see whether anything was going on there.' On the last day of the first-class season, at Hove, Hindley, for once removing his hat, stood up, faced the pavilion flag, and led the small, hitherto subdued crowd in an off-key but spirited rendition of the national anthem. After that, *Wisden's* capsule reviews of the season's few outstanding matches would read simply, 'Cancelled due to the War.'

Although it's often been said that the events of 1914–18 brought an end to the golden age of English cricket, some of its trappings remained largely intact over twenty years later. Even professional matches in 1939 frequently had a distinct country-house flavour to them, particularly those played at the more pastoral venues. In Taunton, a stray pig was known to wander out from the ring of spectators to visit the square. A modern county cricketer would hardly recognise the bustling grounds on which his counterpart often played eighty years ago, seemingly as part of an extended Georgian garden party, with gaudily dressed spectators, and often their servants and pets too, camped out around the park. A finely tuned social etiquette prevailed among the little groups who darted to and fro in between overs, like shoals of tropical fish. In general terms, the game combined a colourful splash of summer pastels with an increasing on-field aggression that worried the anonymous correspondent of the London *National Review*. 'I do not think things have been quite the same for the game since young Ken Farnes of Cambridge bowled short in the University Match of '33, catching the Oxford man David Townsend such a crack to his ear that he subsided onto his stumps,' he wrote.

It would be wrong, even so, to portray the English cricket scene of 1939 as merely a case either of effete young men in cravats behaving as if they had stepped out of the pages of Wodehouse, or, alternatively, of over-adrenalised students attempting to fill the boots of Harold Larwood. There was also a thriving network of good, yeomanlike cricket being played at the league, club, minor county, schools and even workplace levels. This last was 'the true heart of our great summer game,' *The Times* wrote in June 1939. To give just a few of the many regional examples: In 1922, eighteen teams played some form of weekly competitive cricket in the Birmingham Works League; by 1939, fifty-six sides were playing in the league's eight divisions, and fifty-four more were involved in the six divisions of the Birmingham Business Houses Cricket

Association. Elsewhere in the country, the number of workplace clubs listed in the *Sussex Express* rose from seven in 1922 to twenty in 1939. Several large industrial firms such as Pilkington Brothers in St Helens, Lancashire, staged their own keenly contested interdepartmental cricket tournaments each summer. At the Rake Lane ground in Wallasey on Merseyside, Cheshire took on the nearby Unilever Works XI over a bank holiday weekend in 1939 in front of a 6,000-strong crowd.

There were sometimes distinct professional advantages to being a cricketer. Morris Motors in Cowley, near Oxford, was an example of a company known to offer employment opportunities to men who could bat or bowl as well as they could wield a spanner. In May 1939, the sports editor of the *Oxford Mail* wrote that the Morris XI had played with a ruthlessness and efficiency in a Saturday afternoon fixture at Abingdon that had 'quite trimmed the wicks of the lamps of its rivals the Ford Company'.

Apart from the fearful toll soon to be taken by Hitler's war, the *Wisden* obituaries of the day suggest that English cricket's second, or continued, golden age of 1919–39 was fast running out of its own steam. Giants of the late Victorian and early Edwardian eras like the thumping Lancashire batsman Albert Ward, the great Tom Hayward of Surrey and England, and W.G. Grace's last surviving son, the lob-bowling Charles Butler Grace (who succumbed mid-match) all terminally left the crease in the months leading up to the outbreak of war. Neville Cardus thought there was a 'particular omen of loss' in the October 1938 death of the Yorkshire and England stalwart, and later *éminence grise* of the MCC, Lord Hawke. Hawke's speech at the Yorkshire club's annual meeting in 1925, proclaiming 'Pray God, no professional shall ever captain England' was widely taken, rightly or wrongly, as evidence of the crashing snobbery and pervasive air of bumbling still surrounding cricket. ('This is not a game given to sudden frenzies of mindless change,' the author J.B. Priestley wrote.) Hawke may have been taken out of context, as he always insisted was the case, but he came to epitomise a stodgily Victorian image many people still had of the game in 1939. Who can forget the exchange between the two buffers seated next to each other on the train in *The Lady Vanishes* (first released, coincidentally, on the day Hawke died) when one of them speaks lightly of a mutual acquaintance and is rebuked by the other?

'Steady on, old chap, he did play for the Gentlemen.'

'I know – but only once.'

At Chingford in Essex they turned out three separate league teams each Saturday afternoon in the 1939 season, and two more on Sunday. The players appeared wearing the club's colours of chocolate, white and blue, frequently emblazoned on a cravat tied round the waist. The playing area at Chingford was then a rough, rather randomly mown field, with an acrid smell drifting over it from the construction work on the huge twin water-storage reservoirs just to the west. A local player named Syd Spicer remembered, 'There was a sort of marshy feel to the place in general, and it was so flat thereabouts that when a breeze kicked up it often knocked over deckchairs and sent dust and newspapers eddying around like a tornado.' Thistles abounded in the Chingford outfield, which was grazed by sheep; brambled hedges invited lost balls on two sides, and an impenetrable screen of beech trees often made life difficult for the facing batsman at the other end. When you add a timbered pavilion and a backdrop of neatly painted bungalows with a pub at either end you had one of those flawed but agreeable grounds that give English grass-roots cricket its special charm.

Although Chingford later underwent something of a transition, there were no airs or graces to be found there in 1939. The cricketers generally walked to the ground, took their meals together at a bench in the pavilion, and sometimes struggled to find the playing subscription of £2-12s-6d annually. The only note of class distinction anyone could remember locally came when the former Essex batsman-turned-property developer, and later Test selector, Percy 'Peter' Perrin – said to have had 'some of Earl Haig's booming self-confidence with the added charm of a cockney accent' – once arrived at the wheel of his Rolls-Royce to watch a Saturday match.

This was not to be one of the home side's finest performances in the field. After the third or fourth dropped catch of the afternoon session, Perrin strode over to where the twelfth man was sprawled on a mattress in front of the pavilion. 'What the hell is going on, Crafter? It looks to me as if they're nearly all drunk.' 'They are, sir,' Crafter replied. The club had had an unexpected visit that morning from its patron, he explained, and lunch had 'run on a bit' as a result. The patron in question was the local MP, Winston Churchill. Perrin left the ground soon afterwards, but he remains in the record books today as having played more first-class matches as an amateur – 496 – than any other English cricketer. Chingford long remained one of those happily egalitarian, if impecunious, sides that constitute the backbone of the national sport. The club's minutes for 1939 read: 'The General Committee discussed the cost of laying a hard tennis court, as it was felt this would attract new members. To assist in raising funds for this, the Hon. Treasurer was asked to obtain a quotation for the cost of a slide to be shown at Chingford Cinema.'

Perrin later said in a review of the Essex league scene as a whole:

> There tend to be two distinct sorts of batsman on view – those who can move their feet and get into a fair position to play the ball, and those who can't. About ninety per cent fall in the latter category. In bowling, most of the quicker men tend to be young hearties in their early twenties with aggressive personalities. They possess few other qualifications. Yet, allowing for all this, to see the sheer spirit of these games, week after week, in all parts, and at every station of society, is to appreciate the real fibre of England.

Wisden also found space to review the 1939 fortunes of 112 cricket-playing boys' schools in England, and a further seven in Scotland. Most of these were of the fee-paying variety, but there was a modest nod to democracy in the reports of the 'keen hard play' or 'uncompromising grit' at state-funded establishments in places like Wallasey or Stockport. A team of Canadian schoolboys visited England in July and were unlucky with the weather – of their eleven matches, four were abandoned, two were drawn, four were lost and a single game, against King's Canterbury, won. The following month, a British public schools side went out on a return tour of North America. On the day the papers carried the news of the outbreak of war the visitors played a final twelve-a-side, 50-overs match against Bison City in Buffalo, New York. The tourists scored 240 and then bowled out their hosts for 107. Eighteen-year-old Frank Calway from Taunton, lately of Westminster School, opened the visitors' bowling. He took 1-17 in 6 overs with what was described as a 'frantic, sling-shot action', went out to dinner with the two teams later that evening, and attended a thanksgiving service for the departing tourists at Buffalo's St Bartholomew's Anglican Church in the morning. Back home again, Calway promptly volunteered for duty as an ordinary seaman in the Royal Navy and drowned while serving with HMS *Quebec* on Atlantic escort duty in August 1941. He had just turned 20 at the time of his death.

Women's cricket already had a long and varied history by 1939 – the first recorded match was held in July 1745 'between eleven maids of Bramley and eleven maids of Hambledon, all dressed in white' – and the England team's tour of Australia and New Zealand in 1934–35 had established the original three Test-playing sides. The Englishwomen won their first representative match, against Australia at Brisbane, by 9 wickets. *Wisden* somehow failed to mention many of these early international fixtures. Nor did it find space for the Women's Cricket Association, founded in 1926, squeezed as the almanack was in 1939 by its lingering reports of inter-regimental tournaments, or the annual Rugby v Marlborough grudge match at Lord's.

Born in 1899, Marjorie Pollard can lay claim to be the towering figure in the establishment and recognition of British women's team sports, and in particular cricket. Tall, short-haired, lively and bespectacled, she was what the press called a 'modern girl'. Pollard preferred jazz to opera, American musical comedies to the poetic drama of W.H. Auden or T.S. Eliot, and herself wrote articles and essays in a breezy style full of energetically sustained idiom. Her 1934 book *Cricket for Women and Girls*, an early manifesto for gender equality in British society as a whole, would long remain the definitive treatment of the subject. It still enjoys a steady annual sale of some 10–12,000 copies, figures most sports-book authors can only dream of.

Pollard's own playing career was winding down in 1939, but on mid-summer's day that year, the eve of her 40th birthday, she went out to bat at Trent Bridge for the Midlands and North Women in a single-innings match against their counterparts from the East and South. She scored 87 out of a total of 136. Pollard's final representative match came just two months later, when she contributed 20 to the England XI's winning score of 113 against the touring Australians. The war then put paid to any thoughts of further competitive play. Marjorie Pollard devoted much of the rest of her long life to writing and speaking about women's field sports. She was a coach, publisher, film-maker and early television pundit – appearing in the broadcasting box alongside a young Brian Johnston in 1951 – as well. Pollard once said with pioneer idealism: 'We do not wish to follow, we wish to go our own way – to run our own affairs, play our own cricket, and live our own lives.' She died at the age of 82.

With the 1939 first-class season about to start, many English cricket followers wondered whether Yorkshire could achieve a hat-trick of county championship titles and thus lift the trophy for the seventh time in nine years. The only exceptions to this otherwise unbroken run of success had come when Lancashire took the pennant in 1934, and Derbyshire in 1936. The county's early form suggested that they were in no hurry to relinquish their grip on cricket's main domestic competition, with ten wins out of their first eleven starts. Len Hutton, who turned 23 that June, was the leading batsman, but Herbert Sutcliffe, who was twice his fellow opener's age, averaged 51 in championship matches, and at one stage played successive innings of 163, 116, 234 not out, and 175. The veteran went on to complete 1,000 runs by the middle of June, and there was even talk that he might add to his total of fifty-four England caps, the last of which had come in the loss to South Africa at Lord's in 1935. In the end the call never came, but Hutton later remarked of his county colleague that 'Herbert would have continued playing until old age really set in, and he was only bowled out by Hitler.'

In fact, Sutcliffe's first-class career was bookended neatly, if it could be so called, by the two world wars. His county debut was delayed by his service in the army from 1914 to 1919 – he had to wait until he was nearly 30 for his first England cap – and his playing days were effectively terminated when, in August 1939, he became the first Yorkshire player to be called up as a reservist. In general, Sutcliffe was the most serene of batsmen and the most unflappable of characters, the sort, 'Crusoe' Robertson-Glasgow said, 'who would rather miss a train than run for it', and he stood as an acknowledged colossus of English cricket on the brink of the Second World War.

Neville Cardus once wrote of Sutcliffe:

> From the outset he became a pin-up boy in the bedrooms of count-less Yorkshire girls, for this was an epoch in which girls insisted that their glamour heroes should be elegant and eye-catching. Into that dour Yorkshire team, Sutcliffe appeared as some Lothario might have appeared among Cromwell's Ironsides. Immaculately flannelled from his first match onwards; glossy and dark of hair, he was utterly unlike any Yorkshire professional we had ever seen.

Cardus was speaking of the early 1920s, when Sutcliffe had enjoyed a status in the eyes of many impressionable British adolescents hardly less exalted than that of Rudolph Valentino. It was not a young god fans now came to admire in April 1939, but an old pro, getting ready to go through the whole thing again. Sutcliffe still had the strokes, among them a stinging hook that often left midwicket in need of the physio's sponge, but with the years he'd lost some of his fluid ease of movement and replaced it by the priceless knack of staying in. 'As you bowled to him,' Robertson-Glasgow (late of Oxford University and Somerset) ruefully observed, 'you noticed the entire development of every defensive art: the depressingly straight bat, the astute use of pads, the sharp detection of which outswinger could be left; above all, the consistently safe playing down of a rising or turning ball.' Sutcliffe, in short, was the consummate old-stager, who made up in application and willpower what he now lacked in speed and agility. In his twenty-first consecutive season with Yorkshire, he earned a basic £425 (now £11,000) for his four months' work, a figure that with bonuses and incentives may have reached £600. Though much better off than his pub-landlord father had ever been, this was still only in the lower reaches of a typical middle-class income. Even with the proceeds of his successful sports-goods shops in Leeds and Wakefield, he would only have been earning roughly the same amount as a provincial schoolteacher or minor civil servant. As a teenager, Sutcliffe had served as an apprentice bookkeeper in a local textile mill, and his canny eye for the bottom line helped him make the most of what he had, bringing him an at least modestly comfortable lifestyle. He, his wife Emily and their three children (one of whom, Billy, became captain of Yorkshire in the 1950s) lived in an impeccably trim, three-bedroom terraced house in Pudsey, before in time the husband and wife moved into smaller retirement accommodation nearby.

Sutcliffe was as calm and methodical a private citizen as he was a cricketer. He remained a lifelong member of the Congregational Church, spoke in a soft, classless voice Neville Cardus remembered as 'more Teddington than Yorkshire', and set high standards for himself both on and off the field. He took immense pride in his appearance. Perhaps with just a touch of colour, Cardus described him as 'shiny of lock, black as the raven's, with flannels of fluttering silk, and the confident air of super-Pudsey breeding. A deviation from type, a "sport" in the evolutionary process.'

In 1939, Sutcliffe was simply the model professional cricketer.

'Harold Gimblett called on me.' So wrote the Somerset president (and de facto treasurer) Richard Palairet on Tuesday 25 April 1939. It was not the first time he would utter this phrase, signifying an appeal for funds on Gimblett's part, and it was by no means the last.

Born in 1914 in the village of Bicknoller in the Quantock Hills, where his people had been farmers since the Middle Ages, the broad-shouldered, sandy-haired Gimblett's entry into first-class cricket in May 1935 was the stuff of legend. He was already on his way home from an unsuccessful trial at Taunton when the county side found themselves a man short for the match that started the following day with Essex at the Agricultural Showgrounds in Frome. Gimblett was hurriedly sent for, hitching the last part of the way in a passing lorry. He went out to bat shortly after lunch on the first day, with Somerset on 107-6 and bearing the advice from his captain Reginald Ingle to 'watch Peter Smith – he's bound to bowl you a googly first ball.'

Gimblett had never encountered a googly in his limited experience of school or club cricket and had only heard it spoken of in the haziest terms. Nonetheless, he successfully blocked two balls from Smith, a future England Test bowler, and hit the third one for a single. All three deliveries had indeed been googlies. A few minutes later, Gimblett smashed Smith for 15 runs in an over and from then on raced to his 50 in just twenty-eight minutes, bringing it up with a six. He required only thirty-five more minutes to complete his century. Gimblett had by then faced 71 balls and he made his runs out of 130 scored while at the wicket, where his partner for much of the time had been Arthur Wellard, one of the biggest hitters in the game. The debutant eventually made 123 in seventy-nine minutes, including 3 sixes and 17 fours, playing throughout with a borrowed bat. Somerset beat Essex by an innings.

The question everyone asked – including Gimblett – was whether it had all somehow been an aberration, or a kind of glorious fluke? The player seemed to settle the issue beyond doubt when he then top scored with 53 in his second championship match, against Middlesex at Lord's. Just over a year after appearing in the middle order for Watchet in the Somerset leagues Gimblett found himself opening the innings for

England in the first Test against India at Lord's in June 1936, where he scored 11 and 67 not out. It was comfortably the most successful match of his brief international experience. Gimblett was overlooked for the MCC tour of Australia in the winter of 1936–37, and in time his county career settled down into one of fitful brilliance, long stretches of relative anonymity punctuated by a sudden furious eruption – a reflection, some said, of his inner personality – such as the time he destroyed Hampshire with an innings of 141 in two hours, or took 112 off Kent in a game at Folkestone where only two other players on either side reached 20, rather than any pretence of Hutton-like consistency. He finished the 1938 season with an average of 27, which was less than half that of his main rival for the England opening spot.

More ominously, Gimblett may already have been showing signs of the emotional illness that was to afflict him in later life. When he was passed over for the winter tour of Australia, he responded with relief. 'Thank God that's over,' Gimblett supposedly remarked. According to his biographer David Foot: 'His [early] Tests became painful rather than treasured memories; he pleaded silently that he would never be selected again.'

Gimblett was equally unhappy with many of the provisions of his county contract, frequently complaining about being homesick and physically uncomfortable while playing away games – 'kennelled overnight like a dog', he wrote of one northern tour – and often seeking an advance on his wages, or even permission for a special collection box to be taken round to recognise some outstanding innings on his part. Few of these perks were ever forthcoming. Little about Gimblett was typical, but in his all-too-human fallibility in the middle, his regularly aired grievances about his basic working terms and conditions, and in particular his impatience with the 'muckety-mucks who control us for their own gain', he might be said to be characteristic of a certain kind of English county cricketer operating at or fractionally below the highest level in 1939.

Still standing a rung or two further down the professional ladder, the irrepressible teenager Godfrey Evans, travelling round with a huge suitcase decorated by a coronet over the letter 'E' (borrowed apparently from the Derby-winning jockey Eph Smith) was just then starting out as a batsman and occasional wicketkeeper for Kent. He had finished the 1938 season by scoring an even-time 27 in his county's Second XI tie with Middlesex, and a few days later a letter arrived at Evans's family home offering him a contract for the period 3 April–30 September 1939. This 'wasn't notable for its generosity,' the player remembered fifty years later, with a basic £2-5s weekly (£60 today) to start, and a performance-based review promised for mid-season.

Evans had been augmenting his income up until then by a series of light-welterweight bouts in semi-licensed or unlicensed boxing tournaments held in the back rooms of seaside pubs, and as a result of one of these he was sporting a broken nose when he went to see Gerald Hough in his office at Canterbury over Christmas week of 1938 in order to finalise the arrangements for the next season. Hough took one look at Evans and told him he had to choose between boxing and cricket. He chose cricket. Then Hough handed him a £10 signing-on bonus, with the recommendation that he spend this wisely, and Evans took his club secretary's advice by catching the first available train to London and getting himself good and drunk. When he woke up the next morning he had about £2 of his gratuity left, and he promptly invested this as the down payment on a motorbike. To keep fit, Evans took a part-time job for the rest of the winter with the Tickham Foxhounds near his family home in Faversham. 'The basic idea was that I shovelled the crap out of horseboxes all morning, took a nap in the afternoon, had a meal, and then went out on crumpet patrol at night,' he remembered, still speaking fondly of the experience years later.

Evans's teammate Doug Wright provided some context to this last-named activity when he explained, 'Godfrey was like a kid who's never been allowed sweets and is suddenly presented with a lorryload. Cricket was the instrument which pried the lid off the treasure-chest.' Hough recorded in his diary that Evans was a 'brilliant prospect' who 'unfortunately has the mind of a 14-year-old … He will either play for England or go to jail.'

At cricket's purest level, there were also the annual Easter coaching classes held at Lord's under the MCC player Reg Routledge for some

250 enthusiastic young teenagers from 7–26 April 1939. The sun shone throughout, there were morning sessions in the nets with the likes of Patsy Hendren, late of Middlesex and England, magic-lantern presentations in a darkened groundsman's hut smelling of grass clippings, and full-scale practice matches most afternoons on the Nursery End pitch. Looking back on the 1939 season from the dark days of May 1940, the *Morning Post* wrote, 'in retrospect, perhaps those high-spirited young voices of the spring may have been the year's most poignant sporting scene. How many of these hopefuls may be lost in the conflict that now seems to stretch before us like an ordeal?'

While Gerald Hough was helping to spring-clean the Canterbury pavilion that Easter weekend in 1939, some 4,000 miles away in Barbados the West Indies Board – under the chairmanship of 64-year-old, Marlborough-educated Lt Col William Bowring MBE, a Caribbean club cricketer around the turn of the century – published the names of the eighteen players and officials who would tour England that summer. Like many such affairs in that area of the world, it had not been an entirely smooth process. The nucleus of the party had first been announced as early as the second week of March, but there had subsequently been a series of hastily arranged emergency sessions of the selection panel, which in general seem to have displayed all the decorum of a *Fawlty Towers* fire drill. As a result, later in the month the squad was modified to include the 34-year-old Jamaican fast bowler Leslie Hylton, whose omission from the original list had sparked riots on his home island. Hylton's place was eventually secured on condition that it be paid for by public subscription. At the time of sailing the fund for the extra player's expenses was still £400 short, but he nonetheless joined the touring side, while in an effort to cut costs the Board took the last-minute decision not to appoint an assistant to the already cruelly overtaxed team manager Jack Kidney. There was further upheaval when the West Indies' advance man in England, an 80-year-old former

Durham and MCC bowler named Harry Mallett, fell ill and died while negotiating some of the arrangements for the players' local travel and accommodation. Many of these details remained at best half-resolved as a result.

The West Indies party was captained by the 29-year-old Cambridge graduate Rolph Grant, an able all-round sportsman, if not one conspicuously gifted at cricket, who at least met the Board's requirement for a white leader. The fifteen-Test veteran Learie Constantine – a T20 hitter before the idea was born, and still more than useful at the age of 36 with the new ball – had at one time had ambitions on the job, but in the end settled for senior tour professional. He was paid £515 plus a 2 per cent share of any profits, of which there turned out to be none. 'I was dissatisfied, and said so openly, as is my habit,' Constantine recalled. Twenty-nine-year-old George Headley, widely known as the 'black Bradman', later admitted that he, too, had had designs on the West Indies captaincy. 'Rolph Grant inherited the job from his brother Jackie who'd suddenly heard the call to become a missionary in Africa. Both nice guys, pretty poor cricketers,' Headley observed. 'Rolph once told me that his big ambition was to be elected an honorary member of MCC.'

Elsewhere in the cricket-playing world, the Hindus beat the Muslims by 4 wickets in the final of the Lahore Trophy held on 5 March 1939. The *Khyber Mail* reported that the ground at Lahore was 'chock full with denizens of every age, race and persuasion, and they gave both sets of players a good reception.' Organised cricket was also played that spring in the likes of Nigeria, Kenya, Ghana and Ceylon, and even in a series of keenly fought three-day internationals between Chile and Argentina held on a specially prepared corner, decked out with marquees trimmed by patriotic red-and-blue bunting, a cooling sea breeze wafting in from the west, in the botanical gardens of the port city of Valparaiso.

There was a specially arranged match in Melbourne, where the *Age* reported:

Feelings of comradeship were uppermost at the game played here on Saturday between the Australian Imperial Forces and contemporary Test players, but there was also an air of sadness, because it will in all probability be the last appearance, as a team, of the players who fought for their country twenty years ago … There was an impressive scene after lunch, when the Lieutenant-Governor Sir Frederick Mann was met by a guard of honour provided by the Royal Melbourne Regiment. He inspected them and met the players of both sides, who were lined up on the ground. In his oration, Sir Frederick expressed the heartfelt wish that there should be no future conflict like that of 1914–18, which had caused such anguish.

In England that week, the *Yorkshire Post* correspondent Jim Kilburn wrote of the opening of the new season as:

A voyage of most joyous adventure, for it brings promise of the thrilling unknown, together with the prospect of sailing again certain charted and well-loved seas. We go again where we have so often been before to find new paint upon the same pavilion railings, to see new figures tread the old steps well-worn by the feet of the mighty ones of yesteryear.

This is surely the kind of talk that every true cricket lover knows in their bones. It was a time of renewed promise. But even in the hallowed corridors of Lord's, it was not one wholly untouched by shadow. In a meeting of 3 April 1939, the MCC Committee noted that 'it appears desirable to prepare certain rooms as air-raid refuges', with a subsequent order of 2,000 sandbags, and that 'staff, and in particular cricketers, should be encouraged to do all they can to assist in National Service.'

In the cabinet meeting of 19 April, meanwhile, there was a lengthy discussion about whether or not to send a gift to the German head of state on the occasion of his 50th birthday, which ultimately recommended that the king's name be put to a message 'not in the customary form which contained wishes for the recipient's health and welfare, but that His Majesty be advised simply to note the event'.

3

THE BULLDOG BREED

The slightly haphazard travel arrangements of the third official tour by the West Indies of the British Isles foretold a summer of mounting insecurity and crisis, in which plenty of good cricket was also played. On 10 April 1939, the five Trinidad players and the Guyanese batsman Herbert Bayley sailed north to Barbados on the venerable steam packet MV *Columbia*. Their eighteen-hour, 200-mile journey was not without incident. Shortly before dawn on 11 April the boat's captain had decided that one of the successive dark shapes bobbing up in the water in front of them was not a marker buoy, but a mine, and rang the ship's alarm accordingly. At 5.30 a.m., with misty daylight flooding across the Caribbean, Rolph Grant scribbled in his diary: 'Emergency stations. Great consternation. Men on deck in pyjamas. Ship veering wildly, [and] Gomez sick over the side ... Not the greatest start to a long sea-crossing.'

Later that afternoon, joined by a three-man Barbados contingent, the *Columbia*'s passengers set out across the Atlantic. For the most part the tourists were from otherwise different, alien worlds who now found a shared identity in their national cricket team. It took them another eleven days of recurrent storms and heavy seas to reach port in Plymouth, where it was raining steadily. The local *Western Evening Herald* sent a man to cover the event, and their inside-page photograph shows a group of bedraggled-looking sportsmen, each wearing a crested blue blazer, some of them also nervously fingering a felt hat, huddled together under a lone umbrella. Observers noted that the young wicketkeeper-batsman Derek Sealy, a poor sailor, had bent down and kissed the ground as he came ashore.

The West Indians spent their first night on British soil at an unprepossessing guest house on Plymouth Hoe. Sealy later reported that they had been made to feel welcome enough there – although the 'greasy' cooked breakfast had come as a shock, and the water had emerged from the bathroom taps 'like a sort of sticky green hair-oil'. But disappointment had followed when one of the party had enquired about the prospect of visiting the town's municipal swimming baths before setting out for London, and been told that this would only be possible if the West Indians reserved the pool in advance and paid for the water to be completely drained and replaced after they left.

Meanwhile, the tourists' five Jamaican players had set out separately on the Fyffes-line banana boat SS *Tortugero*, docking at Liverpool on Monday 24 April. It was still raining. Two other players, Learie Constantine and Manny Martindale, had long-term English league contracts, and as a result both were already in the country. All sixteen cricketers were reunited at their London hotel on the afternoon of the 27th, which happened to be the day on which Neville Chamberlain's government announced the return of military conscription. The evening papers went on to report that the Polish Foreign Minister Jozef Beck had applied for a grant of £60 million to urgently help rearm his country, but that the mood in Whitehall made this 'nearly impossible' to countenance as Britain's own finances had been so weakened by recent military spending. The Poles were eventually offered a loan of £8 million. Most of the West Indians – though not Vic Stollmeyer of Trinidad, who was suffering from tonsillitis – went on that night to a performance of Ivor Novello's new musical *The Dancing Years* at the Theatre Royal, Drury Lane, where they attracted some curious glances. From their blue blazers the tourists had changed into an assortment of tropical tan suits and fedoras. One of the theatre's other patrons apparently made a racially charged remark to Leslie Hylton when passing him on the way out, and years later Hylton's colleagues still marvelled at the ferocity of his response, like old salts recalling an historic hurricane. As Vic Stollmeyer's younger brother Jeff, a future West Indies Test captain, remembered:

Hylton was a commanding personality but he also contained a fiery temper which had got him into trouble and was probably the cause of his missing the previous tour of England. While playing in the trials prior to that visit, an lbw appeal by him was turned down by the umpire who happened to be the elder brother of the captain-elect. When Hylton threw the ball down in disgust his goose was cooked.

Just before the first ball was due to be bowled of the tourists' first match, a one-day loosener on 1 May against a team of local worthies at Busbridge Hall in Godalming, Jack Kidney assembled his men in their small, bare-walled room in the back of the pavilion. In a throaty voice made scratchy by too many cigarettes and too much coffee over the course of the thirty years that he had been successively a player and an administrator, Kidney made this promise to his side: 'When you go home again in four months' time, you will be the best cricket team in the world.' The room fell silent. Then the 50-year-old manager, always seeming to push the right buttons at the right time, cracked everyone up by pointing out a side window at the Dickensian scene immediately outside of a waterlogged field haunted by a few forlorn-looking spectators hunched together in the rain and saying, 'We're starting right at the top here, boys – talk about atmosphere!' That particular match was abandoned without a ball being bowled. So was the one scheduled for the following day at Park Lane in Reigate. On 3 May, the West Indies at last managed to get on the field of play in a game against Leslie Ames's XI, composed mainly of Kent county players, at Gravesend. Ames himself scored 116 in eighty-five minutes. As a result the home side was able to declare at 278-6, and the tourists replied with 225-3,

Jeff Stollmeyer making 87 before being run out, to earn a draw. After Rolph Grant and one or two of the other fair-skinned players had gone into a roadside pub while on their evening's coach journey to bring back sandwiches and beer for everyone's supper, the West Indians spent that night as guests of the army in a barracks hut at Aldershot.

At Lord's, the 152nd annual meeting of the MCC that day recorded the 'satisfactory' state of the club's finances. There were 6,996 members, an increase of 181 over the previous year, of whom 516 were life members and 228 were abroad. Generous tributes were paid to the late Lord Hawke, 'and to fill the vacancy occasioned by his death, the Committee recommended the appointment of Sir J.E. Kynaston Studd, Bart.'

In other business, the club debated at some length the scheduling of the prestigious Oxford v Cambridge and Eton v Harrow matches, as well as the ticketing arrangements for the Lord's Test. 'If more than 6,000 Rover passes are issued, the available space for the public will be unduly limited,' it was minuted. These were still the days when the English cricket authorities worried about accommodating everyone who wanted to watch the longer forms of the game. In due course there would be roughly 8–9,000 spectators on hand for each day of the university and schools matches, while 58,000 customers paid for admission during the three days of the West Indies Test.*

The county championship season got underway on Saturday 6 May, with four matches played in the south of England, as well as an MCC v Yorkshire fixture at Lord's. Kent were off to a bright start with a 116-run win over Essex at Gillingham, thanks to a brisk first-innings cameo of 62 by Frederick Gerald 'Gerry' Chalk in an otherwise low-scoring game. Born in London in 1910, the tousle-haired Chalk had been a batting prodigy first at Uppingham and then Oxford, for whom

---

* Despite this relatively healthy state of affairs, the relevant MCC Committee had also just considered a request from 'F.M. Cotterell, Clerk of the Works at Lord's, that his wages be reviewed' and decided that this was not possible. 'Subject to satisfactory service, the maximum wage of the Clerk of the Works, exclusive of the value of any flat occupied, should be fixed at £6 a week,' the committee noted.

he scored 108 in the 1934 Varsity Match. His early success seemed to come about without the slightest exertion, so far as anyone could see. Working as a teacher at Malvern, Chalk would go on to appear for Kent on a semi-regular basis during the summer holidays each season from 1935 to 1937, when he was appointed the county's captain. He played full-time throughout the next two seasons, earning something of Mike Brearley's later reputation for astute man-management, if enjoying rather greater personal success with the bat. One correspondent wrote of Chalk in 1939 as a 'man who played the most attractive sort of cricket in a free and happy spirit, and whom I would far sooner see batting than some of those giants of the game, averaging 60 and 70 by masterly but laborious methods'.

Apart from his technical accomplishments, Chalk was a wonderfully anachronistic figure in some of his personal approach to cricket. Godfrey Evans once saw his county captain draw up to the gates of the St Lawrence Ground in the back seat of a 'beautiful but ancient' dove-grey Bentley which also contained 'a chauffeur, a picnic hamper, cocktail shaker, piles of racing form, some binoculars, and a dog the size of a pony'. But Chalk did considerably more than just wave an imperious hand over his players when in the field. His philosophy of cricket was that the game should be played hard, sensibly, and with unfailing goodwill. He was always available to talk to any of his men who sought him out and was invariably generous with both his professional and personal advice. 'Try putting a bit more water in it,' he remarked to Evans, when the young wicketkeeper reeled past him one night in the pub.

Chalk also believed, as he once put it in a letter home, that 'a degree of remove [was] desirable in leadership, where discipline has to be exercised'. A gregarious man off the field, he was notably unsentimental on it. Evans remembered his county captain calling him aside early that season to tell him that 31-year-old 'Hopper' Levett, the side's first-choice wicketkeeper, was 'overdoing it a bit – always a shame at his age', and that the young understudy should be ready to step up into the first team accordingly. When Evans sheepishly asked what exactly his captain meant by overdoing it, Chalk told him with a straight face that in a game towards the end of the 1938 season, Levett, after a heavy night, had taken his place behind the wicket and 'never even blinked' as the first ball sailed past the off stump for 4 byes.

The batsman had then glanced the second delivery down the leg side, where Levett took off to dive and take a spectacular catch, before turning to remark to the slip cordon: 'Not bad, eh, for the first ball of the day?'

It sometimes seems strange that cricket should ever have taken root in the English climate. 'Rain wasted a lot of time on the first two days,' *Wisden* wrote of the three-day Oxford Seniors' match played at the University Parks in late April. There were conditions of 'Biblical flood' during the next two games on the same ground, while for the arrival of county champions Yorkshire on 3 May the Thames Valley sky was a 'pre-deluge shade of grey, with a peppering of jet-black crows swooping around and a softness underfoot that recalled a midwinter's Irish fen.'

The students' captain perhaps rashly invited Yorkshire to bat, and the visitors responded with a total of 322, of which Sutcliffe scored 125 not out. The Oxford eleven then managed 102 runs between them. Yorkshire, composed of ten professional cricketers and the amateur captain Brian Sellers, described as 'a disciplinarian with a fruity sense of humour', won by 10 wickets on the second afternoon.

Two other significant things happened that day. Hedley Verity, recently returned from MCC's tour of South Africa, took 6-73 in Oxford's second innings, proving that at nearly 34 he remained not only a useful bowler under any conditions, but one who on a helpful wet wicket could make the ball rear to the point of being unplayable. And at the death, Oxford's 23-year-old captain and occasional Northamptonshire player Eric Dixon good-naturedly shook everyone's hands and insisted that both teams join him for what became an extended dinner at the town's Randolph Hotel. Neither of these men survived the war.

For their part, Lancashire began proceedings with a comfortable win at Gloucester, but the rest of May was less fruitful. The Red Rose county had the England caps Cyril Washbrook and Eddie Paynter to open the innings, but all too often things seemed to fall off from there. As one critic put it:

Lancashire carried a long tail, but the chief weakness was bowling – in the first place the leg-spinner [Len] Wilkinson, so successful the previous winter in South Africa, seldom gave a glimpse of his real powers. An injured hand affected him early in the season and, compared with 1938 when he took 151 wickets for 23 runs apiece, his victims numbered 88 fewer at an average of 30.

English cricket wasn't then troubled, as it was later, by sports psychologists, but if it had been they surely would have found the 22-year-old Wilkinson to be a suitable case for treatment. Speaking towards the end of his long life, at the time he worked as a local Cumbrian newsagent, he said: 'The only thing I can think of is that I tried to be too perfect, particularly with the googly. I had an England cap and as an England player I was always under pressure to be good.' In his old age, Wilkinson still reminisced about the social atmosphere of 1939:

It was still glamorous to be a cricketer in those days and everyone wanted to know you. It was fashionable to say, 'I met so and so last night at such and such a club.' Another thing that's forgotten: the press left you alone off the field, so we had ample time for mischief.

On top of everything else, Lancashire suffered more than most from the wet weather in 1939. Thirteen of their scheduled seventy-eight days of championship cricket were washed out completely, and many others were badly affected by rain or poor light. When *Wisden* came to report the county's results, they offered the unusual summary:

Played 31, Won 10, Lost 6, Drawn 5, No Decision 9, Not a ball bowled 1, Abandoned through War, 1.

Northamptonshire's playing record showed an at least modest improvement on 1938, when the county had lost fully seventeen of their twenty-four matches and finished the season with a total of 16 points, which was 240 fewer than Yorkshire managed. The side's new captain, 26-year-old Robert Nelson, a Cambridge blue, brought a touch both of collective discipline and personal enterprise to what had previously been a somewhat ramshackle county unit. *Wisden* wrote: 'Sometimes [he] ventured too much in declaring, but brightened several games by his bold policy as well as by his left-handed batting … Nelson, who also scored over a thousand runs by varying defence with forcing play, often pulled a game round or checked a collapse.'

In time, the Northamptonshire county yearbook added: 'Mr R.P. Nelson is coming into his own, and the prospects under his continued leadership are most auspicious.' There was praise in the same publication for the side's 34-year-old leg-spinner Sidney Adams – 'a player we should warmly welcome back, his duties as a councilman permitting' – who enjoyed the distinction of having taken wickets with his first two balls in first-class cricket, including that of Samuel Beckett, later winner of the Nobel Prize for Literature; and also for the 'young Oxford man Mr E.J.H. Dixon, who we confidently expect to strengthen the batting for many seasons ahead'. In fact, all three of these players would be dead within five years.

Despite Northamptonshire's relative improvement on their playing performance in 1939, it has to be said that this wasn't a golden era for the club's fortunes in general. Apart from their wretched championship form (with an unenviable and surely unrepeatable run of 99 successive matches without a victory), they saw their England Test batsman Fred Bakewell's career cut short due to a broken arm suffered in a car crash that also resulted in the death of his 30-year-old teammate and fellow opener Reginald Northway. They had been driving home together from a match against Derbyshire at Chesterfield in which Bakewell scored an unbeaten innings of 241; his injury was as catastrophic in its way as that which ended Colin Milburn's Northamptonshire career thirty-three years later.

Derbyshire began their own 1939 season, like so many other counties, with a crushing win over Oxford University at the Parks. The county's tree-lined ground, overlooked by the twisted church spire of St Mary and All Saints, at Chesterfield, remained one of the most agreeable places in England to watch cricket. In 28-year-old George Pope, one of three sporting brothers, Derbyshire had a genuine all-rounder good enough to score 1,040 first-class runs and take 103 wickets in 1938. Bill Copson was one of those (usually apocryphal) cases of a young northerner emerging from down a coal mine to become a world-class fast bowler, with no apparent intermediate learning curve. But, despite all these attractive qualities, Derbyshire only fitfully played to their full potential in 1939. They finished a lowly ninth in the championship, and in *Wisden*'s headmasterly report: 'The dismissal of the team for 20 by Yorkshire at Sheffield will not readily be forgotten, nor will the startling breakdown which led to defeat by 13 runs from Sussex at Derby.'

Nottinghamshire followed a similar trajectory in early season: after easily disposing of Cambridge University by 10 wickets they settled down to a run of modest success. Twenty-seven-year-old Joe Hardstaff scored 1,818 championship runs in his upright, elegant style, but still gave Neville Cardus the impression 'almost of being bored by normal county play – he needs the spur of danger and responsibility'. Later in his career Hardstaff managed to fall foul of the England captain Gubby Allen, after Allen had tried to prevent his men from staying out late 'to drink alcohol and carouse with low women' during the 1947–48 tour of the West Indies. ('But what else is there to do, Skip?' Hardstaff had enquired.) Notts also had the burly swing bowler Harold Butler and left-armer Bill Voce – a link to the Bodyline era – to open their attack. This pair took 202 first-class wickets between them in the 1939 season.

Warwickshire's batting fortunes depended to a large degree on two men: 24-year-old H.E. 'Tom' Dollery, whose forceful play brought him more than 1,000 runs in fifteen consecutive first-class seasons from 1935 to 1955, and Bob Wyatt, then a veteran of forty Tests and generally thought to be on his way down ability-wise, but still capable of belting 138 against Yorkshire in late August. No one else gave the champions' bowling a worse hammering all season long. Wyatt played his last first-class match only in June 1957, aged 56, and lived to be 93. Having been born in an era when cricket was known without irony as the 'gentle-man's game' and W.G. Grace still captained the MCC, he survived long enough to see a time of lost certainties and frenetic, floodlit slogs played between teams clad in fluorescent tracksuits. 'Shyness became aloofness,' a distinguished critic once wrote of Wyatt. 'Work, status, progress and accountancy were his sole focus.' Nonetheless, Wyatt was a hardboiled, dedicated, eminently sound cricketer – a sort of prototype Geoffrey Boycott – and if he lacked Dollery's populist approach to the game he more than made up for it in application. People would go to watch Wyatt bat as much to see a master technician at work as to enjoy any possible fireworks.

Real indignity befell Leicestershire's 1939 season. *Wisden* wrote: 'The form of the side in 1938 suggested that, after several lean years, they were on the way back towards recovering prestige, but one of the worst years in the history of the club ended with bottom place in the championship.'

Although Leicestershire's failure was comprehensive, the perhaps ill-named 'Foxes' were particularly inept in the field. It was said that between them they put down a total of 26 catches during their open-ing match against Sussex, and that some of the men in the deep walked backwards, rather than forwards, when the bowler began his run-up. When it came to Leicester's batting, the preferred tactic on hitting the ball was for both men to shout simultaneously, and often to then continue shouting loudly during their progress down the pitch, which frequently found them in a mad dash to the same end.

An honourable exception to Leicestershire's shortcomings was the form of their 18-year-old wicketkeeper George Dawkes – 'without doubt the brightest part of the county's cricket', *Wisden* wrote. A stumper in the classical mould, Dawkes would tap his gloves together with a smooth, circular sweep of the arms in between deliveries, before crouching down with a ramrod-straight back that gave one observer the impression 'he always seemed to be standing to attention even when prone.' The teenager took 52 catches and 5 stumpings in his relatively brief 1939 season. Perhaps Dawkes's only real defect as a wicketkeeper, certainly as far as his Test prospects went, was to have been born at almost exactly the same time as Godfrey Evans.

As we've seen, Essex began their championship season poorly, against Kent, and one paper had added the word 'abysmal' to its factual report of the match. Ken Farnes had gone straight from striking fear in the hearts of the South African batsmen during the winter MCC tour to his full-time job as a housemaster at Worksop College in Nottinghamshire. He would not join his county side again until their return match against Kent at Chelmsford in early August, and even then rain prevented any further play after tea on the first day. The amateur Stan Nichols, old enough to have been born in the last century, took up much of the slack with the new ball, finishing with 115 championship wickets at an average of 17. Towards the end of the season, Essex also gave an outing to their 20-year-old seamer Harry Daer. Earning a basic £3 a week from the county, he was a classic case of an outstanding young prospect who never quite settled down into first-class cricket. Daer had taken 3-21 in the first innings and 3-25 in the second on his county debut at Southend in June 1938, and the crowd had called him onto the balcony for a sustained ovation at the close. 'It seemed too good to be true,' the *Evening News* reported, and in fact it was; in Daer's eight remaining matches for Essex he took just 5 more wickets. His highest score in twelve innings with the bat was 17. Daer managed a total of nine first-class appearances in all before signing up for military duty in August 1939. He went on to serve with distinction in the Royal Army Service Corps, and never played for his county again after the war.

A vein of eccentricity ran through Essex cricket as a whole. They were led in the first part of the season by 31-year-old Capt. John Stephenson, a player who made up in exuberance what he lacked in natural ability. Known as Stan because of a passing resemblance to the comedian Stan Laurel, it was said to be 'nothing to see him haring down to Third Man after he had bowled a batsman out, and then return to his position via extra cover … the impression in general was of a dog hot off the leash'. With Stephenson back on active service with the army, the team was led by the hard-hitting batsman (and later garden-seed tycoon) Frederick St George Unwin. When Unwin in turn bowed out because of business commitments the captaincy passed to 29-year-old Denys Wilcox, who in civilian life was headmaster of Alleyn Court prep school in Westcliff-on-Sea, where he counted the young Trevor Bailey among his charges.

These were far from the only characters to be found in the ranks of Essex cricket in 1939. The 49-year-old Guyanese-born Brian Castor served as a supremely efficient if sometimes gruff county secretary, known for his habit of making public address announcements to any stray pigeons who had invaded the outfield. He was paid an annual salary of £450 (about £12,000 today), and in May 1939 the committee voted him a lump sum of £100 to buy a car. Born in 1875, Essex's cricketing vicar Frank Gillingham no longer played at first-class level, but was a constant presence on the county's grounds, where he was known for his habit of wearing a red velvet cap and an overcoat, whatever the weather. Gillingham strongly opposed the London County Council's proposal to allow recreational cricket to be played on Sundays on the grounds that this might lead down the 'slippery slope to competitive sport, and even to the opening of cinemas on the Sabbath'. In 1939 he was appointed chaplain to King George VI.

The 30-year-old Essex all-rounder Peter Smith, who had had the misfortune to be bowling when Harold Gimblett first exploded into life at Frome, was a trim, crisp-haired figure whose bearing might fairly have been described as military even before he signed up to serve in September 1939. Busy, vivacious, garrulous and good-hearted, he had nonetheless had to clutch hard at the remnants of his good humour when, on a non-playing Friday afternoon in August 1933, a message had been flashed on the screen of the cinema where he was sitting asking him to report immediately to the Essex county secretary. The secretary in turn showed Smith a telegram summoning him for international duty against the West Indies in the Test beginning the following morning at the Oval. Curiously, no one seemed to be particularly expecting him when he arrived at the ground. Eventually Smith asked Bob Wyatt, who was captaining England in the match, whether or not he would be in the final XI, and Wyatt had to admit that he had no idea what he was talking about. The telegram had not come from the MCC. Smith had to wait a further thirteen years before another message arrived inviting him to play for England at the Oval. This time it was genuine.

Glamorgan began their first match of the 1939 season only on 13 May, against Nottinghamshire at Trent Bridge. It was a somewhat uneven affair: Notts declared their first innings at 489-7 and the visitors replied with a total of 130 all out. A steady drizzle then kept the players from the field for much of the second day, when a small but vocal Monday crowd congregated around the refreshment tent at the Radcliffe Road end. According to the *Nottingham Journal*, 'frequent laughter emanated from that area when a spectator scored a repartee.' The umpires, who included the one-armed war hero Frank Chester, came out several times to inspect the wicket. One such visit 'brought a fresh round of satirical comment from among the throng', wrote the *Journal*. 'As the ale flowed the general noise dissolved into an occasional chant of "Why are we waiting?" and "We want cricket!"' The match was given up as a draw on Tuesday afternoon.

In those days there was an agreeable air of Welsh eccentricity about the Glamorgan club in general, which often contained three unrelated players with the same surname, as well as the teenaged batting prodigy Allan Watkins, who alternated between playing cricket, sitting his school exams and appearing on the wing for Cardiff City FC, and a swing bowler named Jack Mercer, a Great War veteran who was 46 years old but still good enough to bowl 500 overs in a season.

Glamorgan's captain was the 33-year-old amateur Maurice Turnbull, an accomplished all-purpose sportsman who was a champion squash and hockey player, a fencer, and to this day the only man to have played international cricket for England and rugby for Wales. In addition to all this, he was a scholar of racing form, a shrewd bridge player, knew his poetry and music, scrupulously attended the nearest Catholic church each Sunday, ran a successful insurance business, and wrote two well-received books. To the women of South Wales, Turnbull must have cut a dashing figure with his elegant tweed suit, oiled black hair and slightly disreputable smile, his close-clipped military moustache completing his resemblance to the actor David Niven. He had an eye for the ladies, too, at least up until the moment he married the former Elizabeth Brooke in September 1939. Turnbull was also the Glamorgan secretary, tirelessly raising funds to stave off the threat of bankruptcy from a club elevated to first-class status only in 1921, and frequently galvanising his fellow players and committee members alike with his exhortation, 'We must try to win, even if we lose!' He scored 1,234 first-class runs that season, including a lightning innings of 156 away to Leicestershire in what proved to be the final competitive match of his career. *Wisden* believed that Turnbull in general 'batted in a lively attractive style, and would probably have got many more runs had he not tried to punish the bowling directly he went in'.

On 6 May 1939, as Germany pressed its claim to the disputed port of Danzig, a limited-overs cricket match began in blazing sunshine at the Maori Club's tree-lined Ivydene ground in Worcester Park, Surrey. The visiting Oxshott team beat their hosts by 33 runs. It would have been hard to recognise the bucolic setting, with its modest crowd of men in formal double-breasted suits and women in full dresses, some of them holding parasols, promenading between the perfectly spaced oaks and terraced flower beds, as part of the same world then teetering on the brink of war. The midweek *Sutton Post* remarked that there was a 'lovely, if slightly random' feel to the ground, with a low wooden structure at one end and a row of ancient seaside deckchairs at the other. Never in the very top flight of sports arenas, Ivydene simply presented 'the pleasant vista of a prolonged tea party to a gentle backdrop of play,' the *Post* said.

Opening the batting for the Maoris was the lean, wavy-haired figure of Nigel Bennett, of whom the *Post* wrote: 'The first three balls he faced shaved his wicket. The fourth, dropped in short, sped to the boundary off the batsman's ear. But this was only a temporary reprieve, as the next ball flattened his centre stump.' The 25-year-old Bennett was not a complete duffer, however. He had been the star batsman at Stowe School in the early 1930s and had gone on to score a respectable 38 on his debut for the Surrey seconds against Kent in May 1936. By then Bennett was in the army, where he eventually rose to the rank of major, and his cricketing opportunities were necessarily limited until after the war. It was then that he became an unwitting entrant into the game's folklore by being appointed his county's captain in error.

According to *Wisden*:

Alec Bedser called it simply 'the cock-up', and blamed it on the general muddle everywhere after the Second World War ... Events apparently unfolded like this: When Monty Garland-Wells, Surrey's chosen skipper for the first post-war season of 1946, had to withdraw, the committee decided to offer the leadership to Major Leo Bennett, a well-known and talented club cricketer. While the search was on for Major Leo, Major *Nigel* Bennett popped in to renew his membership after the war. The pavilion clerk took the papers in to the secretary, who happened to have the chairman with him: they offered the captaincy to this Major Bennett, who accepted. He soon revealed his inexperience, twice rolling the new ball back along the ground from the covers for overthrows past a gob-smacked Alf Gover ... In a later match, Bennett asked Jim Laker to open the bowling; when Laker pointed out that he was actually an off-spinner, the captain said 'But you bowl quick too, don't you?'

Nigel Bennett eventually played thirty-one first-class matches for Surrey, resigning his position at the end of the 1946 season with a batting average of 16. The 42-year-old Errol Holmes, another major, returned as county captain in 1947 and Bennett moved to the West Country, where he played club cricket for Taunton. He died in 2008, at the age of 95.

Retrospectively, the early part of the 1939 season seems like one of idyllic serenity, with a strong England team preparing to meet a richly talented and pleasant touring side, among several other attractions. As well as a full schedule of county and club cricket, so far as the weather allowed, there was a busy programme of schools matches. On 23 May Bradfield College crushed St Edward's, Oxford, by 165 runs, thanks in part to a 'rasping' innings of 46 by 17-year-old Ben Brocklehurst. A gifted all-round athlete, Brocklehurst went on to join the Indian Army and was once attacked by a bear, which he 'wrestled to a draw', while posted in Kashmir. After the war he played 64 first-class matches for Somerset and later bought the *Cricketer* magazine. Brocklehurst's approach to the MCC in the early 1970s about their hosting a World Cup did not progress, because the powers-that-be at Lord's thought it 'too commercial' an idea.

In the championship that same week, Kent beat Nottinghamshire at Trent Bridge and then took the train (third class) to Southampton, where they also won against Hampshire. For the first victory Kent owed most to their England batsman Bryan Valentine, who clubbed 201 in just over three hours at the crease. In time Valentine would return from the war, in which he was severely wounded during the Libyan campaign, to take over the county's captaincy from Gerry Chalk.

In the Hampshire match, Kent turned the tables on their hosts by clearing their first-innings arrears and then setting their opponents 288 to win. The home team's response was a calamitous innings of 108 all out. After stumps, an elegantly suited man in his mid-30s with strong cheekbones and a prominent chin knocked at the door of the visitors' dressing room and invited everyone out for a drink, an offer they accepted. Their benefactor was the former Kent and England batsman Geoffrey Legge, who had given up cricket some years earlier in order to go into business with the family paper and pulp-shipping firm. Legge's subsequent success in this field had allowed him to buy a deluxe twin-engine Percival Q6, which he had flown in for the occasion to Southampton's Eastleigh airport from his private airfield close to the Legges' family home at Harlyn Bay in Cornwall. Three hours later, after lavishly entertaining his former county colleagues at the Star Hotel, Legge was on his way to a sales meeting in Paris.

For a cricket team visiting Britain in 1939, a tour didn't start, as it would now, with a token county warm-up or two before plunging into a hectic round of ODIs, T20s and occasional Test matches. The West Indies party that assembled in London in late April was due to play no fewer than eighteen full-scale matches before they met England in the first Test at Lord's two months later. The side's preparations continued with a three-day game against Lancashire at the 3,000-seat Aigburth Park in Liverpool. Founded in 1807, it was another of those agreeable, slightly run-down provincial grounds, with a log fire burning in its pavilion hearth, some weather-stained municipal benches, and a little green press box perched over the fine-leg boundary where E. W. Swanton had the feeling 'a strong gust of wind would deposit one in the street below'. A pudding of a pitch found the tourists groping with unfamiliar problems, and their captain Rolph Grant had to retire after being struck on the knee early in the match. Rain fell on the third day, and as a result the final session lasted just forty minutes. Headley filled most of this time by an unbeaten innings of 76, but the West Indies never seriously attempted to make the 247 needed to win. They closed at 142-3, and the *Liverpool Post* said that the small crowd went home 'damp but generally contented with a contest between two well-matched teams. Honour had been satisfied'.

Approaching his 30th birthday, George Headley was clearly in a class of his own at Liverpool, and for that matter in very nearly every other forum where cricket was played. On his previous tour of England in 1933, he had scored 50 in the first Test at Lord's, 169 not out in the second Test at Old Trafford, and before he could get going at the Oval in the third Test he was stumped while trying to deposit the Lancashire spinner 'Father' Marriott over the legside gasometer. Headley finished that series with an average of 66.28. He was largely uncoached, and arguably a more 'natural' batsman than Bradman, with whom he was often compared. No one ever hit a shot further at the Sydney cricket ground than Headley did when he smacked the medium-pacer Stan McCabe over the Ladies' Pavilion and into nearby Driver Avenue during a tour match against New South Wales in 1930. *Wisden* judged Headley to be the best batsman of the 1939 season, 'technically quite as accomplished even as W.R. Hammond'. Charles Fry, the former England captain turned journalist, wrote that Headley's 'middle name should be Atlas', suggesting that he carried the team on his back. Despite his habitual modesty, the West Indian was well aware of his popular reputation – 'If I rest for a match, the local spectators are hurt and I take stick in the press,' he remarked at one point in the long 1939 series.

In Headley and Learie Constantine, the West Indies had two of the finest examples of the proverbial swashbuckling calypso cricketer who ever played the game. Both men also relished a good challenge and would go to some lengths to meet it. Headley loved to bat on wet wickets, which was just as well in the England of 1939, and later in the summer he went berserk in a match against Nottinghamshire after a small knot of Saturday afternoon spectators, under the handicap of the rough local ale, started up a racially insensitive chant. The result was an unbeaten innings of 234 scored in just over five hours. Constantine for his part admitted that he would sometimes bowl a bouncer at an English batsman for the 'sheer fun' of annoying the crowd. Bradman once said of him that he was as dangerous with the ball as Larwood had been, especially if 'teased or provoked in some way – such taunts were inevitably self-defeating on the perpetrator's part'.

Constantine later remembered in this connection that:

A deep fissure of intolerance then ran through much of the cricket-playing world. There may have been a veneer of civility and acceptance in polite society, but it was a very different thing when you found yourself trying to enrol in bed and breakfast lodgings in rural England. Many in the white majority were reluctant to accept the concept of all races being on equal footing; and where discrimination was officially proscribed, some took the law into their own hands to inflict it.

This was a reference, perhaps, to the urbane Jack Kidney's conversation with the stupendously unintellectual manager of the Plymouth municipal baths, among other such incidents.

In later years, Constantine was at pains to make the distinction between the 'friendly and often warmly hospitable' reception the West Indians had received from most ordinary cricket lovers the length and breadth of Britain, and the 'localised racial hatred' they sometimes encountered in hotels and restaurants.

> The old bugaboos of black men preying upon white women and being morally devious played into people's fears. We were fine so long as we restricted ourselves to playing sport. The problems began when one of our chaps tried to assert himself as a true character rather than as a jolly little calypso cricketer.

When Constantine later came to reflect on which of his 1939 West Indian teammates could fairly be described as such a character, he found he was somewhat spoilt for choice. We've seen how the fiery Jamaican seamer Leslie Hylton had joined the side as a last-minute addition only after riots had broken out at the news of his omission from the original party. There had already been some lively interplay between Hylton and the British public even before the cricket began when the West Indies had attended a musical in London. This was not an entirely isolated social lapse on the player's part. In general Hylton seems to have been of the 'brilliant but bolshy' fast-bowling school, whose impulsive, sometimes tempestuous nature tended to make him a popular target. There was the time, for instance, indignant at an unsuccessful LBW appeal, when he threw the ball 70 yards into an unoccupied section of the stands at Northampton. In the tour's next match, at Derby, Hylton flung a handful of dirt into the face of the home batsman George Pope (after, he said, Pope cursed at him for bowling a bouncer), and just a few days later he had to be dissuaded from wading into the members' seats at Lord's before he could confront another heckler there. Constantine once said of his hot-headed West Indies colleague that he was 'known, and generally admired, for his passionate nature and aggressive, never-say-die outlook', which was undoubtedly true, if perhaps inaptly phrased when it came to the player's private life. In October 1954, Hylton was sentenced to death for the murder of his wife Lurline (the daughter of Jamaica's former Chief of Police) and went to the gallows at the island's Spanish Town Prison on 17 May 1955, at the age of 50. He remains the only Test cricketer to have been executed.

Elsewhere in the West Indies party there was the 28-year-old wicket-keeper-batsman Ivanhoe 'Ivan' Barrow, also from Jamaica, who can be said to have laboured under the twin handicaps in the prevailing climate of 1939 of being both mixed race and Jewish. In July 1933, at Old Trafford, he became the first West Indian to score a century in a Test match in England, while George Headley, at the other end, remained stranded on 99. After the first Test in the 1939 series Barrow gave way to the side's second-string wicketkeeper, Derek Sealy, who had his own place in cricket history as a result of having made his international debut just after his 17th birthday, which still gives him the distinction of being the young-est ever Caribbean player to represent his country. Both Barrow and in turn Sealy bravely elected to stand up to the bowling of their col-league Manny Martindale, who had taken a leaf from Harold Larwood's book and liberally bounced the English batsmen during that same Old Trafford Test in 1933. 'The home side were discomfited,' *The Times* had been forced to admit, as Wally Hammond left the field with a bruised jaw, and Les Ames went out to replace him audibly humming 'Nearer My God to Thee'. Martindale finished with 14 wickets in the three-match series, which was more than the other nine West Indian bowlers managed between them.

Also on tour in 1939 were men like Carlos 'Bertie' Clarke, a 21-year-old leg-spinner from Barbados who stayed on after the cricket to read medicine at Guy's Hospital in London. Although popular and successful in his postwar career as a Northamptonshire GP, the local press reported that Clarke had eventually 'been forced to accept the hospitality of the Crown for three years' due to the illegal termination of a pregnancy. The doctor emerged from prison to play English league cricket until well into his 60s, finishing his career with an appearance for the Old World XI against Old England at the Oval in September 1983.

Joining Clarke in the West Indies side that last pre-war summer was the 27-year-old American-born batsman Ken 'Bam Bam' Weekes, cousin to Everton, who as his sobriquet implies liked to get on with it in the middle; 19-year-old Gerry Gomez, an all-rounder who also played top-level football and tennis and who went on to be an important rallying figure in developing the world-beating West Indies sides of the 1980s; and his fellow Trinidadian Jeff Stollmeyer, 18, who would similarly enjoy a distinguished second career in cricket administration and who died in September 1989, aged 68, as a result of being shot while confronting intruders to his Port of Spain home. Taken as a whole, these were not men who were reluctant to express an opinion. When in May 1939 Ivan Barrow tried to show his solidarity with the plight of Europe's Jews in an article he proposed to submit to the *News Chronicle*, his team manager blocked it. 'Mr Kidney says I must hold it to after the tour,' Barrow wrote to his friend, the *Jamaica Gleaner* executive Michael De Cordova. 'I wish I were free!'

Barrow later remarked that, while proud to represent his country on an overseas tour, 'You could argue that we toiled under a slave's terms and conditions, although a slave would probably have had better overnight lodgings than we did.' The West Indies board's boilerplate contract called for their three full-time players, Headley, Constantine and Martindale, to each be paid a basic £500-575 for his services, along with a £50 kit allowance and the faint prospect of a share of any profits. As a result, they earned around £4 a day, or the equivalent of £1,460 a year, which would translate as roughly £105 and £38,000 in today's money. All sixteen cricketers were able to claim £250 apiece for their personal expenses incurred on the tour, from which they were expected to bear the cost of any additional blazers, caps, flannels or boots they might require over and above the standard issue. If a West Indies player happened to crack his bat or tear his trousers in the course of a match representing his country, it was down to him to make his way to Jack Hobbs's sportswear shop in London's Fleet Street or one of its regional counterparts and buy himself a replacement.

George Headley later admitted that the confidence he exuded on the field of play was achieved only by means of 'constant worry'. By that he meant that he was concerned not just about the opposition bowlers, on whom he kept elaborate notes, but about 'basic matters of sustenance for my wife Rena', who was back home in Jamaica heavily pregnant with their son, the future West Indies batsman Ron Headley. The man widely acknowledged as cricket's greatest living batsman alongside Bradman and Hammond slept fitfully during the England tour, and by his own account was 'constantly turning things over in my mind'. Racially abusive fans found it increasingly easy to get under Headley's skin. He was tired and on edge most of the time, and later said he'd been 'virtually sleepwalking' when in late May he scored an unbeaten 116 against Essex at Chelmsford, after 'a night spent tossing and turning at a local fleatrap'.

On Saturday 13 May, the West Indies began what was intended to be a three-day match against the MCC at Lord's. Denis Compton, English cricket's brilliant but chaotic *enfant terrible*, scored 115 on the first morning and had a brief stand with Yorkshire's Norman Yardley before, somehow inevitably when batting with that particular partner, Yardley was run out. MCC finished the day on 435-7, with 104 coming in the last thirty minutes, and rain then prevented any further play. There was an official dinner for both teams on the miserably wet Monday night of 15 May. The story later circulated that Leslie Hylton, after drinking perhaps more wine than was advisable, had at one point shouted down the table at Bill Edrich, 'Hey, shortarse, I'm coming after you in the Tests!' This account may or may not be apocryphal, but in any case Hylton never had the chance to do as he's alleged to have promised. Despite scoring 2,186 first-class runs at an average of nearly 50 that season, Edrich was ignored by England.

From Lord's the West Indies took the train to Cambridge, where play was again delayed by steady rain on the first morning. When proceedings began after lunch, Headley scored an unhurried 103 against the university attack, which was led by Patrick Dickinson and Udayasinhrao Gaekwar, both Indian-born, and Alan Shirreff, who was flying with the

RAF just over a year later in the Battle of Britain. Despite following on, the students held out for a draw. There was another bibulous dinner that night at the University Arms hotel, where high spirits prevailed. According to Ivan Barrow, everything went well enough until someone asked Shirreff to pass the soup and, anticipating his future career, 'he airlined it'. Barrow himself then ducked under the table, where he found Bam Bam Weekes already in residence. Someone else bowled a series of bread rolls down the tile floor. Before long it seemed as though the room had become the scene for one of those P.G. Wodehouse tales where Bertie Wooster consorts among friends with names like Pongo and Oofy and Catsmeat, with Jack Kidney acting the part of the imperturbable Jeeves when it came to getting everyone safely home and rousing them from bed in the morning with tea and kippers, and a treacle-and-red-pepper concoction that Barrow said 'tasted like axle grease' to rinse away the hangovers. The *Cambridge Evening News* reported merely: 'The students' steadiness in their second innings helped to save the match, which was played in a good spirit throughout.'

Kidney's restorative must have worked, because the West Indies were in action at 11.30 the next morning against Surrey at the Oval. Batting first on a wet wicket, they scored 224, the future England captain Freddie Brown taking 8-94 with mixed spin and seam. In the end it came down to a winning target for Surrey of 201, which they reached in the final session for the loss of three wickets. Leslie Hylton had match figures of only 1-82, and it may have been for this reason that he reacted poorly to the idiocy of a middle-aged man standing at the door of the Oval pavilion who bared his teeth and clutched himself under the armpits like a monkey when the West Indies players walked past. Hylton was angered, Ivan Barrow felt, because the spectator in question 'did not treat him with the elementary respect the white man accorded the coloured brother back in Kingston'.

In the championship, Yorkshire took on Gloucestershire at Park Avenue in Bradford – not only a study in contrasts between the business-like approach of the home side and their more volatile guests, but also a relatively rare first-class outing for the starkly utilitarian ground at

Bradford which finally closed its doors to professional cricket in 1996. Batting first after a lengthy rain delay, Yorkshire scored 253, with a Maurice Leyland century. The great left-hander was then approaching his 40th birthday and had made his county debut nearly twenty years earlier. Often more effective for England than Yorkshire, Leyland had scored an unbeaten 187 at the Oval in 'Hutton's Match' against Australia in 1938. He was a handy outfielder, too, and sometimes amused the crowd and himself by bowling 'chinamen' (left-arm off-breaks), a term he's widely credited with inventing.

Leyland's century at Bradford helped Yorkshire's captain Brian Sellers to declare on the third afternoon, leaving 100 minutes for play and 189 runs as a Gloucestershire target. Bill Bowes's first over cost 10 runs, his second was a maiden, and then Gloucester's Charlie Barnett went mad and hit the bespectacled seam bowler back over his head for six into a whelk stall. Shortly after that Hedley Verity appeared in the attack, but for once to little avail. After a few minutes of reconnaissance Barnett went down the track to him, missed – and was not stumped, the 40-year-old England Test keeper Arthur Wood comically fumbling the ball. Jim Kilburn of the *Yorkshire Post* wrote that it was now that 'the crowd's cold unhappiness could first be felt.' A few minutes later Barnett edged Verity's arm-ball to Herbert Sutcliffe at slip, and Sutcliffe, by general consensus one of the best close fielders in England, dropped it. This 'brought a fresh round of acerbic comment from those grouped at the bar', Kilburn noted. Although Barnett perished on 90, his team-mates saw Gloucestershire home by 6 wickets with five minutes to spare. Wally Hammond was unbeaten on 29 at the close. It was one of only two home defeats Yorkshire suffered all season, and whatever Sellers said to his men immediately afterwards in the dressing room seems to have worked because they won their next seven matches on the trot, five of them by an innings.

Stationed prominently in front of the beer tent on the last evening at Bradford was a broad-faced, 41-year-old man named George Gibson Macaulay. He had bowled right-arm seam and off-spin for Yorkshire, and on eight occasions for England, between 1920 and 1935. Blessed with a caustic wit, Macaulay had not been slow to offer advice to his former county colleagues from beyond the boundary rope. Verity, who did not enjoy one of his more productive matches, going for 33 off 3 overs, at one point trotted in with his neat, tiny steps and bowled a ball that skewed away far down the leg side for byes. An unmistakable voice from the crowd called out, 'Could tha not keep it on the cut grass, lad?' Kilburn later wrote that there had been 'appreciative laughter, not least from [Verity] himself, at this repartee'.

Macaulay had first played county cricket as a 22-year-old trainee bank clerk, when he appeared for Yorkshire as a shock fast bowler. Under the influence of George Hirst and Wilfred Rhodes, he cut his pace but developed his line and length to such effect that in June 1921, at Hull, he captured 7 Derbyshire wickets for a total of 12 runs. Eighteen months later he took a wicket with his first ball in Test cricket. Macaulay reached the top of his form in 1925, with 211 dismissals at an average of 15. He was everything that could be expected of a Yorkshire professional cricketer. Kilburn wrote not only that 'his run-up was half-shambling, his steps short and his shoulders swaying ... making for a fearsome, lumbering approach like that of a rugby forward', but that batsmen in general were his 'mortal enemies'. Crusoe Robertson-Glasgow described Macaulay as an unusual man, 'fiercely independent, witty, argumentative, swift to joy and anger'. Although titanically aggressive in the field, with a habit of catapulting a ball straight at an opponent's head, he would also applaud a skilful shot played off his own bowling. Summing him up, Robertson-Glasgow described Macaulay as 'a glorious foe; a great cricketer; and a companion in a thousand'.

Macaulay had married the former Edith Hay, who was three years older, in 1919. They had no children. He played his last championship match for Yorkshire in June 1935, by which time he was racked by lumbago that he treated with various homemade remedies in which beer played a not insignificant part. In September 1936 he opened a sportswear shop in Leeds, but this quickly collapsed leaving its proprietor £1,807 in debt, the equivalent of £50,000 today. As a result Macaulay appeared in West Yorkshire's bankruptcy court in

February 1937. He blamed 'competition' from other businesses for his downfall. However, the court also heard testimony that Macaulay never kept accounts, and never accepted that he was in financial difficulty. The *Guardian* report of the proceedings adds the detail: 'The respondent denied that he spent his whole life in public houses drinking.'

The following May, Macaulay was appointed the professional at Ebbw in Wales for the 1937 season. He spent 1938 and 1939 playing for Todmorden in the Lancashire League, and appeared for them in a match at the Centre Vale ground on the day after watching Yorkshire lose 20 miles away at Bradford. Macaulay took 3-43 in the single-innings win against Haslingden. His last appearance in the league came against Accrington on Saturday 2 September 1939, that long day of suspense between the rape of Poland and the formal declaration of war, recording figures of 0-18 and leaving the field, the *Telegraph* wrote, with 'the bowed gait of a man twice his age'. He had taken 1,837 first-class wickets and scored just over 6,000 runs in his fifteen-year career. Although he could easily have avoided service on the grounds of age, Macaulay promptly volunteered for the RAF, and in early 1940 was appointed Junior Messing Orderly, responsible for serving the officers' meals, at Sullom Voe in the Shetland Islands. This was not a job ideally suited to a man who already had pronounced views on the inequities of the British class system.

Yorkshire's unexpected loss at Bradford handed an opportunity to their arch rivals Middlesex – the one side by popular reputation stuffed full of stout-hearted professionals, the other the domain of blazered toffs with double-barrelled names and an ancient nanny in the attic – to challenge them at the top of the table. The southerners seized their chance with a 2-wicket win over Essex at Lord's. A draw seemed the most probable result with Middlesex facing a target of 224 in only two hours' play, but the 6ft 4in Wiltshire-born 'Big Jim' Smith, whom some credited with the furthest-carrying six in history, at Lord's in 1937, when he played a shot that cleared the Old Grandstand on the north side of the ground, hit up 45 in quarter of an hour, and victory came with two minutes to spare.

Middlesex went on from there to beat Northamptonshire at Lord's, Denis Compton and Bill Edrich adding 179 in just over two hours, but then, like Yorkshire before them, lost at home to Gloucestershire. Hammond scored 60 and 71 for the visitors. The end came with ten minutes to go on the suddenly warm final evening. The police took up station on the Tavern boundary, Arthur Wilson, the visitors' wicketkeeper, made the winning shot, and the crowd, except for a few sunbathers, trickled away past newly installed signs at the Grace Gate advising, 'In the event of an air attack, cover from shrapnel and debris should be obtained under the concrete stands.'

That same week, Lancashire, fourth in the table, drew with sixteenth place Somerset at Old Trafford. Harold Gimblett came out of his shell to score 108 in two hours, while his fellow opener Frank Lee defied the home bowlers all day for an unbeaten 155. Lancashire went on to draw with Oxford University and to lose successively to Warwickshire and Yorkshire in their remaining fixtures of May 1939 and found themselves suddenly floundering at eighth place in the table as a result. The traditional Whitsun Roses Match, held that year at Old Trafford, was a massacre. Lancashire at least got off to a reasonable start with a first innings of 300. In a comic touch, the *Guardian* newsstand pitched at the ground's Warwick Road end on the Saturday evening of 27 May read 'Nutter Goes Mad', referring to the home batsman Bert Nutter's achievement in scoring a rapid 85. On Bank Holiday Monday, Yorkshire responded with 528-8 declared, with centuries from Herbert Sutcliffe and Arthur Mitchell. The third and final day belonged to Bill Bowes. He took 6-43 off 19 overs and Lancashire lost by an innings.

During this same period Nottinghamshire, in mid-table, drew with Glamorgan, lost to Kent, and then won at home against Surrey. Rain was a persistent theme in all three fixtures. The ruddy-faced Claude Lewis of Kent was taking a lot of wickets with his left-arm spin and finished the summer eighth in the national bowling averages. He achieved little more, at least in terms of raw numbers, during the remaining twelve years of his career. After his playing days, he became successively Kent's coach and scorer, finally retiring at the age of 80. Shortly before his death, Lewis, one of those men whose lifelong devotion to cricket does not necessarily stem from statistical success on the field, was awarded the British Empire Medal for services to the sport.

Nottinghamshire checked their vertiginous slide down the championship table with a hard-fought win over Surrey at Trent Bridge in late May. The best cricket came on the last day. Needing 263 to win, the home side were in some bother at 48-3 when George Gunn joined Joe Hardstaff in the middle. They were still there four hours later when Gunn hit the winning runs. Both these solidly named players showed what Neville Cardus called a 'phlegmatic concentration' on the job at hand, leavened by an occasional 'fine clumping hit when the chance arose' and a willingness to 'fairly hurl themselves around in pursuit of a single' that prefigured the running in today's one-day cricket. Notts now sat at ninth in a championship table led by Yorkshire and Middlesex, with Essex, Kent, Worcestershire, Surrey, Gloucestershire and Lancashire coming up behind.

At Hove, meanwhile, Sussex comprehensively beat Glamorgan in what amounted to a lively game of lower-table leapfrog. The visitors scored a sorry 94 in their 38-over first innings, the last 8 wickets going down for 49 runs. Being the scorer for Sussex in 1939 was often complicated by the presence of two sets of nearly identical brothers in the first five of the batting order: John and James Langridge followed in turn by Harry and Jim Parks. Between them these four now put on 296, and Glamorgan batted for a second time against arrears of 356; they lost by an innings and 79 runs.

The visitors then climbed in their small convoy of cars and drove nearly 200 miles north up pre-motorway roads to Kettering, where they reached their local boarding house just before midnight. Maurice Turnbull recalled that a 'cold collation of sweating pink mutton and a plate of vivid blue and yellow sugared cakes, with a jug of lemonade' had awaited them on the sideboard. Nearby was a sign requesting that overnight guests not 'agitate the chain of the Water Closet after 10 p.m.' to ensure 'calm on the premises'. The place 'smelled obscurely of all the ghastly things of boarding school' added Turnbull, who as a teenager had attended Downside. The professional players slept three to a room that night and were greeted at first light by a tub of 'indeterminate bubbling grey liquid' that may have been porridge, and a greasy cup of lukewarm tea apiece. 'On that note we set off en masse to play championship cricket,' Turnbull said.

At 11.30 on the morning of Wednesday 24 May the Glamorgan eleven was duly on the field at the Town Ground for a three-day match with Northamptonshire. It was yet another of those provincial English cricket venues with certain physical limitations, among them a pronounced cross-slope to the pitch and a heavy roller that had first seen service during the reign of Queen Victoria. Set against this, the place had a 'quaint Midlands charm', Crusoe Robertson-Glasgow allowed, sitting there 'solid, ample and serene' with a branch railway line to one side and a clump of tall trees to the other. In a low-scoring match the visitors were left chasing 168 to win. *Wisden* wrote: 'Glamorgan went for the runs steadily until Turnbull, going in third wicket down, hit up 51 in 35 minutes ... With two successive sixes off Buswell he brought the match to an end in sensational fashion.' Following that the Welshmen again took to their cars and drove another 200 miles through the night back to Cardiff, where on 27 May they began a keenly awaited match with the West Indies.

Hampshire for their part began a dismal run of six consecutive championship losses, going down to Worcestershire, Middlesex, Kent, Lancashire, Yorkshire and Lancashire again in the space of just twenty days. It was hard to argue with *Wisden*'s verdict that the county 'lacked real fighting spirit', although there was an exception to the rule in 31-year-old John Arnold, who finished the season with 1,467 first-class runs at an average of 35. He had played a lone Test for England against New Zealand in 1931, scoring 0 and 34, and enjoyed no further international recognition. Hampshire's opener Neil McCorkell and the left-handed Donald Walker also at least fitfully contributed with the bat. Watching them in the middle at the United Services Ground in Portsmouth, the local *Chronicle* once wrote that 'The two seemed to be the mirror image of one another, and looking from one batsman to the other and back again you might have thought they were twins who

would never be separated in life.' Sadly, this proved to be an only modestly gifted prediction of future events, because Walker died in 1941,
aged 28, while McCorkell lived to be 100.

Northamptonshire continued to be the running joke of English
county cricket, at least up until the moment they hosted Leicestershire
at Northampton's Wantage Road ground in late May. We've seen that
even under their enterprising young captain Robert Nelson the team
had still managed only to draw one and lose three of their first four fixtures, most recently at home to Glamorgan. The *Daily Echo* praised the
club's 'useful Colonial', the New Zealand leg-spinner Bill Merritt, but
criticised the side's lack of batting depth and called their much-vaunted
recruit from Sussex, Bill Greenwood, 'the official flop of the line-up'.
('I was hurt by that remark,' Greenwood later told E. W. Swanton in a
radio interview.) The wicketkeeper-batsman Ken James was another 'sad
story', the *Echo* believed, while a clown's red nose could just as easily
have adorned the all-rounder Jack Timms, whose 'risible' medium-pace
bowling accounted for just thirty-one victims at an average of 41 all
season. There was a bright spot in the middle-order form of 23-year-
old Dennis Brookes, the winner of a sole England cap after the war, but,
as the *Echo* remarked, 'no one involved was entirely blameless for the
prolonged disgrace'.

Fortunately, Northamptonshire had forgiving fans. There were no
fewer than 6,152 paying customers packed into the small County
Ground on the Monday afternoon of 29 May to see their team reverse
their fortunes in dramatic fashion by beating Leicestershire by an
innings and 193 runs. It was the home side's first championship success
in a sequence of exactly 100 matches, dating back four years, and it
surely remains one of the most unintentionally impressive records in
any major sport. That evening's headline 'NORTHANTS CRICKET
WIN' was a sort of pre-JFK moment, news so viscerally shocking that
the individual would never forget where he or she was when they heard
it. At the close on a suitably sunny and warm bank holiday, hundreds of
spectators invaded the pitch, removing the stumps and swallowing up
the players. A few minutes later they were massed under the pavilion

balcony shouting 'Speech, Speech!' The baby-faced Robert Nelson obliged. Dressed in his immaculate white flannels, a blue blazer and a striped cravat, he was said to have faced the crowd and 'raised his arms in a quieting gesture like Moses parting the water … The hordes below immediately fell silent.'

'We are naturally pleased to have broken our spell of bad luck,' Nelson announced in a level, classless voice, betraying no sign of the performance anxiety that he said always afflicted him on such occasions. 'We hope further victories are in store,' he added, with a broad grin. That concluded Nelson's public remarks. Even the non-drinking players had gotten 'thoroughly crocked' that night, the young captain admitted. No one present could have guessed that the county's next success in the championship would in fact come only in July 1946, when they beat Glamorgan at Rushden by 4 wickets, and that Nelson himself would not be alive to see it. The innings win against Leicestershire at least helped Northants to rise off the bottom of the table, a position they had occupied in five consecutive seasons.

If anyone gave Robert Nelson a run for his money as a progressive young county captain it was Gerry Chalk of Kent. The 28-year-old Oxford blue may have been only modestly gifted when judged by the highest first-class standards – finishing the 1939 season with a batting average of 29 – but he possessed a cool head and an acute cricketing brain, as well as the priceless ability to make every man on the team feel as though he alone were the captain's favourite. When, in late May, Kent drove up the coast to play Hampshire at Southampton, Chalk took the county's talented but sometimes oddly diffident Test opener Arthur Fagg aside and told him that the wicket that day might have been expressly made for him, and that he knew for a certain fact after having visited them in their dressing room that 'these Hampshire buggers are fucking terrified of bowling at you'. Fagg, whose previous eight knocks of the season had brought him a total of 86 runs, promptly went out and smashed 149 to help set up a win for the visitors on the third afternoon. Kent then lost their next match, on a green pitch away to Derbyshire at Ilkeston, by 5 wickets. Since the opening firm of

Fagg and 22-year-old Peter Sunnucks was still underperforming, Chalk politely asked Sunnucks to take a well-earned break and promoted himself up the order for the county's next match against Sussex at the Angel Ground in Tonbridge. He scored 198, helping Fagg to put on 171 in two hours. Kent won by an innings. When Glamorgan appeared at Tonbridge to begin a match the following morning, Chalk called Sunnucks over and told him with a warmly encouraging smile that he thought he could do most damage if he batted at number six. Sunnucks later remembered that 'the skipper could make you feel as though you were walking on a red carpet all the way from the dressing room to the middle, and that the other lot's bowlers were positively shitting themselves just to see you come out.' It took Sunnucks some moments before he realised that he had actually been demoted in the order. The previously ineffectual batsman scored an unbeaten 54 at nearly two runs a minute in the draw with Glamorgan.

When it came to Kent's wicketkeeping position, Chalk and his committee found that they were spoilt for choice. Hopper Levett remained the man in possession, while in 33-year-old Les Ames the county had arguably the greatest batting wicketkeeper the game had yet produced. In April 1939 Ames had told his captain that he was suffering from back trouble and now preferred to play solely as a batsman, going on to score 1,846 first-class runs in the season at an average of 46. Waiting in the wings behind these two sometime England Test stumpers, meanwhile, Kent also had a young tearaway bowler on their books named John Pocock. He, too, increasingly took on the wicketkeeping duties for the Club and Ground XI when he failed to progress in his career as a second Larwood. On occasion, even the opening bat Arthur Fagg liked to pull on the gauntlets.

Despite this embarrassment of riches, Chalk had kept his eye closely on Godfrey Evans as the teenager continued to periodically appear for the county's second eleven. Later in July, Chalk gave Evans his chance to graduate to the senior team against Surrey at Blackheath. He was there solely as a batsman, scoring 8 in his only innings, although the real point of the exercise had been to give him a taste of life at the top.

A week later, Levett was away on duty with the Territorial Army and Evans made his first-team debut behind the stumps against Derbyshire at Gravesend. Norman Harding, a bowler of better than medium pace, sent down the second over. The first ball cut back off the seam, clipped the inside edge of the Derbyshire captain's bat and jagged down the leg side. Evans took off like a bird in flight and caught it. The next week's *Kent Messenger* ran an action photograph of the dismissal on the front page. Les Ames, standing at short leg, strolled up to the young keeper and said, 'You may never make a better catch than that.' Gerald Hough wrote a note in the club's minute book remarking that 'Evans did grand work' on his debut in the position he would soon make his own, and that 'considering his youth and natural exuberance he should be able to build a considerable career for himself'. Hough added, in a more private assessment: 'One just prays he will keep his feet on the ground.'

While the Northamptonshire players were nursing their hangovers following their historic win over Leicestershire, the touring West Indies were in action against Glamorgan at Cardiff Arms Park, then little more than a tree-lined meadow with a wooden stand at either end before being bulldozed to make way for a 65,000-seat stadium thirty years later. Maurice Turnbull scored a run-a-ball 60 in Glamorgan's first innings of 377, but the real hometown hero was the burly 26-year-old all-rounder Wilf Wooller. A sportsman par excellence, Wooller, coming down from Cambridge with a degree in anthropology, had already been capped eighteen times for Wales at rugby, played centre forward with Cardiff City FC, represented his nation at squash, boxed a bit, and casually turned to county cricket to fill in time during his annual holiday from his job as a shipping clerk in the Cardiff docks. He was an immediate success for Glamorgan, taking 5-90 in his maiden bowling spell against Yorkshire. Wooller was as ruthless on the field (where he liked to stand at short leg, exchanging pleasantries with the batsman) as he was genial off it. He went on to captain Glamorgan from 1947 to 1960, became full-time secretary of the club in 1961 and was elected its president thirty years later. When you add the fact that Wooller was also an outstanding and often controversial journalist, with decided views on the apartheid regime in South Africa, served as an England Test selector for seven years, and had the most heroic of all possible wars, you were left with one of the great renaissance men anywhere in mid-twentieth-century Britain. Wooller scored 111 in two hours in the 1939 match against the West Indies, which Glamorgan won by 73 runs.

As we've seen, Yorkshire had triumphed easily in the Roses Match played that same week at Manchester. Despite the result, the Lancashire treasurer can't have been too unhappy: there were 41,848 paying customers through the Old Trafford turnstiles over the three days, and 'street fakirs' selling red and white rosettes, official or unofficial programmes, scorecards, team photographs and 'Eddie Paynter novelty hats' could be found lurking in many corners in and around the ground. Dawn on Saturday 27 May saw hundreds of spectators of all ages lined up to buy tickets and, as the *Guardian* reported: 'Oranges and nuts were sold as at a village fair, and the raucous voices of the vendors were heard on every side. Brightly iced buns commanded an enormous sale among the younger bystanders.'

Despite the relative windfall of the traditional Whitsun derby with their rivals from across the Pennines, Lancashire, like every other first-class county, still struggled to foot their bills. The club showed an operating profit of just £3,100 in 1938, and by the following spring was writing to appeal to its members to consider adding a 'gift or subvention' to their annual subscriptions. It was much the same story at Derbyshire, where the minutes for 1939 note that 'the wet summer was of disastrous consequence at the gates'. Even the comparatively affluent London clubs were financially strapped. The Surrey committee were worried about meeting an estimated £250 bill for repairs to the Oval pavilion roof, without which a 'wholesale collapse thereof may ensue', while Walter Robins, the 33-year-old secretary at Middlesex, regularly engaged the MCC authorities in discussion about the exact terms of his county's lease of the playing facilities at Lord's. The essence of 'The

Agreement' (as it was known in the MCC minutes) was that Middlesex paid £900 (around £25,000 today) to host roughly a dozen matches on the ground each year, along with a small percentage of ticket sales and other revenue. Robins, a once and future county captain, and holder of nineteen England Test caps, spent a significant amount of his time in the summer of 1939 walking up and down the pavilion stairs, accounts book in hand, from his office to the nearby MCC committee room.

Under the circumstances, it's not surprising that many professional cricket clubs and individual cricketers, like their Edwardian predecessors, turned to wealthy patrons to supplement their incomes. Nottinghamshire, for one, were generously subsidised by 56-year-old Sir Julien Cahn, an eccentric Welsh-born businessman of German-Jewish descent who had made a fortune in the hire purchase furniture trade. Dark eyed, with a bushy moustache and a bulbous W.C. Fields nose, it was said he 'lived for cricket and sex', in so far as he made a distinction between the two. Between 1929 and 1939, Cahn invested the fabulous sum of £20,000 (£650,000) a year in the facilities at Trent Bridge, paying the annual subscriptions for 800 new members of the Nottingham club in 1935 alone. In time he installed his own full-scale cricket ground at his stately home at Stanford Hall near Lutterworth in Leicestershire (another county he helped bankroll), where he hosted regular Sunday afternoon matches during the summer months. Cahn was the John Paul Getty Jr of his day. Those lucky enough to come into his orbit were inundated with cash and other perks. Following stumps at Stanford Hall the players would each be handed an envelope stuffed with crisp £5 notes and then entertained to a lavish dinner followed by a performance in Cahn's private theatre, complete with a Wurlitzer organ that went up and down on a hydraulic platform in front of the stage. There were generous additional bonuses for any cricketer who made a special contribution with bat or ball. Not surprisingly, by 1939 there was intense competition on the county circuit to catch Cahn's eye.

The author Duncan Hamilton, writing in his biography of Harold Larwood, adds the detail:

Cahn also arranged and paid for winter tours (with Fortnum and Mason hampers for the players) and always captained his own team. The visiting tourists would be invited to play his own XI, and Cahn had ten nubile 'ladies' waiting for them. There were only ten because 'the bugger' who got Cahn out wasn't to be included in the pleasures of the bedroom. Cahn wore inflatable pads, which were pumped up by his general factotum-cum-butler. Deliveries flew off them like a tennis ball thrown against a brick wall.

On 31 May 1939, Cahn hosted a two-innings match played at Wardown Park, Luton, between his own invitation XI and Bedfordshire of what was then called the 'County Championship – 2nd Division'. For once the sun shone brightly, the ground hummed, the pitch looked perfect and there was a brass band to welcome the players on to the field. The New South Wales all-rounder Harry Mudge was one of four visiting Australians in Cahn's team. 'The game was pretty well over in the first hour,' he recalled. 'Their quick bowler hit Sir Jules on the pads plumb in line. The ball shot back off them to somewhere near extra cover. Not out. The same thing again when he banged the ball to slip and the guy there fairly hurled it down as if it was red-hot. That set the tone for the contest.' The eventual scores were Sir Julien Cahn's XI 375, Bedfordshire 120 and, following on, 192. At stumps both sides got into a fleet of waiting black cars to be driven 50 miles up the road to Lutterworth. 'There was a bit of business that night in the old boy's heated swimming pool, which we shared with some local ladies and two performing seals,' Mudge recalled.

Back in the more austere world of everyday English first-class cricket, where the players waiting their turn to bat were known to relax to the big-band strains of Glenn Miller or Tommy Dorsey on the dressing-room wireless, there were increasingly grim news reports about the so-called Pact of Steel, or the latest German threats to central Europe. When parliament returned following the Whitsun break, Neville Chamberlain told MPs that if 'Herr Hitler should act unilaterally over Poland, we will have no alternative but to honour our guarantee to come to that country's support'.

4

'WE ARE THE PILGRIMS, MASTER'

When *Wisden* came to name Bill Edrich of Middlesex and England as one of its Five Cricketers of the Year in 1939, the almanack tempered its praise for the 23-year-old player's all-round prowess with the verdict, 'No other cricketer has ever been so persevered with in the face of continued non-success as a run getter.' After being dismissed in consecutive South African Test innings for 4, 10, 0, 6 and 1, *Wisden* reminded its readers, 'Edrich, his detractors now howling with glee, most dramatically came back into his own when he produced a magnificent 219 in that never-ending match at Durban.' It somehow seemed characteristic of a player who got by as much on sheer willpower as natural ability, and whose canny opportunism on the field was matched by the equally impressive self-destructive skills he often showed in his private life.

Both sides of the Edrich enigma were on view when the West Indies tourists came to play Middlesex at Lord's early in June 1939. The visitors batted first and scored 665. There were centuries for Jeff Stollmeyer and Derek Sealy, while George Headley lingered for just five hours over his chanceless innings of 227. On the Saturday the West Indies scored 491 runs for the loss of 3 wickets, and their eventual first innings total was the second highest ever hit at Lord's. Edrich later remembered that he had gone to some pains not to catch the eye of his captain, the 32-year-old Anglican vicar of Willian and occasional cricketer Rev. Tom Killick, and thus avoid becoming the next sacrificial bowler in the firing line. In the end he was called on for just 5 overs, finishing with the respectable figures of 1-24.

When inevitably it came time for Middlesex to follow on, 482 behind, Edrich entered into one of those stately periods he sometimes indulged in when the bowlers, like serving wenches, seemed intent merely to please him. He cut Martindale for a four that ricocheted back off the Tavern fence nearly as far as the aggrieved bowler's hand. A similar blow followed two balls later. When Rolph Grant finally dispensed with his slips, Edrich promptly carved Constantine's next ball through the newly vacated area for another four. He was not generally a man to take the attritional approach at the wicket, nor one to settle for a compromise in the face of overpowering odds. In the end Edrich scored what Neville Cardus called a 'magnificent but reckless cameo' of 51, displaying his 'fighting attributes [in] defying the bowlers by sheer grit and guts', which was at least enough to help delay the inevitable West Indies victory until the third day. The batsman himself later admitted that he had been suffering from a bilious hangover during his innings and had wanted simply to 'get on with it rather than spew up on the Lord's pitch'.

From there the Middlesex players drove 150 miles over increasingly rustic roads to Frome, where on 7 June they began a three-day match with Somerset. Edrich scored 71 and 0, Compton hit an unbeaten two-hour 103 in the final run push, and the visitors won by 5 wickets. Somerset's 37-year-old all-rounder Arthur Wellard, a good enough opening bowler to have been selected in that role for a Test against Australia, said of Edrich:

He was a little slinger whose preferred style was to hurl the ball down just as fast as he could. It usually came off the deck like bloody streaked lightning. As a batsman you had a double problem to cope with, because Edrich would fling himself halfway down the pitch after delivering, muttering at you all the way, and if you came out of your crease to play him you were always liable to meet the little bugger head-on in his follow-through.

Finding that he had a few hours to spare before driving back to London on the evening of 9 June, Edrich joined some of the Somerset players at the bar of Frome's Old Bath Arms hotel. In 1939 there was no such thing as respectable press interest in a cricketer's private life, and no question of a camera following him as he entered or left a pub. Investigative journalism (or muckraking, as it was then called) remained in its infancy. So Edrich was relatively free of the threat of public scrutiny when, in rapid succession, he drank himself first into a state of euphoria, then of belligerence, and finally of total coma, at which point Wellard and some of the other Somerset team located a wheelbarrow in which to push their distinguished opponent back up a side street towards the car park on Styles Hill where Middlesex's Laurie Gray, Ian Peebles and Jim Sims were waiting in Gray's antiquated but functional Austin Seven. 'It was a bloody long drive home,' Jim Sims confirmed. 'Bill was soon back in his merry state, and I had to shove a handkerchief in his gob when he started singing arias from *Madame Butterfly*.' Roughly twelve hours later, Edrich went out to play for Middlesex against the county champions Yorkshire at Lord's: he scored 1 and 9, and the visitors won by an innings.

At Tonbridge that week Kent's Gerry Chalk played his career's best innings of 198 against Sussex, while his teammate Leslie Todd contributed 143 from the lower order. In the next match against Glamorgan Todd added a further 115 not out. At that stage Chalk invited his newly prolific colleague to bat at number five in the county's next game away to Leicestershire. Todd scored 54 in his only innings. All this time he was also taking wickets with his left-arm bowling, which he could vary from orthodox spin to lively medium pace: 8-90 against Derbyshire on a damp wicket at Ilkeston, 3-33 on a batsman's paradise at Tonbridge, and match figures of 5-80 in Kent's win at Leicester. Todd bowled particularly effectively with the new ball later in the season against Lancashire at Old Trafford, mixing prototype-Derek Underwood floaters with other deliveries that reared up at the batsman's ribs. He was often genuinely fast, twice knocking the bat from Cyril Washbrook's hands. Jim Kilburn wrote of him that season: 'Whether hopping or sprinting to the wicket, his approach was always the signal for a dead hush in the crowd.'

Born in London in 1907, Todd overcame the early shock of being hit over the eye by Harold Larwood at Trent Bridge in May 1930 to play a total of 437 matches for Kent over a twenty-three-year career interrupted about halfway through by the war. He took over 80 wickets in five consecutive seasons, completing the double in 1937. Despite these achievements, Todd was not always regarded as a model teammate. In fact he could be a nightmare to deal with. The writer E.M. Wellings, admittedly known to occasionally dip his pen in vitriol, once described Todd as 'the most perverse, most infuriating cricketer of his generation', while even the more benign Crusoe Robertson-Glasgow conceded the player's temperament was 'a little suspect'.

Fifty years later, Les Ames recalled his own 'highly mixed' emotions about his Kent colleague during that last pre-war season, calling him 'ambitious and thoroughly selfish', if also a 'very capable performer on his day'. When not batting or bowling, Todd used to 'lumber around in the deep', Ames remembered. A good catcher, he was not otherwise greatly gifted in the field. 'If he happened to chase a ball to the boundary, another man would always follow him, waiting halfway back to the wicket, in order to collect his underarm throw and pass it on to the wicketkeeper,' Ames said. Todd had apparently also made some 'indelicate and objectionable' requests for better terms from the Kent committee. 'He was a stroppy bugger,' Ames added, 'but on his best days he was a useful bugger.'

Les Todd served with distinction in the Second World War, following which he returned for another five years with Kent. His benefit season in 1947 brought him around £1,500, or roughly £30,000 today. Todd blamed the eye problems that brought about his eventual retirement from cricket on the blow he had received from Larwood twenty years earlier. He went on to become a well-regarded umpire of the old school, but died, aged just 60, in August 1967. Ames remarked that Todd could be an 'awkward sod [who] always thought the boys upstairs in the committee room were a load of tossers who knew bugger all about cricket' – a not wholly unjustified view of some county authorities of the era – but added: 'I prefer to remember him in his sunny days, a big-hearted lad bounding down the pavilion steps at Canterbury before a tough match and telling us, "Come on you shower of shit – We'll murder them!"'

While Kent played Sussex during the sunlit Tonbridge week of June 1939, Yorkshire were disposing of Hampshire by an innings and 129 runs under heavy skies at Sheffield. Herbert Sutcliffe scored 116 and Len Hutton an unbeaten 280 in a partnership of 315 in just over four hours. You could have taken these two players, added in a couple of bowlers and a wicketkeeper, and they would have given a game to most county elevens in 1939. The northern side was winning match after match, often by crushing margins, and an article in the *Cricketer* that July asked simply: 'Why is Yorkshire supreme?' Forty years later, Hutton believed that it had largely been down to the team's balance of youth and experience: 'You had Herbert in his mid-forties and me in my mid-twenties. Verity was about 35 and [the off-spinner] Ellis Robinson was nearer my age, and he could bat a bit, too – he once put the Glamorgan fast bowler out of the Arms Park at Cardiff.'

'No one was unfriendly at Yorkshire,' Hutton continued in his reminiscence of the 1939 season. 'But they were never a sentimental club. No one ever jumped up and down if you scored runs or took wickets. It was your job. You had a feeling of being in a team of professionals.'

Derbyshire, meanwhile, demolished Worcestershire at Chesterfield, with the Pope brothers, Alf and George, both former miners, taking 12 wickets between them. The weather spoilt the county's next fixture against the West Indies. Thirty-one-year-old Bert Alderman, a right-handed batsman, occasional wicketkeeper, and former inside-left at Derby County, scored a rapid 90. Bad light probably saved the tourists from defeat, leaving them on 54-6 in pursuit of 150. The Derbyshire players then drove 160 miles through heavy rain to the Woodbridge

Road ground in Guildford, where on a waterlogged pitch they anni-
hilated a twice-collapsing Surrey by an innings and 43 runs. Alf Pope
took 6-44 in the first innings, and his younger brother George 5-46 in
the second innings. Despite stoppages, the game was all over before tea
on the second day.

There was a remarkable match around this time at Trent Bridge,
where Nottinghamshire beat Essex by 8 wickets. The small and trim
Jack O'Connor, who was fast approaching his 42nd birthday, scored 194
during a stay of five hours for the visitors. The opener Charlie Harris
replied with 196 for the home team. John Stephenson, the Essex captain,
still somehow juggling cricket with full-time army duties, then made a
possibly over-sporting declaration which set Nottinghamshire a target
of 238 in just over two hours. They knocked off the runs in 99 minutes,
with an unbeaten 93 from their sometime Test opener Walter Keeton.
Taken as a pair, Crusoe Robertson-Glasgow wrote, there was a 'comic
disparity' between the county's first two men as they came out to bat:
'Keeton strung up, concentrated, quick-glancing; Harris serenely dis-
trait, revolving idealistic strokes against an attack that would not occur;
lagging sometimes a pace or two behind, like a boy with a parent on an
unwilling Sunday walk.' Between them, Keeton and Harris scored 3,002
first-class runs in 1939.

In the normal course of affairs a three-day cricket match between
Glamorgan and Gloucestershire starting on a wet Wednesday morning
in Newport would qualify only as a sort of routine courtesy call by one
county side on the other. However, this particular fixture took on an
explosive aspect. The home team scored 196 in their first innings, their
opener Arnold Dyson unluckily stranded on 99 not out when he lost
his last three partners in an over. Gloucester's Walter Hammond had
meanwhile announced in the dressing room that he was indisposed
with lumbago and would prefer not to bat for the time being. Hearing
of this, Wilf Wooller, who had previous form with the brilliant but iras-
cible England captain, remarked over the tea interval that it was 'fucking
typical of Wally to sit on his arse and sulk' rather than to come out and
entertain the small but loyal crowd who had paid their entrance money

in large part to see this cricket icon in action. In time, Wooller's comments duly made their way back to the visitors' dressing room.

Hammond, it's true, did not always exert himself when taking part in a relatively inconsequential early-season fixture with the likes of Glamorgan. But now, stung possibly by Wooller's rebuke, and further stimulated by the offer of a cash win-bonus by Gloucester's president and all-round patron Sir Stanley Tubbs, he decided to let fly. Perhaps, with the rain blowing away and the pitch looking better and better for batting, he simply sniffed runs.

Anyway, it was carnage. The increasingly vocal crowd huddled around the Rodney Parade marquees were treated to a masterclass in controlled aggression. Hammond, all baggy cap and narrowed gaze, strode out to bat an hour before the close on the first day. At stumps he had run up an unbeaten 55. The next day he cut loose in a five-hour innings of 302, with 2 sixes and 35 fours, equalling the highest individual total ever made from Glamorgan bowling. At one stage he lofted a shot out of the ground and through a window of the nearby Corporation Road power station, a carry of some 130 yards. As a result, Hammond was able to declare Gloucestershire's innings at 505-5, giving the visitors a tidy lead of 309 on first innings. It wasn't quite enough. Dyson and his batting partner Emrys Davies went on to record 255 for Glamorgan's first wicket, and the match ended in a draw. It has to be said that Wooller's criticisms had proved spectacularly counter-productive on this occasion.

Hammond's purple patch continued in Gloucestershire's next match, at home to Surrey, where he scored 135 and brought up his 1,000 runs for the season in only his eighth match. Gloucester won by an innings. He then had a rare lapse against Sussex, managing only 33 and 8 on a damp wicket at Worthing, did little against Yorkshire at Bristol beyond letting the off-spinner Tom Goddard bowl the home side to victory with figures of 6-61 and 7-38, but then returned to form with consecutive innings of 153 not out at home to Kent (Goddard equalling a world record by taking 17 wickets in a day) and 207 against Essex at Westcliff.

While *Wisden* commended Hammond's 'masterly' leadership of Gloucestershire in 1939, others such as the Cambridge-educated Basil

Allen, his predecessor as county captain, did not approve. The author David Foot quotes an exchange of views between Allen and the MCC stalwart Sir Pelham Warner during the annual Gentlemen v Players match at Lord's:

'Basil, that Wally Hammond of yours really is a wonderful chap, isn't he?'
'If you want my honest opinion, Plum, I think he's an absolute shit.'

In general, Allen seems to have been one of those who felt that there was a touch too much of the cavalier in Hammond's approach to the job, and that, while undoubtedly a great batsman, he was also a 'moody bugger [who] took no interest in other people, unless they happened to be pretty girls'. As we've seen, the 36-year-old England captain by now led a somewhat enigmatic home life. Married since 1929 to the former Dorothy Lister, the daughter of a wealthy Yorkshire textile merchant, he was currently involved with both his future second wife Sybil and also, apparently, several other parties. An elderly Gloucestershire lady named Ursula Wicks remembered some years later:

I knew Wally Hammond from 1937–45 and for much of that time we hoped to marry. His wife had agreed to divorce him when he was sent abroad in 1940 but it was not [yet] possible ... He would never talk about cricket and could be moody and silent but, through it all, there was no doubt of his love for me.

Meanwhile, the real heart of English cricket – some would say of English life – continued to beat on the club, village and school grounds up and down the country. At a (for once) fine and dry Cambridge on 7 June, the university began a three-day match with the army. The 30-year-old batsman Charles Packe, formerly of Leicestershire and now the Royal Fusiliers, scored 145 in just over an hour at the crease during the sunlit second afternoon. It proved to be his final appearance in first-class cricket. The following day, a gaunt 35-year-old listed on the scorecard as 'Dunglass' – the future Sir Alec Douglas-Home – went out to bat for the Lords and Commons XI in a single-innings match at Eton College. The author J.B. Priestley said of the batsman (who scored 7) that he resembled 'a prematurely hatched bird, whose Adam's apple danced up and down a narrow neck adorned by a tightly-wrapped MCC cravat'. Dunglass had made ten first-class appearances between 1924 and 1927 and remains the only prime minister to have played cricket at that level.

Later that week, Julien Cahn's team went on to play Leicestershire's Club and Ground XI at West Bridgford. Cahn himself turned up, a dapper, monocled figure, in a burgundy Rolls-Royce complete with a full-scale cocktail cabinet folded into the boot. The weather had at last settled, with puffy white clouds high overhead and a cool breeze ruffling the nearby trees. When play began there were runs for most of Cahn's side, except Cahn himself. After scoring 7 in somewhat jittery fashion, he played on to the opposition's 17-year-old tearaway bowler Cyril Drake. Drake knew full well that the hire purchase tycoon would generously provide female company after the match for ten of his opponents, but not for 'the bugger' who personally dismissed him. The first 5 balls of the over he bowled to Cahn had duly passed far down the leg side. The sixth, also wide, took the inside edge of the bat and flew back to clip the top of middle stump. Cahn took a long look down the pitch at the offending bowler and then began to walk off. 'Hold on,' Drake shouted. 'It was a no ball … I didn't bowl you. You're not out.' 'Yes, I fucking well am,' said Cahn, reaching down, as if to illustrate the point, to release the air from his inflatable rubber pads. In addition to his disappointment later that night back at Stanford Hall, Drake would go on to play just seven more matches for Leicestershire, retiring at the age of 18 with a total of 19 wickets at 31 each, while with the bat he managed 43 runs at an average of 5.37, and a high score of 13. He died in 1992, aged 70.

Those who spend time around cricket come to appreciate the difficulty of making it to the top level. Scores of young boys – and increasingly, girls – dream of striding out in front of a packed house at Lord's. In 1939 most or all of them would have played some sort of organised schools cricket, where the process inevitably begins of some prospective stars moving ahead and others falling behind. By the time a young man of eighty years ago had managed to break into the county game he would have already vaulted past thousands of his contemporaries who had started out thinking that they, too, would play cricket for a living.

Tony Pawson, born at Chertsey in August 1921, was invariably self-deprecating when he later came to talk about his cricket career. It was the way he was brought up. But it was a lie. Pawson was one of those players, about equal parts raw talent and iron will, who was a superstar as a young man without ever quite going on to reach the very highest level. He was also a classic case study of an up-and-coming cricketer of his uniquely ill-fated generation. Pawson had just turned 18 when the war broke out. When it was all over he was nearly 24, and had lost what should have been his most productive early sporting years. He later remembered the strange feeling of emerging from the army with a longing to resume normal life, which 'largely meant cricket', co-existing with an equally firm conviction that, after seeing front-line service with the Rifle Brigade, and in particular 'picking up bits of one's friends' following an all-out assault on the Germans' deeply-entrenched position at Tunis in April 1943, 'playing games would somehow never really seem important again'.

On 13 June 1939, Pawson opened both his school's batting and bowling while captaining Winchester in an away match at Marlborough. He scored only 3 but did better with his right-arm spin to end with a haul of 5-27 off 22 overs. Nine days later Pawson hit 107 in just over an hour's batting at home to Harrow. In Winchester's next game he managed only 15 against Eton, but then bowled 13 thrifty overs for figures of 1-38, as well as catching the Eton number five Alastair Coats by holding onto a full-blooded drive while crouching under the batsman's nose at short-leg, and then, having done the really hard part, throwing in what seemed to some a slightly gratuitous somersault or two before emerging to toss the ball high into the air, the picture of a happy if untypically histrionic young cricketer.

By September 1939, said *Wisden*, Pawson was not only 'in a class by himself at Winchester' but qualified as school cricket's 'batsman of the year' – a cutter and hooker 'with a vigilance in defence beyond his years'. After the war he went on to represent Oxford University and Kent, although his guiding approach to sport, as well as his status, was amateur. Just a few months older than his demobbed county colleague, Godfrey Evans remembered that Pawson had sometimes announced that he was missing a particular match to go fishing. 'You had to admire the guy's neck. His attitude was "I've been through the war and seen my mates being blown to bits in front of my eyes. You won't spoil my fun again."'

Pawson also won a blue at football, appeared on the wing in two matches for Charlton Athletic, scoring on his league debut against Spurs, and won an FA Amateur Cup-winners' medal at Wembley in 1951. He had steadied his nerves before this last occasion by downing a large whisky in the dressing room. Pawson appeared for Kent intermittently until 1953, once actually found himself playing in front of a full house at Lord's when he went out to bat for MCC against the South Africans, later became the cricket and football correspondent of the *Observer*, and somehow also made time for a successful business career as personnel director of Reed International. Trim, white-haired and beatifically laid-back, he exuded what amounted to an almost zen-like calm amid all the beery exuberance of the typical 1970s cricket press box, where the prevailing ethics would have caused comment at a particularly louche Rolling Stones party. In 1984 Pawson went on to become the world fly-fishing champion. Four years later, at the age of 66, he was awarded the OBE for services to angling. Towards the end of his long life he remarked that, but for the war, he might well have found himself on the full-time county cricket circuit by 1940 or 1941, and 'realistically one might even have played a Test or two before the selectors realised their error'. Pawson sometimes balanced the seraphic quality everyone knew and loved about him with a salutary inner steel. He once wrote in an essay about his hero Douglas Jardine: 'Whatever your attitude to a game, if you play at any level, you should play to win, with every fibre of your being devoted to doing well.' Truly the last of a breed, Tony Pawson died in 2012, at the age of 91.

There were several other young cricketers in the 1939 crop who went on to distinguish themselves in sports careers or elsewhere. The Brighton College captain Ian Philips later appeared as a successful all-rounder for Northamptonshire before becoming a long-serving local headmaster. The teenaged prodigy Norman Gibbs was thought to be one of the most promising cricketers of his generation, and on the fast track to England honours, but appeared to lose interest in the game after the war, when he went into business as a property developer. He died under mysterious circumstances in 1975, when the small plane he was piloting crashed on a remote Scottish island. Robert Higgins – known as 'Hee-Hee' because of his infectious laugh – played his last match for Cranleigh only in May 1940, when he scored 80 and took 4 wickets in his school's win over Brighton; he died just four years later, aged 23, when his Lancaster bomber was lost over Holland. Alan Fairbairn of Haileybury went on to play twenty-one times as a left-handed bats-man for Middlesex, making a dramatic start by hitting centuries in both his first two matches – a feat unmatched in English cricket – but gave up the game for business in his late 20s. Finally, Kenneth Campin of Bedford Modern was another young player with a tragically short interval between representing his school and dying in action; in his case while serving as a bombardier with the RAF in January 1945. The above list is far from exhaustive.

There was one venerable name from the Edwardian age of cricket, no less a light than Jack Hobbs, also to be found playing just below the first-class level in 1939. The Surrey and England master batsman was then 56 and divided his time between the demands of his London sports shop along with his charity work and occasional journalism. With his 197 (some say 199) first-class centuries made between 1905 and 1934, Hobbs had surely earned his retirement. But now he was coaxed back by his friend the lawyer Henry Grierson to appear for his nomadic Forty Club in a series of matches with the aim of developing and encouraging youth cricket.

The result was that Hobbs went out to bat at the Rugby School ground just after lunch on 3 June 1939. He scored 75 runs in classic style, having previously bowled 5 overs of gentle medium pace whose distinguishing characteristic was width rather than line or length. The following week Hobbs was back in action against the Military College at Minley Manor in Hampshire. He contributed 27 to the Forty Club's total of 264-3 declared, following which the young army cadets replied with 47 all out. Hobbs added 83 in the next match, against Bloxham, and rounded off his season with a run-a-minute 77 against Kimbolton School in Cambridgeshire. Granted that these were often teenagers bowling to him, he still showed what the *Cambridge Daily News* called a 'thoughtful and highly determined and polished approach' at the wicket, whether 'taking the slows apart' or 'driving the quicks almost with negligence'. Hobbs explained his latter-day cricket philosophy to the same paper: 'When you are playing an innings it is the most important thing in the world. When you are out, nothing could count less.'

Covering affairs for the *Daily Telegraph*, 37-year-old Crusoe Robertson-Glasgow was one of those present to reverentially watch Hobbs ('as though Zeus had lightly descended for an afternoon from Olympus') walk out to bat against Rugby. It was as if the gods of cricket had met on that otherwise unassuming public-school games field. Robertson-Glasgow was a sharp and graceful writer who was as a rule less interested in recording the dull prosaic facts of a game than in capturing its whimsical or occasionally absurd atmosphere, an aspect to which he in no small degree personally contributed. The title of his 1933 collection *The Brighter Side of Cricket* was clearly his own aphorism. Crusoe's press box colleagues knew him for his exuberance, his taste for a drink, his casual dress, his seemingly effortless and lapidary prose style (of a lively wicket at Southend he once wrote, 'the pitch, like Jezebel, was fast and unaccountable') and not least his cavalier way with deadlines. He was an ineffably British *bon vivant*. E.W. Swanton, his fellow correspondent on the *Telegraph*, later remembered: '"RC" laughed loud and often, producing a noise that rang out like that of a handful of coins tossed onto a hard counter-top.'

Reminiscing further in his 1977 book *Follow On*, Swanton added:

A solemn schoolmaster once preposterously proposed that Crusoe be banned from Vincent's Club in Oxford during term-time as a provoker of undue hilarity. The motion found no support. For Crusoe made no enemies except priggishness and pomposity. When Crusoe entered the Parks, where under some captains a certain over-earnestness was inclined to develop, it was as if the sun had broken through.

Certainly the lithe, sandy-haired Robertson-Glasgow exuded a kind of manic good cheer as he toured the outlying English cricket grounds of 1939, a well-thumbed copy of the morning's *Sporting Life* and a hip flask to hand, producing his scintillating pen portraits of the game's great and good. Walter Hammond was never better captured in print: 'There was the effect on a match of his presence alone; the influence on a bowler's feelings of the sight of Hammond taking guard at about 11.50 a.m., when lunch seemed far and the boundary near.' Or, as he wrote of the contrasting styles of Herbert Sutcliffe and Patsy Hendren: 'Sutcliffe is the megalo-psychic; denying, by attitude, the existence of good luck, or, almost, of the bowlers themselves; Hendren, democratic, busily and gladly sharing the enjoyment and stresses of batting with spectators, umpires, scorers and dogs.' No wonder that Swanton once remarked, 'Crusoe's art was pure and his fun riotous. We were all mere plodders by comparison.'

In 1939 Robertson-Glasgow was already suffering from what is now referred to as bipolar disorder. But the condition wasn't widely accepted at the time, when alternating bouts of depression and mania tended to be stigmatised, ignored or, at best, self-medicated. Many sufferers, like Crusoe himself, simply melted into society and dealt with their demons in secret.

In fact Robertson-Glasgow seems to have been grappling with the disease even while appearing in the 1920s as a fast-medium bowler and occasional batsman for Somerset, to all outward appearances the model of a swashbuckling amateur cricketer of the old school. He was said to have suffered a first breakdown in 1924 and a second in 1931, when he attempted suicide. He cut his throat, and the scar never healed. The black mists descended again following his father's death in 1938. It's an extraordinary reflection of Robertson-Glasgow's dual nature that in July 1939, while continuing to turn out his convivial and sparkling essays on cricket and other topics, he should have been found sitting alone one night in a darkened room at the Mermaid Hotel in Yeovil. He had gone to the town in order to cover the Somerset v Lancashire championship match taking place at the nearby West Hendford ground. It was his 38th birthday, and downstairs a small group of friends and colleagues waited for him to join them for a celebration meal in the hotel's oak-panelled dining room. But Robertson-Glasgow found himself unable to face the occasion. Instead, he reportedly spent the evening sitting alone on his bed, staring at a sharp-pointed letter opener on the nearby bureau. What would it feel like, he wondered, to stab it through his left palm? Like others, Robertson-Glasgow was appalled by the 'horrible shrill screech' of Hitler's voice piping out from the radio wherever he went that summer, and already alarmed at what sort of 'debased world' he could expect to live in after the inevitable war. By the time Crusoe came to write his memoir *46 Not Out*, published at that age, the mask of permanent geniality was occasionally allowed to slip to reveal his true revulsion for the 'hollow man', the crass product of a 'grimly uniform' post-war society. 'Stupid figures,' he remarks of sports careers – and by extension, of people's lives – judged by the accountancy of mere numbers. 'How I loathed them, and loathe them still. What a mess mathematics make of man, damning his generous currents, frowning on joyous fallibility, pursing the dry lip at admirable error.'

Robertson-Glasgow was only part of a tidal swell of apprehension and 'full-scale bloody terror' that steadily overtook even professional optimists like the teenaged Godfrey Evans by around midsummer of 1939. Although the war itself seemed to be postponed time and time again, Evans recalled:

It was impossible to lead a normal life. I went back one night to my father's house at Faversham after playing for Kent seconds, and we were just sitting down to eat when someone from the council knocked at the door with a clipboard in his hand and started reading off all the facts and figures about the effects of chlorine-bomb attacks and the best way to make yourself vomit and not swallow your tongue in the process, and how many gas masks did we think we might need when it came to it, etc., etc. *Not* the ideal way to unwind after a long day's cricket, I can tell you.

Evans's near neighbour and fellow young hopeful at Kent, John Pocock, had a similar experience:

I was in and out of the county seconds, and when I was out I quite often lent a hand driving a delivery van around the countryside between Maidstone and Canterbury for the family bakery. So I saw a fair amount of that part of the world. You always got an earful about Hitler: 'We've got to stop him now'; 'Bloody well stop him'; 'String him up like the bloody Kaiser' [a false memory, since the last German emperor was then living in comfortable exile in Holland], as well as stuff like 'We bloody nearly bought it the last time this happened' and 'Oh, God, not again!' One old lady I visited wanted to buy the entire vanload of bread off me. She was worried about starving to death.

The unmarried E. W. Swanton was another of those living in the same general area as Evans and Pocock who found himself leading a double life in what he called that 'strange twilight summer'. By the middle of June, Swanton's boss at the BBC, 'Lobby' de Lotbiniere was in discussion with his counterparts at the MCC about the prospect of televising the Lord's Test later in the month. It was a conspicuously relaxed process compared to the often feral atmosphere that surrounds today's high-stakes sports-broadcast negotiations. 'We lunched at the Langham,' Lobby remarked to his board in a memo of 16 June. 'Afterwards there was a brief skirmish about whether or not we should propose an "inclusive" arrangement to also cover the University and Public Schools matches. This was swiftly agreed.' As a result, the BBC would pay a fee of just 50 guineas (£1,400 today) for the combined ball-by-ball radio and television rights to the first Test against the West Indies, while 'further exchanges' were to take place 'with regard to other suitable fixtures on the Lord's list'.

While Swanton was preparing to join the small commentary team in its somewhat wobbly perch craning out at a diagonal over the Lord's boundary like a more modest Berghof, he was also in training with the Bedfordshire Yeomanry, 'being mucked about much like every other Territorial formation of the day'. There was a touch of *Dad's Army* about some of the unit's early exercises. 'Our first role was an essentially static one,' Swanton wrote in his book *Sort of a Cricket Person*:

> We had no transport to speak of, defending the coast of Norfolk and Suffolk from any landing from the other side of the North Sea. It was an unexacting role. After Norfolk we repaired north to the borders of Scotland where our training and equipment were due to be completed.

Swanton remembered that in between times he had warmed up for the Lord's Test by providing some 'very basic' and 'by modern standards, very slow' radio commentary during Surrey's match against Oxford University played from 21 to 23 June at the Oval. It proved to be a miserable experience. 'Quite honestly, it could have been November,' Swanton said. 'It was colder and darker than at any cricket match I'd ever seen, and they were all trooping on and off for bad light or rain at hourly intervals. There was no play at all on the first day and not much on the third either, I recall.' In the time that remained Surrey scored 234 and the students replied with a creditable 133-1. Oxford's wicketkeeper Peter Blagg was singled out by *The Times* for his 'exemplary glovework' and 'spirited display throughout'. Lt Blagg died just three years later while serving with the Royal Fusiliers in Burma, aged 24.

Apart from that, probably the chief distinguishing feature of the match was that it marked the first ever senior team appearance for Surrey of the 20-year-old Bedser twins. *Wisden* wrote:

Eric Bedser created a fine impression while staying nearly an hour, but the pitch afforded Alec no chance of proving his ability as a bowler. These two tall, dark boys resembled each other so closely that it was impossible to distinguish between them, especially when they fielded together in the slips. Surrey officials predict a great future for them.

That richly fulfilled promise – particularly so in Alec's case – co-existed with a dourness, or perhaps just a commendable dedication, in the Bedsers' approach to the business of playing cricket. The brothers' county colleague Alf Gover saw 'a propensity for pensiveness and solemnity … They did extremely well on the field, but you wouldn't catch them propping up the bar afterwards. It was all strictly business. Really, they were Yorkshire cricketers.'

Set against this, Godfrey Evans always remembered a match between Kent and Surrey seconds at Folkestone during the early part of the 1939 season. 'Eric and Alec were both big, burly guys with the exact same features, and we took one look at them and said, "How are you meant to tell these buggers apart?"' Since the brothers also dressed and spoke alike, frequently finishing each other's sentences, a certain amount of confusion reigned in their circle that was particularly pronounced during the twins' early days on the county circuit. At Folkestone, said Evans:

There was this annoying little sod in the hotel trying to sell us life insurance. All Brylcreem and brothel creepers, a real spiv. You don't think of the Bedsers as a barrel of laughs, but they soon got a routine going with this guy, I remember. They were sitting there both dressed in a matching blue jacket and grey flannels, and every now and again one or other of them would get up and go to the gents. When he came back people would stand up to let him push past them, and in the confusion the Bedsers would change seats without the insurance guy noticing. It was like a shell game. So when the salesman tried to pick up the conversation he thought he'd been having a few minutes earlier, Eric would say with a straight face, 'You must have been talking to my younger brother.' The guy would protest, 'But didn't you just tell me that you were interested in buying a policy … ?' 'No, no,' Eric would say, 'That was Alec.' Then Big Al would pull the same stunt – 'Are you sure you're not confusing me with my brother?' The insurance guy finally reeled out, a broken man. Old Gerry Simpson – he'd been playing for the MCC in W.G. Grace's day – nearly died laughing. He was purple in the face and his tongue was rolling around outside his mouth. Anyone who didn't know better would have thought he was having a stroke. So much for the Bedsers not having a sense of humour.

This was a rare moment of levity, and further proof that cricket can be better than life, during a time of deepening public fear and confusion in Britain as a whole. In east Kent, Gerry Chalk and his young wife Rosemary now began to wonder about the wisdom of him signing up to fight while she stayed home alone on what would be the direct path of Luftwaffe planes crossing the North Sea to bomb London and other targets in the south-east. In the event the Low Countries fell, Kent was also uniquely vulnerable to the threat of a German invasion. As in 1914–18, the fear of enemy landings on the British homeland persisted very nearly up to the last months of the war, in this case just in time to give way to the terror of the V-1 and V-2 attacks.

'All sorts of rumours were flying about and by around June 1939 people talked about nothing else,' said Rosemary Chalk, who stubbornly remained in Canterbury until her husband joined the Honourable Artillery Company, at which point she spent more of her time with her extended family, the cricket-playing Foster dynasty of Worcestershire. Gerry Chalk noted sardonically that one of his own chief concerns during the summer of 1939 was the steep rise in 'war risk' insurance premiums, and that this had caused the young couple to 'fork out an extra ten bob a month so one could be covered against the Germans bombing us to bits'.

Few cricketers or cricket clubs were immune to war jitters. At Lord's on 12 June, the secretaries of the MCC and Middlesex again discussed the terms of the contract governing the county's use of the Lord's playing facilities. A note in the minutes adds: 'Following the exchange, Mr Walter Robins asked that an additional clause be added to The Agreement to

cover the possibility of a National Emergency interfering with cricket.'
By then official notices were plastered on the walls outside the ground
giving details about the future issuing of identity cards, the registering
of eligible adult males and the latest thinking about air-raid precautions.
'You'd have to have been blind and deaf to be surprised when the war
finally broke out,' Godfrey Evans remarked. One sunny day at the Bat
and Ball ground in Gravesend, the young wicketkeeper saw a party of
schoolboy spectators walking towards him, each holding at the end of
a piece of string a small cardboard box. As the group passed by, Evans
realised that the boxes, which had looked like containers for sandwiches
at a day's cricket, were, in fact, gas masks. 'Another moment one had a
distinct sinking feeling,' he later admitted.

These were far from the only signs of a growing intrusion on what
Neville Cardus called the 'happy, sane, healthy' life of an English cricket
season. Rupert Howard, the former county batsman who was now secretary of Lancashire, already had a War Department bulletin on his desk
advising him that no unnecessary lights were to be left on at Old Trafford
after close of play, and that the ground itself was on the list of possible
temporary billets for units of the Royal Engineers 'during any future
period of national emergency'. Howard's counterpart at Yorkshire, John
Nash, noted in his minute book of 24 July that there was a 'natural fear
of the unknown', and that as a result some people were reluctant to leave
their homes even to watch cricket. Although there were good crowds for
the visits of Worcestershire and Warwickshire in the first half of August, by
the time Essex appeared at Sheffield on the 19th of the month the ground
was a 'cavernous, dark place with barbed wire strung up at the gate, and
the chief noise one of the clatter of passing trams, along with the inces-
sant nearby banging of factory presses'. William Taylor at Derbyshire put
it more succinctly: 'August was a disaster. First the rain, then the Huns.'

War preparations and precautions closely corresponded with the
tempo of the 1939 season as a whole. The first civil defence circulars,
with particulars of the digging of trenches and the provision of fallout
shelters, went out in the week of 8 May, just as a poor MCC team,
rendered vertebrate only by Bill Edrich's batting, were losing to the

county champions Yorkshire in the traditional curtain-raiser at Lord's. In late June, with the West Indies Test series about to begin, Hitler chose the moment to announce: 'England is our enemy, and the showdown with her is a matter of life and death', before going on to speculate on what the showdown might be like – 'Holland, Belgium and France will be overrun, and we must then burn our boats … it will no longer be a question of right or wrong, but of to be or not to be for 80 million Germans.' This was the point where people had begun knocking on the doors of English houses to discuss the benefits of gas masks. Two months later, the warning signs were unavoidable, with bomb shelters, barrage balloons, and a Territorial Army officer like Lancashire's 27-year-old team captain Lionel Lister hurriedly forced to leave a match in progress at Northampton in order to board a requisitioned corporation bus bound for troop exercises on Dartmoor. His rations for the eight-hour journey consisted of a small tin of pilchards.

For Sussex, the season continued with that trademark mix of individual charm and collective irresponsibility somehow never far removed from south coast cricket of the day. At Horsham in early June the home team made heavy weather of beating an injury-hit Warwickshire. The Sussex all-round hero was Jim Langridge, the older of the two Langridge brothers, who took 8-37 in the match and threw in a whirlwind knock of 87 in the second innings. Other than that it was a somewhat listless team performance, and the *Argus* correspondent wrote: 'None of the side threw in the ball with conviction, while some of the movement in the field recalled that of the ploughman homeward plodding his weary way.' John Nye, the Sussex left-arm seamer, alternated between long accurate spells and what the paper called 'sudden descents into chaos'. The Warwickshire batsmen took him for nearly 7 runs an over. Langridge aside, the other Sussex bowlers were unobtrusive to the point of near invisibility. Warwickshire could count themselves unlucky in that three more of their men – Santall, Dollery and Wyatt – broke down in the field, all of which helped Sussex, after slumping to 45-4, reach their mark of 206 to win on the third day.

The next morning, the Surrey players arrived in little groups of two or three, huddled together in the drizzle as they hurried through the gate, their captain Monty Garland-Wells joining them by taxi, at the same ground. Alf Gover took 7 wickets in the match and his brother-in-law Eddie Watts, known more for his enthusiastic seam bowling than his batting, hit a quick 66 in Surrey's first innings. It all came down to the visitors chasing 221 to win in the final four hours. After thirty minutes the Surrey opener Stan Squires, somewhat unluckily, was caught behind off his arm, giving the umpire a hard look as he strode past him on his way to the pavilion. Sussex, having tasted blood, brought the field in to crowd the new batsman Tom Barling. For about half an hour the tactics looked as if they might pay off – two 'heaven-shaking' shouts for LBW rousing the crowd around the refreshment tent at the Railway End – but cleverly as a succession of Langridges and Parkses bowled the pitch was against them. Barling finished on 88 not out, his batting partner Laurie Fishlock adding an unbeaten 107, and Surrey won by 9 wickets with time to spare.

Sussex never so much as got on the field for their next match, against Lancashire at the Aigburth ground, Liverpool, where after a week's heavy rain the pitch wasn't so much wet as it was better suited as a habitat for local waterfowl than for playing cricket. From there the players drove 250 miles down narrow and often flooded country roads to Worthing, where, as we've seen, they at least got into the middle against Walter Hammond's Gloucestershire. Sussex collapsed from 42 without loss to 124 all out on the last day, and the visitors won by four wickets. There were some disparaging remarks in that evening's *Worthing Herald* about a recent performance of *Tannhäuser* at the State Opera House in Munich, where 'two undraped young females, one posing as Europa astride a bull, the other depicting Princess Leda in a most immodest congress with a swan' were apparently added to the dramatis personae for the benefit of 'the leering Herr Hitler'. The same paper also had some strong words about the new German friendliness towards the Soviet Union. A Sussex supporter named Laetitia Stapleton travelled back with some of the Gloucester players to London, where the cricketers were due to change stations before catching the late train to Bristol. During the journey she handed Hammond her copy of the *Evening Standard* and asked him if he would help her complete the crossword. The England captain took the paper, appeared to write energetically on it for some minutes, and then silently handed it back to its owner. Miss Stapleton found that he had doodled some 'quite accomplished' cartoons of barrage balloons and searchlights across the page, then added in the words 'Bloody War', before drawing a vivid red circle round the phrase.

Hampshire meanwhile continued their own fitful season, in which they managed to win only two matches out of the fourteen where they had led on first innings. Rain spoiled any chance of a finish in the game against Nottinghamshire in the middle of June at Portsmouth. The southern team then showed its most perverse side in its away fixture with Essex. Starting their second innings on a flat pitch with a lead of 56, Hampshire were soon reduced to 37-3, with, said *The Times*, the home bowlers 'openly frolicking' (if such a term can be used in the context of a damp Tuesday morning at the Old County Ground, Brentwood) at each success. The visitors eventually succumbed for 96, Ray Smith taking 5-34 with a combination of right-arm swing and fast off-breaks. Left 153 to win, Essex got home in less than two hours with 5 wickets in hand.

Hampshire fared no better in their next match, against Middlesex at the Victoria Recreation Ground in Newport, Isle of Wight. The visitors batted first and started slowly, at least until a red-eyed Bill Edrich, seeming to pass from the maudlin to the euphoric with no apparent transitional stage, suddenly cut loose against the spinners. He was well supported at the other end by Jack Robertson. Before long the small Carisbrooke Road scoreboard was turning over like a fruit machine. Edrich finished with 118 and Robertson with 97 out of the Middlesex first innings total of 261. Hampshire replied with completed innings of 93 and 143. The home side 'showed little resolution', *Wisden* harrumphed, 'and Creese apart, shaped poorly against a varied attack. Smith, in the first innings, and Peebles, in the second, bowled splendidly.'

Although Middlesex then had four days off before travelling up to play Lancashire at Old Trafford, Edrich himself had only three hours in hand before catching the train back to London, where he was due to represent the MCC at Lord's the following morning. He spent the short time available to him first in the snug bar of the Cask and Crispin pub in Newport, then in exploring a Great War tank parked nearby, followed in turn by extensive tours of the respective buffets of the Portsmouth ferry, and that city's Sally Port hotel, before finally allowing himself to be steered onto the Waterloo-bound express. By now Edrich's marriage to his first wife Betty – 'the prettiest girl in north London', he'd once called her – was already dissolving. Too much cricket, too many nights on the road away from home, perhaps too convivial a manner with his many female admirers had all taken a toll. Later in the season, Hopper Levett briefly came back from army exercises to once again take over Kent's wicketkeeping duties from Godfrey Evans in a match against Middlesex at Canterbury. Fifty years later Levett remembered being 'quite struck by the amount Bill put away' each night at the bar of the town's Parrot Hotel, 'let alone what happened upstairs later'; a notable tribute from a man himself not unduly bound by bourgeois proprieties.

After disposing of Hampshire, Essex stayed on at Brentwood for the visit of Cambridge University – a more socially stratified fixture than it might be today, with all eleven students and their four fellow amateurs on the home side each rating a courteous 'Sir' from the umpires and the other seven players making do with a grunted 'Frank' or 'Stan', as appropriate. *Wisden* wrote of the match:

> Essex won by an innings and 6 runs. On Saturday, when 19 wickets went down for 288 runs, Carris and Sharp were the only University men who shaped confidently. R. Smith kept a length and made the ball break back. Essex in turn were given many uncomfortable moments by Webster, fairly fast, and Dickinson, medium pace, six men falling for 49 runs before O'Connor and P. Smith stopped the collapse.

All four of the young students named in the report went on to play county championship cricket. Unmentioned by *Wisden*, the Cambridge number four batsman John Blake similarly represented Hampshire in fourteen first-class matches from 1937 to 1939, managing 325 runs at an average of 13, with a high score of 48. He made his final appearance on a civilian cricket field in early August 1939 at Canterbury, neither bowling nor taking a catch, and scoring no runs. Later that month, Blake enlisted in the Royal Marines, where in time he reached the rank of captain. The author Evelyn Waugh remembered him as a fellow pioneer commando – 'talkative, good-natured, quite fearless, loved equally by all ranks' – with a ringing laugh and a comma of dark hair flopping across his face. In June 1944 John Blake fell in action on the island of Brač in German-held Yugoslavia. He was 26.

Essex were captained against Cambridge by the 28-year-old plant-seed magnate Frederick Unwin, as we've seen one of three players who shared the county's leadership duties that summer. On the face of it a complex and somewhat peculiar arrangement, it turned out to be a great success. Essex finished fourth in the table and proved good enough to beat Yorkshire by an innings in a late-season match at Sheffield. The side were still without the services during June and July of their philosophically minded seamer Ken Farnes, who was finishing off the summer term at Worksop. He returned to the county to play against Kent at Chelmsford in early August, just in time to flatten Gerry Chalk's middle stump on the first afternoon before tropical rain set in for the next two days. Crusoe Robertson-Glasgow thought Farnes the sort of bowler 'who can suggest even by his run up that the batsman would do well to stay firm', and Bill Edrich ruefully said of facing him in the Gentlemen v Players match at Lord's: 'I tried to play back, a defensive back stroke while turning my head and lifting my hands. The next thing I knew was that someone was saying smoothly, "Have some water, there's no hurry."'

Farnes was unusual among the cricketers of 1939 in being equally dedicated to the claims of the body and the mind. A physical culture buff with a slightly disconcerting habit of showing off his stomach muscles for the benefit of his teammates in the dressing room, he was also a devotee of the Edwardian poet and playwright James Elroy Flecker, who composed lines such as those engraved on the clock tower of the Special Air Service barracks in Hereford:

We are the Pilgrims, master; we shall go
Always a little further; it may be
Beyond that last blue mountain barred with snow
Across that angry or that glimmering sea.

In a 'burst of light' while reading one night in his Durban hotel room during the timeless Test of March 1939, Farnes had experienced the revelation that 'beauty and value are inherent in all things, even the most lowly and untalented'. Moreover, he noted, this value 'surely proclaims the presence of God'. Farnes had attained this insight as a result of his study of the Bengali poet Rabindranath Tagore, and his 'profoundly sensitive, fresh and beautiful' verse collection *Gitanjali*. Published in English in 1912, the work offered a philosophy both sublime and complicated – truth was universal, Tagore wrote, all humankind and nature were one, and, paradoxically, the most intense sound on earth was that of total silence. 'Let all my songs/ Gather together their diverse strains/Into a single current and flow to a sea of stillness/in salutation to thee', Tagore wrote in his *Poem 103*. As a result both of this and his other readings, Farnes (though not averse to more earthly, female charms, as his diary makes clear) espoused certain beliefs rarely associated with the average English fast bowler of the 1930s, let alone his modern counterpart. Rather than go into a syncopated frenzy on taking a wicket, for instance, he often had some consoling words for the departing batsman. Len Hutton remembered that he had once been bowled by Farnes, and then informed by him while on his way back to the pavilion that the names and distinctions that human beings apply to their triumphs and disasters are merely an illusion. ('I thought he'd been drinking,' Hutton told me.) Farnes later wrote that Tagore's poems struck him as 'literally an uninterrupted contemplation of God', adding: 'Each soul is holy because it is part of God, and the body is merely a shell. The aim of life is to look beyond the shell and see the holiness within.'

In another striking passage, Farnes would write in his autobiography *Tours and Tests* of leaving the field after Essex's dismally wet county championship match against Kent 'basking in a glow of pure contentment' quite unrelated to any developments in the middle. In the brief time he had left to him after returning from South Africa in the spring of 1939, his life and his career would be saturated with his new faith.

June was one of the more consistent periods in Warwickshire's fortunes, though not in a way the county's supporters would have wished. They drew four of their seven matches during the month and lost the rest. The team's England leg-spinner Eric Hollies took 31 wickets in those twenty-one days' cricket but got little support. Warwickshire's right-arm seamer Kilburn Wilmot managed only 33 scalps all season, and of his opening partner, Danny Mayer, Swanton wrote: 'Either the pitches were too slow for him, or he for them', although in fairness Mayer also took 8 wickets in the losing cause against Sussex at Horsham, and no fewer than 11 later in the month against Worcestershire at Birmingham.

Warwickshire continued to lean heavily on Tom Dollery with the bat: in one purple patch in June he scored innings of 25, 170, 63, 70, 18 not out and 117 in the course of four consecutive matches at Edgbaston. The actor Alan Bates remembered that as a young boy he'd been taken to Burton-on-Trent that summer 'chiefly to see Copson bowl for Derbyshire and Dollery bat for Warwickshire', the ignition point of a lifelong love affair with cricket that many believe found its apogee in 1971's *The Go-Between*, with the film's lavish exploration of the coded hypocrisies of English life as mirrored in a country-house match, although Bates himself always spoke more fondly of his performance seven years later in *The Shout*, which features a similar contest held between the staff and inmates of a lunatic asylum.

Further down the Severn Valley, Worcestershire were dealing with what the county secretary called 'the anger, pain, grief and desolation' of events that transcended cricket. On the Sunday night of 28 May, a car carrying five of the county's players was in collision with a stationary lorry on a road near Margaretting, a small village just outside Chelmsford. It was the rest day of an away match with Essex, and the cricketers were on their way back to their team hotel after a round of golf and dinner. The lorry was partly pulled off to the side of the narrow road and its driver was underneath it doing repairs when the car hit it from behind at around 50 miles per hour. Worcestershire's 29-year-old wicketkeeper-batsman Syd Buller suffered a concussion and multiple broken bones in the accident and missed the next ten weeks' cricket. The players' small car had been so badly overcrowded that Worcester's popular opening batsman Charles Bull had been sitting on Buller's lap in the front passenger seat. He was killed instantly. Bull had easily passed 1,000 runs in each season from 1934 to 1937, seemed to be on his way back to form after missing much of the previous year's cricket through injury, had at one time been an international table tennis champion, and was universally liked and admired on the county circuit. He had just turned 30 at the time of his death.

Worcestershire's heavy defeat by Essex was hardly surprising under the circumstances, and it took the county several matches to regroup. In early June they were thrashed by Somerset at Taunton, where Harold Gimblett hit an unsentimental 129, and then lost by 315 runs away to Derbyshire. After that Worcestershire managed to draw with Northants, largely thanks to an unbeaten 212 by their middle-order batsman Harold 'Doc' Gibbons, who was then pressing hard for England selection. Further draws followed with Glamorgan and Warwickshire before, at the end of June, Worcester recorded their first victory in the seven matches since Bull's death when they beat Gloucestershire at a New Road ground where there were 'many black costumes on display', the *Empire News* reported, and the pavilion flag still flew at half-mast. Gibbons scored another century and the seamer Reg Perks, a veteran of the timeless Test, took 9 wickets in the match while on his way to 159 victims at 20 runs apiece in the season. Perks's then 2-year-old cousin became the schoolboy cricketer (and future Rolling Stone) Bill Wyman.

While Syd Buller recovered from his injuries, 21-year-old Hugo Yarnold, who had begun the season as an assistant groundsman and scorer, took his place behind the stumps for Worcestershire. Both players later became distinguished Test match umpires. Yarnold used to talk about the thousands of miles county cricketers piled up on the back roads of England every summer, and once wrote that 'Getting from Point A to Point B [was] one of the biggest drawbacks of the job.' He was killed in August 1974 while driving home from officiating at a match between Northamptonshire and Essex at Wellingborough when his car crashed into a lorry. He was 57.

The umpires in the first Test between England and the West Indies at Lord's, 'Tiger' Smith and Fanny Walden, formerly of Warwickshire and Northants respectively, were each paid £18 (£480 today), plus third-class rail fare, for their three days' work. They earned their fee, because the match began on 24 June in conditions so cold and dark that the *Daily Mail* gave its cartoon of the event the caption 'Winter Sports'. There was also to be a series of closely disputed catches for the officials to adjudicate on the third morning before England chased victory in the final session. The venerable north London ground, then already in its 126th consecutive year of use, was almost unrecognisable from its modern successor. In general the whole place was flatter and airier than it is now, although with two utilitarian-black cooling towers soaring up on the road outside the Grace Gates. The old north grandstand with its pillared balconies gave Neville Cardus the impression of a 'grand yet faded music-hall'. Despite the weather, some 60,000 spectators paid for admission over the three days. To date it remains the only one of the 140-odd Lord's Tests to contain 8-ball overs.

The generally sombre mood of the crowd, as a north wind played around the ground on the first day, can hardly have been lifted by the periodic announcements issuing from the loudspeakers positioned in the stands. 'Will you serve your king and country in this hour of their need?' they asked, before going on to encourage all able-bodied men to register immediately with the military authorities. During the lunch interval, Hammond, the England captain, broadcast a similar appeal through an old-fashioned tin megaphone nearly as big as he was, while hoardings around the ground asked, 'National Service – are YOU playing?' As Cardus wrote: 'These were not on the whole joyful tidings', adding of Hutton and Compton later in the match that their batting gave promise of 'their character and of the part they will play in more searching engagements of the near future'.

There was an eminently solid look to the England line-up at Lord's. Hutton, Compton, Hammond and Paynter were all at or near their prime, Copson and Bowes made for a new-ball attack ideally suited to the conditions, and Yorkshire's veteran wicketkeeper Arthur Wood had all the necessary attributes of a top-class stumper bar youth. The spin-bowling duties fell on Doug Wright and Hedley Verity, who already had 59 and 82 first-class wickets respectively in the season. It was a sign of England's available resources that there was no room in the side for Bill Edrich, the hero of Durban just three months earlier, who promptly set about savaging the Hampshire bowling for his two-hour century at Newport while his sometime colleagues were in action 100 miles away at Lord's.

The West Indies side, when announced just before the toss, was not without surprises. For a start, Vic, the elder of the Stollmeyer brothers, was absent ill, opening the door to his 18-year-old sibling Jeff to make his Test debut. The Cambridge blue John Cameron, a jobbing all-rounder whom *Wisden* described as 'not reliable with bat or ball' was preferred to Tyrell Johnson, a left-arm seamer whose achievements included taking a wicket with his first ball of the tour at Worcester, where he finished with figures of 3-28 and evidently would have done even better if his teammates had held their catches. The swashbuckling Peter Bayley, whose recent innings of 268 for British Guiana against Barbados remained a Caribbean domestic record until the 1990s, was also overlooked, Rolph Grant solving the problem of finding capable opening batsmen by promoting himself up the order. Both the West

Indies' specialist wicketkeepers played, Ivan Barrow donning the gauntlets (in what proved to be his final Test) and Derek Sealy settling for the outfield. Leslie Hylton, the explosively aggressive 34-year-old seamer omitted from the original tour party, opened the bowling.

The West Indies side wasn't only notable on technical cricketing grounds. It also deserves a place in the reference books for the unmatched series of curious or exceptional – and sometimes brutally violent – events surrounding its individual members. The eleven players who successively went out to bat on that wintry June Saturday at Lord's included both a future convicted murderer (Leslie Hylton) and a murder victim (Jeff Stollmeyer), as well as an imprisoned illegal abortionist in the form of Bertie Clarke, who, putting this setback behind him, went on to win the OBE for services to medicine. Apart from being one of the game's greatest batsmen (and eventually the first black man ever chosen to captain the West Indies) George Headley remains the only Test match player to be born in Panama, while his teammate Bam Bam Weekes was similarly unique at the time in hailing from the United States. Derek Sealy was just 17 on his international debut, and still remains the West Indies' youngest ever representative cricketer. Ivan Barrow is thought to be the only Jewish player to have scored a century in a Test match. Learie Constantine went on to become chairman of the League of Coloured Peoples, a high commissioner, and the first black man to sit in the House of Lords. When you add the fact that there was both a future war casualty and a POW, as well as a suicide victim, and a wicketkeeper fast approaching his 41st birthday, in the England side, which was captained by a man allegedly losing his mind to syphilis, and that the umpires at Lord's included in 5ft 1in 'Fanny' Walden comfortably the smallest man ever to represent England at football and in his colleague 'Tiger' Smith the world's eventual oldest living Test cricketer, you surely have the ingredients for a cracking pub quiz.

The tourists' captain Rolph Grant, Trinidad's heavyweight boxing champion, won the toss at Lord's and batted. *Wisden* wrote:

The pitch, which had been completely protected from rain, was lifeless … Without becoming too venturesome, Grant drove and cut both Bowes and Copson well until he played a half-hearted defensive stroke and fell to a smart left-handed catch at short-leg. Then Headley joined Stollmeyer and for a long time the English bowlers were mastered. Before lunch the light became very bad and the batsmen must have been severely handicapped, especially when facing the dark background of the pavilion.

Stollmeyer fell for 59, but Headley went on to score 106, the occasion demanding discretion, in four hours and ten minutes. West Indies were dismissed for 277. Bill Copson, the flame-haired Derbyshire strike bowler, making his Test debut at the age of 31, took 5-85 as part of a haul of 146 wickets for only some 15 each in the season.

On Saturday evening, England finished at 11 without loss. No one then played competitive cricket on a Sunday, so the two teams relaxed as best they could in the atrocious weather. There may have been no desolation more total than a wet British Sunday prior to the 1994 relaxation of the trading laws. The Englishmen were staying at the Charing Cross Hotel in central London, while the West Indians lodged at a bed and breakfast establishment behind Paddington station. By all accounts there seems to have been some heated discussion among the tourists about the best tactics to adopt when play resumed on Monday morning. Learie Constantine, who had made his professional debut as long ago as 1921, recalled: 'I was roundly condemned as old-fashioned when I tried to put some gunpowder into the cricket – the general thinking was negative.' An anonymous younger colleague, confirming that there were both 'technical and financial matters kicked around at the table', told a reporter: 'I don't listen to Learie when he is talking cricket, but when he talks money I pay attention.'

On Monday, in warmer weather, England took their score to a solid 147-3 without ever quite closing off all hope for the bowlers. At that stage Compton joined Hutton at the crease. 'There now occurred some vital incidents which turned the game in favour of England,' it was reported. Both batsmen were dropped off a series of chances, and both then rode their luck to score centuries. Hutton's 196 came in 337 minutes and included 21 fours; Compton's 120 took 133 minutes with 16 boundaries. If some Martian force were to destroy the whole of Test match cricket, leaving only these two innings, we could clone from them every salient detail of top-class batting: Hutton textbook straight and severe, murderously efficient in dispatching even the fastest bowling and in reducing the trundlers to complete insignificance; Compton powerful, unorthodox and seemingly engaged in a carefree knockabout on the beach for the amusement of himself and the spectators. They were clearly the two outstanding batsmen of their generation, Hutton the one you'd want if your life depended on it, Compton the one more likely to inspire lines of poetic enchantment. Between them they put on 248 for the fourth wicket in 140 minutes and Hammond declared the England innings at 404-5.

Facing arrears of 127, the West Indies, it seemed, were content that wickets should not be lost, rather than the tempo accelerated. Headley was again the hero, with an innings of 107 in just under four hours, the first player ever to score two centuries in a Lord's Test. Norman Preston, writing in *Wisden*, was suitably impressed but still believed the batsman 'was not the same dashing player that England knew in 1933. He had the weight of the world on his shoulders.' As Douglas Jardine wrote in the *Daily Telegraph* at the time, 'It was a case of "Headley out, West Indies out".'

The end result was that England needed 99 for victory, and they knocked the runs off in seventy-five minutes with 8 wickets to spare. Perhaps the only real disappointment on the home side was Harold Gimblett, who scored 22 and 20 in what proved to be his final appearance in a Test. Following stumps there was a muted celebration in the England dressing room, some of the team needing to hurry off to join their county colleagues in places like Cardiff or Nottingham for the next round of championship matches starting in the morning. When Denis Compton (who had the luxury of staying on at Lord's to play for MCC against Oxford University) saw Gimblett standing alone at the end of the bar, the Somerset player burst into tears. 'I'll never make a Test match batsman,' he said. Compton uttered some conventional words of support, but he had only limited experience of the reality of clinical depression. In those days the standard response in such cases was to offer a slap on the back, often fortified by a stiff drink. Gimblett's brief second innings at Lord's seemed almost like a microcosm of his life. In a manic start he clubbed the first two screamingly fast balls he faced from Leslie Hylton for four and six, but then seemed to lose heart and tamely allowed himself to be bowled by a relatively innocuous straight ball from Martindale. Three weeks later, Gimblett duly learnt that he had been dropped by England. 'It's all a mess,' he wrote to a relative after hearing the names of the team read out on the radio, 'and so cruel how they do it. Wonder if you have any idea.'

E. W. Swanton climbed down from his 'distinctly invigorating' perch at Lord's – 'swaying aloft in the first day's breeze like a lookout up the mast of some Conradian schooner' – and thought the experiment of ball-by-ball broadcasting of the Test 'generally a success'. In time the BBC sent the MCC a cheque for the agreed 50 guineas for their use of the Lord's facilities. Swanton's experience in Durban had given him 'a unique slant on the challenges of covering a cricket marathon,' he remembered, adding that, 'with little human support or other resources to speak of', he had simply had to 'get through some of the *longueurs* of the West Indies Test' as best he could. 'I think at one time I may have resorted to reading out the slogans on the advertisements one saw propped up around the ground,' he admitted.

While the England players dispersed up and down the country following the Test, the West Indies decompressed with a two-day fixture against part-timers Norfolk at the Lakenham ground in Norwich. As always in that county there was a generous quota of Edriches on hand, Bill's older brother Eric and younger brother Geoff both playing and their 16-year-old sibling Brian coming up from his digs in Canterbury, where he was trying to break in with Kent, to serve as twelfth man. The Norfolk XI also included three of the brothers Rought-Rought, Desmond, Rodney and Basil, the last of whom would be captured while fighting in France less than a year later, making several subsequent escape attempts from German camps, the last of them successful, returning to play cricket after the war, and dying at the place of his birth only in 1995, at the age of 91. Bam Bam Weekes scored 123, with 15 fours and a six in the match at Norwich, which was drawn.

The West Indies noticeably raised their game in their next fixture, against Nottinghamshire at Trent Bridge. Batting first, the home side made just 149 in an innings that barely lasted into the afternoon session. The Notts opener Walter Keeton bravely hooked a Leslie Hylton bouncer for 4 in the first over. The next ball Keeton tried it again and was helped from the pitch for treatment by two ambulance attendants. Headley in turn followed his two centuries at Lord's by an unbeaten innings of 234 in five and a half hours. Vic Stollmeyer had to leave the crease with his own score on 73 due to a recurrence of his tonsillitis, but Derek Sealy added a rapid 115 and allowed Rolph Grant to declare at 510-3. Nottinghamshire managed 267 in reply, losing by an innings and 94 runs. Learie Constantine was apparently unhappy with Grant's captaincy in the match, and more especially with Grant's request that he bowl for long stretches uphill into a stiff breeze. The one-time bodyline merchant duly cut his run, spinning the ball at speeds varying from slow to gentle medium, and finished with figures of 8-117 in the match.

Back at the county ground, Taunton, 'Young' Frank Lee (already in his twelfth year at Somerset, but the last-born of three cricketing brothers) went out with Harold Gimblett to open the side's innings against Hampshire. They scored 28 and 9 respectively, but the Argentinian-born Peter McRae added 107 from the middle order and Mike Bennett, standing in as captain while the usual skipper 'Bunty' Longrigg was away on business with his family's law firm in Bath, declared at 490-8. Hampshire followed on 169 behind. They looked doomed at 100-4 in their second innings, but their batsmen Len Creese (86) and Don Walker (90) saved the day in an unbroken partnership of 177. Towards the end Gimblett came on to bowl his occasional medium-pacers and promptly had Walker 'caught' at slip by McRae off a no-ball. All three men involved in this incident later died violently. Arthur Wellard had meanwhile engaged in some typically free-spirited hitting in the one Somerset innings, smashing 7 sixes in his brutal knock of 87. 'He murdered anything pitched up to him,' the Taunton *County Gazette* wrote. 'Bouncing a ball off the top deck of the pavilion, or planting it in one of the outlying snack stalls, was all part of the job – Our Arthur simply "butchered" all sorts of bowling, not only loose or mediocre stuff but the best.'

A lesser batting talent but Wellard's equal as a cricketing character was Somerset's 34-year-old all-rounder Rollo Meyer, known far and wide on the county circuit as Jack, and at Millfield School, which he co-founded, as 'Boss'. In fifteen years of intermittent county cricket, fitted in around the demands of school teaching, Meyer recorded a top score of 202 not out against Lancashire at Taunton in 1936, although legend insists that the double century was obtained only after an offer to contribute handsomely to the Lancashire beneficiary's fund. His bowling, an uncategorisable mishmash of spin and swing, was good enough to eventually yield 408 first-class wickets at around 25 each. Meyer's essential attitude to cricket was described by his brother Horace: 'He took the game seriously but he could smile at it, and poke it in the ribs.' Somerset once took the field on a damp morning in 1939 with only ten men until Meyer appeared under a large red umbrella. He often carried a racing form book in the back pocket of his whites, studying it at intervals during the day's play. Once dropping a catch off Arthur Wellard's bowling, he reached into another pocket: 'Sorry, Arthur, here's a quid.' Meyer, in short, was one of those peculiarly English cricketers of the time who combined the highest intellectual and moral standards with a marked degree of childlike levity. Immediately volunteering for RAF service on the outbreak of war, he died in March 1991, just short of his 86th birthday.

Kent finished the month in style, beating Leicestershire by 161 runs in between showers at Tunbridge Wells. Arthur Fagg scored 64 and 131 for the home side, and Norman Harding took 9-47 in the match, which turned out to be the best figures of his short career. A game that started under skies more black than blue ended with the Leicester batsmen complaining about being dazzled by the sunshine bouncing off the windscreens of cars parked around the boundary. Kent were now fourth in the table.

Godfrey Evans was still energetically pressing his claim for promotion from the county's Second XI, where he sometimes appeared alongside Brian Edrich. Both young hopefuls kept plugging away in junior matches where the number of players sometimes exceeded that of spectators. According to Gerald Hough, Evans was often the last player to arrive at the ground in the morning and the first into the pub in the evening, 'but in between times it was clear he was a huge talent with a strong sense of destiny'. After turning out for the Kent reserves in front of a thin crowd at Sittingbourne that month, the teenager gravely informed his county secretary that he intended to be England's Test wicketkeeper 'by the end of next season, or at the latest the one after that'.

Evans's impressive levels of pride and self-confidence were matched only by the intensity of his social life. Sometime late in June, Hough had a quiet word with Les Ames to ask the veteran player if he would keep an eye on the richly talented but headstrong young stumper. Six years earlier, Ames had been keeping wicket for England against Australia at Adelaide when the home team's Bert Oldfield top-edged a short ball from Harold Larwood on to his forehead. The batsman suffered a fractured skull. Assessing the 'murderous' atmosphere in the crowd, which had then begun baying for English blood, Ames had quickly agreed with Larwood that in the event of a pitch invasion, they would divide up the stumps – 'You take middle and leg, I'll take off' – for their personal protection. So this was not a man easily rattled by most circumstances. Even so, Ames remarked shortly before his death in 1990 that:

Policing Godfrey Evans and his pals was a job that required a high degree of tact, quite apart from the sheer stamina of keeping up with them. Overdoing it in the pub was one thing. You got used to that. What really caused trouble was when young Godders in his cups took a shine to some woman, whoever she might be, and let her know it in no uncertain terms. I remember he broke the ice with an attractive older lady he bumped into at a midsummer ball we held in Kent by asking her what colour her knickers were. She turned out to be the wife of the Bishop of Dover.

As events would demonstrate, Evans and his peers would soon face unforeseen obstacles to their future careers, and, as the young wicket-keeper put it, these had 'bugger all to do with playing cricket'.

George Headley, the 'black Bradman', who finished the West Indies' 1939 tour of England with 1745 runs at an average of nearly 73.

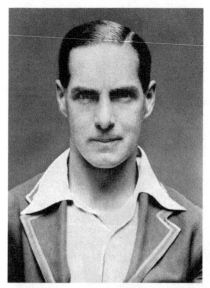

Herbert Sutcliffe of Yorkshire and England, seen
both in his Rudolf Valentino pose and standing
with his county teammate Percy Holmes in front
of the Leyton scoreboard after their world-record
stand of 555.

Len Hutton and Walter Hammond, the two greatest English batsmen of their respective generations. In August 1939 they played out the last rites of Test cricket for the next seven years.

18-year-old Godfrey Evans behind the wheel of his first car. Evans's county secretary Gerald Hough wrote that the young wicketkeeper had a great career ahead of him. 'One just prays he will keep his feet on the ground,' Hough added. (Author's collection)

Yorkshire's Bill Bowes (l) and Hedley Verity, the county's two leading bowlers in the 1939 season.

Bill Edrich, who began 1939 by scoring 219 in the timeless Test at Durban and ended it in training with the RAF.

Denis Compton in uniform. A man who always preferred direct action, he later waded in to 'whack' some offensive American servicemen.

Well-dressed spectators queue up to enter Lord's in July 1939. (John Gay/Historic England/Mary Evans)

WEST INDIES CRICKET TEAM, ENGLAND, 1939

Standing:- W. Ferguson, G. Gomez, J. B. Stollmeyer, L. G. Hylton, T. Johnson, C. B. Clarke, H. P. Bayley, E. A. V. Williams
Sitting:- G. Headley, I. Barrow, R. S. Grant, J. M. Kidney, J. H. Cameron, L. N. Constantine, E. A. Martindale
Front:- K. H. Weekes, J. E. D. Sealy, V. H. Stollmeyer

The West Indies touring party to England. Standing: William Ferguson (scorer), Gerry Gomez, Jeff Stollmeyer, Leslie Hylton, Tyrell Johnson, Bertie Clarke, Peter Bayley, Foffie Williams. Sitting: George Headley, Ivan Barrow, Rolph Grant (Capt), Jack Kidney (Manager), John Cameron, Learie Constantine, Manny Martindale. Front: Ken Weekes, Derek Sealy, Vic Stollmeyer. (Mary Evans/Pharcide)

Kent CCC in 1939. Seated are Hopper Levett, Bryan Valentine, Gerry Chalk, Leslie Ames and Les Todd, all five of whom immediately volunteered for war duty. (David Robertson/Kent CCC)

Gerry Chalk, Kent's enterprising young captain. 'He was unflappable,' Godfrey Evans remembered. 'You'd go out to bat with him at something like 150-7, chasing 400, and he'd say, "We'll knock these runs off tonight".' (David Robertson/Kent CCC)

Eric and Alec Bedser, the double-act of English county cricket.

Arthur Fagg, the prolific Kent and England opener.

The West Indies' leg-spinner Bertie Clarke, who later shrugged off a three-year jail sentence to win the OBE.

Harold Gimblett. His spectacular debut for Somerset in 1935 was matched by his dramatic departure from the county nineteen years later.

Learie Constantine warms up.

Ken Farnes appeals for run out against Don Bradman in a Test at Melbourne.

Harold Pinter, who as a cricket-obsessed 8-year-old joined the small but distinguished crowd at an amateur match played at Lord's in August 1939.

Stanford Hall, the eccentric Sir Julien Cahn's country seat in Leicestershire.

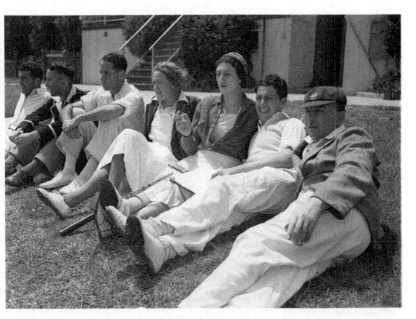

Players and spectators relaxing at a club cricket match, August 1939.

Alf Gover takes another wicket for Surrey in 1939. The batsman walks immediately. (Grenville Collins Postcard Collection/Tom Gillmor/Mary Evans)

A women's team of 1939. As a whole, women cricketers were still viewed as having less athletic skill and less commitment to their sport than the men. However, the female players were more interesting than the men for their 'journey' to the top.

London carries on shopping in 1939.

Sussex and Yorkshire play out the last first-class match of the season, at Hove on 1 September 1939. The Wehrmacht had invaded Poland that morning. (Rob Boddie/Sussex CCC)

The official announcement of hostilities two days later.

Lord's at war.

The Duke of Gloucester shakes hands with Denis Compton as he meets an England XI in front of the Lord's pavilion during a match against The Dominions in August 1943. To the right of Compton are Harold Gimblett, Alec Bedser, Leslie Compton, Trevor Bailey and Tony Mallett.

Geoffrey Legge, cricketer, businessman, racing-car enthusiast and pioneer aviator, who became the first English Test player to die in the war. (Alex Legge)

Gunners of the Surrey and Sussex Yeomanry temporarily leave their weapons to play an improvised game of cricket in Italy, 1943.

The Kent honour party to France, 1989: Godfrey Evans is in the middle of the back row, Hopper Levett and Les Ames are seated centre. (Author's collection.)

5

HIGH SUMMER

The typical MCC cricket committee of the 1930s was not known for its spirit of excessive adventure, but the men at Lord's did risk one modest experiment when they decided to start the 1939 Oxford v Cambridge match on a Saturday rather than the traditional Monday. During the three days of play, some 16,000 people each paid 2s for admission to the ground, and members brought the total attendance on the first afternoon, when the weather began to warm up, to around 10,000. It says something for the popularity of this staple of the English social season of the time that a subsequent note in the MCC minutes read: 'The initiative of starting on a Saturday failed completely in its appeal to the general public. There will be a reversion to the usual Monday plan in 1940.'

The Oxford captain Eric Dixon won the toss on the damp morning of 1 July and announced that his team would bat. They scored 313 runs, Dixon himself furnishing 75 of them. Cambridge folded for 157. The Oxford seamer Gwynn Evans began short but despite his moderate pace got the ball to lift at the batsmen's ribs. He finished with figures of 4-55 off eighteen 8-ball overs. *Wisden* wrote: 'Dixon, after managing his bowling discreetly, did not enforce the follow-on and Oxford, in the best weather of the match, built up a strong position. Lomas showed perfect form, making up for lack of power with beautifully timed strokes in his innings of 91.' Set an eventual target of 430, Cambridge missed out by only 46. The future Surrey batsman Pat Dickinson scored a century, and there were runs for John Blake and Arthur 'Podge' Brodhurst in the middle order. The Oxford wicketkeeper Peter Blagg, though unsuccessful with the bat, brought off a nimble one-handed catch low to his left to dismiss Studd, the Cambridge captain. There were twenty-five minutes left for play.

As we've seen, Eric Dixon, aged 25, Peter Blagg, aged 24, and John Blake, aged 26, would all fall in the Second World War. The Oxford opener John Lomas died in December 1945, aged 27, after being invalided out of the Royal Navy. Six other players who appeared in that last peacetime university match never returned to organised cricket after 1945. Some were too scarred in body or mind, others simply moved on to other things in life. The notion of young undergraduates all but rushing headlong from the dappled shadows of Lord's to the front line of a war might appear absurd to us today, but for the second time in twenty-five years that is exactly what happened. By all accounts, the students who signed up in 1939–45 fought with the same unflinching gallantry as their counterparts in 1914–18.

At Leeds that week Yorkshire comfortably beat Surrey, with Hutton scoring 151 and 81, bringing up his 1,000 championship runs for the season in the process, and Verity taking match figures of 8-56 to similarly pass his 100 wickets. The crowds were large, and Yorkshire donated half the gate money to the Civil Defence Service. Hutton remembered that there were 'suddenly a lot more men in uniform' to be seen in the stands, and that driving home that night he passed by 'some soldiers trying to pump up a barrage balloon, and not making a very good job of it' in a park just north of Headingley. Verity, for his part, had more pressing matters on his mind than the details of local civil defence measures. His wife Kathleen, whom he had known since they were children in Leeds, was in poor health and struggling with the demands of raising their two young sons. Her doctors had recommended an extended holiday in a warm climate, and Verity had planned to take the family back with him to Cape Town over the winter of 1939–40. This now looked an increasingly remote contingency. With reality sinking in that he would quite possibly be leaving home to fight a war rather than to coach cricket in South Africa, Verity began to put his affairs in order. After writing to John Nash, the Yorkshire secretary, about the investment of some funds and taking out a life insurance policy with the North British and Mercantile office in Bradford, the 34-year-old professional cricketer told his sister Grace of his misgivings about the world situation. 'This is no chuffing garden party,' he said. 'This fellow, Hitler, means it if we don't stop him. We have got to stop him.' Verity summed up his own credo in a letter to his sons Wilfred and Douglas. 'Always remember to do what's right,' he wrote, 'and to fight for what's right if necessary.'

On 5 July, Verity was in the Yorkshire side to meet the West Indies at Harrogate. Rain played havoc with the cricket on the first and second days and washed out play entirely on the third. In between cloudbursts there was time for the tourists to score 234 and for Yorkshire (without Hutton and Bowes, both away representing the Players at Lord's) to reply with 114. Constantine alternated between long accurate spells of wrist spin and sudden bursts of pace generated by his smooth, high action, keeping his maroon cap jammed down on his head through-out. He finished with figures of 5-28 in the one Yorkshire innings. Two months short of his 38th birthday, Constantine kept himself fit by a combination of diet, daily 3-mile runs and some improvised weight training that often involved dragging an item of furniture around his team hotel. There was a moment at Harrogate when he took off in the covers like a sprinter, collected the ball, seemingly no bigger than a cherry pit in his huge palm, and in one fluid action threw down the stumps in the same split second that the batsman, hurriedly abandoning his leisurely trot for a shallow dive, just slithered home. The Yorkshire club had arranged for a brass band to parade around the field during the tea interval on the third day, but in the event both the entertainment and the cricket itself were abandoned in the torrential rain.

There was a small upshot to the game involving a decision that was unsentimental, even by Yorkshire standards. It proved to be the last first-class match ever played by the county's middle-order batsman George Wilson, who was out for a second-ball duck. At the age of 23 he decided simultaneously with his committee that he would never make it at that level, and that his best bet in life was now to join the staff of a Leeds bank. Over the course of four seasons Wilson had played 15 matches for Yorkshire and scored 352 runs at an average of 17, with a top score of 55. By all accounts it was a muted departure as the young player collected his belongings and simply walked off through the gates in the rain. The club never contacted Wilson to thank him for his service, and only Verity bothered to keep in touch. Wilson later admitted that he was hurt by the way it ended, 'but that was the reality of life at Yorkshire back then'. It would not be the last time a talented but underperforming county cricketer went back to civilian life without a word from his former employer.

From there Yorkshire went on to host Middlesex at Bradford, a contest that left undecided the burning question of whether it was the hard-as-flint north or the effete, soft south with the better team. More rain washed out the first day, and Yorkshire eventually managed a score of 171 on what Hutton (who made 72) called a 'suet pudding' of a wicket. The visitors replied with 292, Edrich lingering most of the day over his 69. Yorkshire at least upped the tempo in their second innings but were prisoners of circumstance. Neither side could overcome the handicap of a deadly slow pitch and an outfield so sluggish that the ball hit there generally stopped dead in a spray of mud. It's a testament to the enduring appeal of Yorkshire cricket that on the wet but playable Monday there were some 9,000 spectators, and a collection raised £150 for Arthur Wood's benefit.

As a symbol both of the British class system and the strength in depth of English cricket, it would be hard to top the annual Gentlemen v Players match. Already in its 134th year on the sporting calendar, it was played at Lord's from 5 to 7 July 1939. E.W. Swanton saw 'everything fine in the land' epitomised by this parade of wage-earning professionals and what Fred Trueman later characterised as 'twats in cravats' nominally claiming only expenses. The social aspect of the fixture was that most calculated to impress the ordinary observer. Despite the drenching rain, a mile-long procession of cars and taxis snaked its way up St John's

Wood Road before the start, and the ground itself was adorned with a ring of fruit and sweet stalls, picnic areas, tea tents and champagne bars attended by liveried waiters and young women in starched white aprons. Some of the Gentlemen wore striped ties around their waists as they took to the field, with one or two salmon-pink scarves peeking out under all the Panama hats and other multicoloured headgear. The scene lacked only a Lowry or a Renoir.

The Players batted first, allowing Harold Gimblett to perform another of his glittering cameos at the crease by hooking and driving his way to 52 before hitting over a straight ball. Denis Compton added 58 and Tom Dollery 70. Ken Farnes was down from Worksop for the week to open the Gentlemen's bowling. Making the ball rise disconcertingly on the damp pitch, he finished with 5-78 in the Players' completed innings of 270. Bill Copson, the professionals' number ten, had only just put on his pads when he heard the shout: 'You're in, mate.' As Copson walked out of the Long Room the incoming batsman Doug Wright passed by him holding a bloodied handkerchief up to his nose. Wright looked at his teammate and said, out of the side of his mouth: 'He's fucking quick, Bill.' That concluded the technical exchange. Copson lasted one ball as Farnes, making his first appearance of the summer, took 3 wickets in an over.

Gerry Chalk opened the Gentlemen's reply, and later confirmed that this had not been a congenial experience, the weather being 'blustery and grey, with bits of muck whipping up into your face as Bill Bowes pounded in to bowl'. Hammond, wanting to turn his own bowlers loose as quickly as possible, declared at 158-7. The tactic seemed to be working with Gimblett and his captain Eddie Paynter both quickly back in the pavilion, but the England firm of Hutton and Compton realised 141 runs in eighty minutes, allowing Paynter in turn to declare at 202-4. Challenged to score 315 in three and a half hours, the amateurs fell 161 runs short. Several players were rendered *hors de combat* during the chase, and that trenchant, red-blooded cricketer Wally Hammond later informed the MCC secretary, Col Rowan Rait Kerr, that the experiment of using rock-hard Australian balls in the match had on the whole proved unsatisfactory, Hammond perhaps adding an intensifier or two to underscore his point. In the sort of quick-change just then becoming familiar to British film audiences following the adventures of Superman and his alter ego Clark Kent, Ken Farnes went direct from terrorising the professionals' batsmen to teaching sixth-form geography at Worksop College. Like many bachelors of quickly advancing years Farnes was haunted by the fear of loneliness, and his diary speaks not only of his deep-held spiritual beliefs but of his marital prospects with any one of several young women listed.

While most of the players hurriedly left Lord's to return to their counties on the evening of 7 July, Gerry Chalk had only to take a taxi across London to the Oval, where he was due to lead Kent in a match against Surrey the following morning. He remembered having been 'roughed up' by a number of rising balls bowled by Bowes and Copson at Lord's. 'I could barely get out of bed the next day,' he admitted. 'It took me forever to get dressed, and I breakfasted off black coffee and aspirin. Of course Surrey won the toss and batted, which meant I was stuck out in the field all day instead of having a nice bath. Cricket can be cruel sometimes.'

Still, Chalk had his moments.

One such came in Kent's next match, against Somerset at Maidstone, where Chalk scored a lightning 73 and then skilfully deployed his bowlers to bring about victory by 8 wickets, despite Arthur Wellard having characteristically hit 3 consecutive sixes off Doug Wright as well as taking 8-96 with the ball. Generally unimpressed by other cricketers, Wellard later remarked that in a certain mood the Kent captain was the best batsman in England in 1939, and apparently unaware that the bowling was intended for anything other than his personal enjoyment.

Chalk spent more of his time after that away on army duty, but he was back later in August to hit 124 against Sussex at Hastings and an unbeaten 115 against Yorkshire at Dover. He fell just 6 runs short of adding yet another century in his last match of the season, in the home victory against Lancashire. Godfrey Evans was fully launched in the Kent side by then and remembered:

Chalk was an odd bird, with his MCC blazer and his bloody great ice-cream swirl of hair, and as a young player you didn't get too close to him. But he loved his cricket. He was unflappable. You'd go out to bat with him at something like 150-7, chasing 400, and he'd say: 'Now, Godfrey, we'll knock these runs off tonight and have time for a good dinner.' I wanted to tell him to get his hair cut but I didn't dare. Chalk never held a post-mortem if we lost a match. He was always looking ahead. I admired that in him.

Hampshire's 8-wicket victory over Northamptonshire in early July is worth mentioning chiefly because it was the home team's first championship success of the season, and also marked the last appearance by their 34-year-old seamer John Steele, an army chaplain who went lame in the field and never played competitively again. Earlier in the summer Steele had taken 6-62 against Warwickshire at Portsmouth, and a few days later sent back Ames, Chalk and Valentine in four balls while facing Kent at Southampton. Hampshire's left-handed batsman and occasional wicketkeeper Don Walker was now coming into form. He took 54 and 90 not out off Arthur Wellard and the rest of the Somerset attack at Taunton, 66 against Sussex at Portsmouth, and then an unbeaten 108 against Surrey on the same ground. 'The Don', as he humorously introduced himself, had a rare zest for life. John Steele said of him, 'he communicated to all he met his vitality, optimism, faith and his simple belief that life was there to be lived', while on a more technical note *Wisden* added: 'Sound in defence, with unlimited patience, he brought off good strokes all round the wicket and generally gave every indication of a successful career.' Tall, dark and cleft-chinned, with a passing facial resemblance to the young Cary Grant, whom he sometimes impersonated, Walker was also now playing his last season of county cricket.

As the Edriches and others proved, it wasn't unusual to see family members playing together in the same cricket team in 1939. But Sussex took this to new heights when in early July they went into the field against Lancashire at Hove with no fewer than three sets of brothers in their ranks. The Langridges and the Parkses were joined in turn by

Walter 'Tich' Cornford, an enthusiastic wicketkeeper-batsman, and his younger sibling Jim, who bowled right-arm seam. The former, aged 38 and standing just 5ft tall, had played four Tests for England, including a match at Auckland in 1930 which contained 47 byes or leg byes in the New Zealand first innings. It was unkindly said that when Cornford crouched down behind the wicket under his floppy grey hat that he resembled an ancient tortoise that had inadvertently strayed onto the field. He took two catches and a smart stumping in the one completed Lancashire innings at Hove. The visitors followed on 301 behind, but rain ensured a draw.

Testimony to cricket's nationwide popularity, especially as the prospect of war now asserted itself, came in a match played between the Royal Artillery and Royal Engineers on 10-11 July at Lord's. It rained torrentially on the first morning and Pelham Warner, for one, said he didn't think there was any way the teams could get on the field, and that even if they did, no one would come to watch them.

Warner then looked on from his seat in the committee room as play began at 11.30 a.m., as scheduled, and 6,000 spectators streamed into the soaked ground.

The match itself, which was drawn, proved to be a near-idyllic respite from what Warner called the 'sterner contests' awaiting the soldier-cricketers in the times ahead. There would be a total of seven war casualties among the two sides. Twenty-nine-year-old Warren Zambra, from Petersfield in Hampshire, opened the Artillery bowling, taking 2-55 in 10 overs. According to Warner, Zambra was the life and soul of the post-match dinner at the Café Royal. 'There was about that young man an ebullient air, an expression of the sheer joy of playing sport among friends … by every word and deed [he] might have been a boy on a long holiday, without a care in the world.'

If this was a mask, it was one that Zambra kept firmly in place during his participation in almost every significant theatre of the land war over the course of the next five years. By then a lieutenant colonel and holder of the MBE, he fell in the attritional fighting around the medieval town of Gradara, on the Adriatic coast of Italy, in September 1944. He was 34.

Zambra's younger brother Roger, also a cricketer, had been killed while serving with the RAF in October 1940. Difficult though the show of high spirits at Lord's and afterwards may have been, it never faltered. 'Mr Zambra told me simply that he was proud and happy to be playing there, and that whatever happened in the future it was an achievement he would hold dear for the rest of his life,' Warner remembered.

Twenty years earlier, *Wisden* had published a photograph showing King George V being introduced to the members of the Eton and Harrow sides before their annual encounter at Lord's. The captain of Harrow that 'relieved yet forlorn summer' of 1919, as the caption put it, was W.A.R. Collins, the future publisher Sir William Collins, while the Eton eleven contained both the future MCC luminaries Gubby Allen and Ronnie Aird, and the Sussex and England XI bowler Clement Gibson. By then the fixture was already in its 115th year and firmly established as a date on the English social calendar. Fortunately, His Majesty had already left the ground by the time Eton won the match on the second evening, following which a fight broke out 'of some proportion', as *The Times* noted, between rival followers of the two schools seated in the Tavern stand. The next year before play began Eton's captain Wilfred Hill-Wood warned his players and their young supporters that if there was a repeat occurrence the match would be taken away from Lord's. The peace seems to have held as a result, and the cricketer-playwright James Barrie wrote:

> I went to the Lord's match, 15,000 tall hats – one cad hat (mine); 15,000 stiff white collars, canes, shiny faces … The ladies comparatively drab, fearing rain, but the gents superb, colossal, sleek, lovely. All with such a pleased smile. Why? Because they know they had the Eton something or the Harrow something. They bestowed the something on each other, exchanged it with each other as the likes of me exchanged the time of day.

Little about the occasion had changed by 1939, except that there was now a television camera mounted on a tripod next to the pavilion and several more spectators dotted around the place who were guilty of the once-impossible tastelessness of not wearing a hat. In general the fixture kept up its ritual wonderfully well. E.W. Swanton was present and remembered sitting with his friend and Oxford near-contemporary 'Buns' Cartwright, who was then 39 but seemed considerably older.

'"Buffer" does not in any way fit the eccentric personality of Col Cartwright,' Swanton wrote:

> Other terms will occur to those who knew him … He never followed a profession or business career, though he served at one time as a judge's marshal and government Patronage Secretary. With his beetling brow and fierce military moustache he was a formidable figure at the best of times. How he must have seemed from the other side of a desk in the palace of Westminster is a comical thought. It was, on the face of it, a peculiar appointment.

Crusoe Robertson-Glasgow was also among the packed house at Lord's for the start of play on 14 July 1939. There was more than a touch of awe in Swanton's memory of his fellow correspondent. 'Crusoe resembled an elemental agency of some hitherto undiscovered sort – a benign agency, to be sure, not destructive like an earthquake, but still a very potent force that was only subject to its own natural rules.'

While that was undoubtedly true, it was emphatically not the impression Robertson-Glasgow gave just a few nights later at a reception held by Joseph Kennedy, the US ambassador to Great Britain, at his official residence near Hyde Park. Neville Chamberlain had made a statement that week on the 'tinderbox of Europe' and, more particularly, the disputed control of the city of Danzig, to a hushed House of Commons. The ambassador's 22-year-old son John Fitzgerald Kennedy thought the 'wispy-haired old boy' whom their mutual friend David Ormsby-Gore brought to the house 'a curious study … He shuffled in, shoulders stooped, greeted a few with a limp shake, then heavily sank into a chair and remained in the prone position thereafter. His reputation as an orator preceded him, but we saw no evidence that night.' Crusoe did, however, spring to life when his host the ambassador informed the room that in his opinion the current international crisis was at root all about capital. 'I have advised Neville to propose a settlement that will bring Hitler economic benefits more important than the territorial annexation of Danzig,' Kennedy proclaimed, in his distinctive Boston accent. 'To put in a billion or two now will be worth it.' At that point Crusoe had risen from his seat, fixed the ambassador with a hard look, and announced, 'We may fail in the fight against fascism, but we shall not negotiate with it. Good night!'

Back at Lord's there were scenes of feverish excitement on the sunlit evening of 15 July. Harrow won finally by 8 wickets, their 17-year-old captain Tony Lithgow finishing proceedings with three successive straight drives to the pavilion fence. His team had needed to score 131 in just over two hours, and it was their first victory in the great schools' grudge match since 1908. Lithgow was an individualist, with a shock of unruly dark hair and large black-rimmed eyes that gave him the impression of having just stepped from the prize ring. 'He played his own game,' Robertson-Glasgow wrote of the young batsman, who went on to serve with distinction in the Black Watch, surviving the war. 'The faster the bowling, the more he liked it and the harder he hit it.'

Wisden added of the finish at Lord's:

> The crowd invaded the field and carried both Lithgow and his partner Crutchley in triumph to the pavilion. Then for 20 minutes an ordered assembly, numbering about 8,000, cheered the heroes. The victorious team, with Hendren, their popular coach, appeared on the balcony; the Harrow school song was sung and there followed a free fight for top hats. Not for 20 years had the meeting of Eton and Harrow ended with such a frenzied scene.

The proudly Anglo-Irish Patsy Hendren, of solid yeoman stock and the holder of 51 England Test caps and 170 first-class centuries, later remarked that after being 'cheered to the skies by the young gentlemen in their tails and toppers' on a midsummer's evening at Lord's, life was all downhill from there.

Certainly no one seemed to doubt that there had been an exhilarating display of youthful high spirits that day at cricket's headquarters, and that for the most part this had been entirely decorous, although the MCC later reported in a private note:

> The Secretary disclosed that while the material damage resulting from the ragging after the Eton and Harrow match had been insignificant, an elderly lady spectator had been knocked down and fractured her arm. The Headmaster of Harrow had written indicating that he thought the school should take steps to eliminate ragging on future occasions. The committee agrees.

It perhaps speaks to the deference then afforded the great rivals of public school sport that Middlesex moved their home match against Nottinghamshire to the Oval in order to make Lord's available for the young cricketers. The chief characteristic of this unusual arrangement was an unbeaten innings of 312 by the Notts opener Walter Keeton. Carrying his bat through 435 minutes at the crease, he hit a five and 28 fours in what proved to be the highest individual score of the season. In two completed innings, Middlesex made a total of just 58 more runs between them. Keeton had been born in 1905 in the small mining community of Shirebrook in Derbyshire, and attended the local colliery school before, at 15, he laced up a knapsack, slinging a pair of football and cricket boots over either shoulder, and set off from home to seek work. In time the young sportsman made his way to the mecca of venturesome youth, Mansfield, where he became apprenticed to a shoe manufacturer. Keeton's family eventually followed him east to Nottinghamshire and settled in the mining village of Forest Town. Walter Keeton remained in the area for the rest of his life and died there at the age of 75.

Keeton first played for his adopted county in 1926, but since Notts then operated not so much a youth as a full-scale senility policy it was another five years before he became the county's regular opener alongside the eccentric Charlie Harris. Between them they put on a three-figured partnership no fewer than forty-five times over the years. Keeton was, though, a nearly man when it came to international selection. Probably his greatest defect as an opening batsman was to have run into form just as Hutton and Washbrook established themselves at the top of the England Test order. By July 1939 Keeton had managed a single appearance for his country, in the drawn match against Australia at Leeds in 1934, in which he made 25 and 12 and Don Bradman scored 304.

The selectors promptly dropped Keeton as a result, and he suffered a further setback that winter when he was knocked down and seriously injured by a lorry near his home. Defying medical opinion, he was back playing for his county side in June 1935 and remained the team's most productive batsman in each of the next three seasons. While his opening partner Harris was seen as enigmatic, as likely to block a full toss as to knock an unplayable delivery out of the park, Keeton was thought solid and steady, with a particular mastery of the on-drive. He was also a brilliant fieldsman, as befitted a sometime inside forward for Nottingham Forest. Keeton had finished 1938 with two centuries and an average of 30, which was poor by his standards, but he already had some 1,500 runs at over 60 by the halfway point of the summer of 1939. In short, he was the model professional. Keeton was married to his teenaged sweetheart Florence Russell, despite which he was said to 'cut a dashing figure to the ladies at Trent Bridge with his crinkly dark hair, sharp eyes and lean, clean-cut jaw'. Nottinghamshire paid him a basic salary of £400 to tide him over from early May to late September each year, and like many players he supplemented his county income by an interest in a local sports shop. Robertson-Glasgow said of him, 'Walter was a quiet soul, with a wonderfully convivial side he reserved for his family and friends … He took great pride in his lone England cap, and whenever possible had himself photographed in it.'

After a brief lull at around the time of the Eton-Harrow match, the weather got even worse during the middle of July. Derbyshire could get on the field for only ninety minutes during the first day's play against Yorkshire at Chesterfield, and for a total of four hours in the two remaining days. Essex were similarly stymied in their match with Surrey at Colchester, although ultimately they turned the conditions to their advantage. The county's leg-spinner Peter Smith took 7-47 on a drying pitch and the home side won by 10 wickets. It was the same tale at Southampton, where Hampshire drew with Glamorgan, and at Yeovil, where Somerset and Lancashire managed just 190 minutes' play over the scheduled three days.

Perhaps no one in England was more disgruntled with the atrocious weather that July than Sir Julien Cahn, the eccentric hire-purchase tycoon with his own cricket team. Cahn had assembled a side that was due to play a full-strength West Indies XI over two days at the West Bridgford ground near Nottingham. By modern standards it might seem a curious way for the tourists to prepare for the all-important second Test against England, which was due to start immediately afterwards. Cahn's side included a number of visiting Australian and New Zealand club players, and its bowling was opened by 36-year-old John Hall, who could boast a lone county championship appearance for Nottinghamshire in 1935, and Vic Jackson, an occasional New South Wales all-rounder and (just as important a credential to his host) *bon vivant*, who tragically lost his life in January 1965 when he was involved in a traffic accident at a level crossing.

Cahn himself captained the side, batting at a perhaps optimistic number six in the order. The ground had been lovingly prepared for the occasion, and all week a butler in full regalia and a host of waiters, maids, caterers, gardeners, carpenters and electricians had been hard at work erecting a huge marquee at the Loughborough Road end, in time filling this with tubs of palms and exotic plants, and plates of brightly coloured cakes laid out on two long trestle tables said to have been groaning with luxury. There was also a champagne cup and a young lady rather incongruously dressed as the Statue of Liberty (a reference, apparently, to Cahn's recent expansion into the American market), sporting a papier mâché headpiece and a matching ruffled green robe of noticeably more sparing cut than the original, ornamented at the waist with roses of teal blue and pink. Two groundsmen and a boy had meticulously laid the pitch, which, on the face of it, looked good for thousands of runs.

Unfortunately, it didn't just rain on the first day of play. The cricketers and spectators had a mini pop-up tropical storm to contend with, and Cahn's crew had to hurriedly tear down the marquee as it strained at its moorings and remove its contents as best they could to the ground's more sturdy and capacious pavilion, where the facilities included a full-scale badminton court. No cricket at all was possible that day, and when the West Indies finally got to bat the following morning only Headley, with 61 out of a total of 197, proved the master of conditions. At 1.30 p.m. a colliery brass band squelched around the outfield, the somewhat soiled-looking Statue of Liberty marching ahead of them, periodically twirling her torch high above her head. Cahn's XI went in after lunch and had time to reach 121-4 before the storm clouds returned. It had not rained so much, they said, during fifty years of local club cricket.

After the disappointment of the actual sport, the players were entertained in characteristic style that night at Stanford Hall. Cahn himself felt a touch of his recurrent lumbago coming on and so interacted with his guests from his electric wheelchair. Lady Cahn not being in residence, a young nurse who appeared to have been sewn into a flesh-coloured costume that Vic Jackson noted appreciatively 'only accentuated her natural upholstery' attended him throughout the evening. After dinner there was mixed bathing for those who wanted it in the heated outdoor pool, which they shared with Cahn's pair of trained seals, while others preferred an exclusive screening in the sunken art deco cinema of *The Wizard of Oz*, which their host had somehow procured three weeks in advance of its official release. At some stage in the proceedings several more nurses appeared on the scene. The future Lord Constantine disdained both the swimming and the film but remembered being taken to inspect the miniature bats and mounted cricket balls on the living room mantelpiece, each with an elaborate inscription of some particular feat on Cahn's part. Without any apparent connection of thought, someone had placed a large painting of an erotically posed lady on the wall immediately behind this display. 'The twin icons of Sir Julien's life, perhaps,' Constantine later said. It was a long night, and the West Indies tourists eventually reached their Manchester hotel only late in the afternoon of Friday 21 July. It was perhaps just as well for their prospects in the match that it was again raining heavily at the time play was due to start in the Test the following morning at Old Trafford, and that only half an hour's play was possible during the day.

Earlier that week, Yorkshire had been in action, if it could be so called, against Sussex at Scarborough. A thick mist wafted in to the ground from the sea, meaning that the players in the middle could see one another in ghostly outline, but nothing whatsoever of the outfield or the spectators. Hutton, who scored 177 and 57 not out in the match, later remarked: 'Only when a boundary shot hit the fence did the crowd know we were playing and we were reassured of their presence by their applause.' Bill Bowes took 7-54 in the first Sussex innings and Yorkshire won by 10 wickets.

On 19 July, the great turn-of-the-century Surrey and England all-rounder Tom Hayward died of cancer at the age of 68. To some it was another sign that the long summer twilight of the golden age of cricket was fading into history. Hayward had been only the second batsman to reach the milestone of 100 first-class centuries, following W.G. Grace. He had performed the double of 1,000 runs and 100 wickets in the 1897 season and scored 3,518 runs in the summer of 1906. Hayward's funeral on 22 July filled the Mill Road Church in Cambridge, the town where he was both born and died, to the rafters. The Surrey and MCC secretaries both sent flowers, and there was a wreath from Jack Hobbs with the inscription: 'To my old boy, from his broken-hearted friend.' Many cricket clubs up and down Britain (though not the two Test sides sitting in the rain at Old Trafford) chose to observe a minute's silence before they started play that day.

Hayward's old county club played Kent at Blackheath that week. It was another rain-soaked draw, although there was time for Surrey's 26-year-old middle-order batsman Jack Parker to score 96. Though never gaining international recognition, Parker was good enough to be named a member of the MCC side scheduled to visit India in the winter of 1939–40, only to see the tour cancelled due to the war. Gerry Chalk was back from army training to captain Kent in the same match. He was so popular with his men that when he went off to fight barely more than a month later they held a 'Good Luck, Skipper' party, and gave him such gifts as two monogrammed shirts, a suitcase and a fishing rod. Godfrey Evans was then just coming into the Kent senior eleven. 'Life was pretty good,' he later reflected, 'and most of us thought it would stay that way in the future. When we waved Chalk off it felt to us just like we were saying goodbye for the winter. We were sure everyone would be back to play cricket again in April.'

Walter Hammond was seventeen years older than Evans, and perhaps as a result less sanguine about current world affairs. 'Oh Christ,' he remarked, when the news broke on 19 July that the German foreign minister had been in discussion with the Soviet chargé d'affaires in Berlin about a possible pact between their two countries. 'Now the cat's among the fucking pigeons.' In the fatalistic spirit he habitually adopted even in peacetime, Hammond often drank to excess, and there were occasionally awkward results. Harold Gimblett remembered that Somerset had played a championship match against Gloucestershire later in the season, and that at the close England's renowned Test captain had stood and waved from the upper pavilion deck, 'invok[ing] the spectacle of the king looking down on his humble subjects from the palace balcony'. The imperious image had been somewhat dented only when one of the nearby stewards tidying up after the match had managed to drop the leg of a heavy iron bench on Hammond's foot and had him hopping in pain. Gimblett believed that 'Wally [had] gotten himself nicely soused' even before play had begun on the shortened third day of the match, although set against this it should be remembered that the Somerset player had recently been dropped from the Test side and may have borne its captain a grudge as a result.

In any event, Hammond was duly present at the Ashley Down Ground, Bristol, on the morning of 19 July for the start of a county championship match against Hampshire. This was an 'amazing' contest, *Wisden* wrote. Thanks to the rain only fifty-five minutes' play was possible on the first two days, but on the third morning a sort of speed-cricket game broke out. Hampshire were skittled out for 103, and Hammond then declared the Gloucestershire innings with a lead of 1 run. Next the England off-spinner Tom Goddard ran riot with figures of 8-36, shooting the visitors out for 66 in little over an hour. Gloucester in turn needed 66 to win in seventy minutes and managed to lose 5 wickets before scrambling home. Hammond's first innings of 30 was the top individual score of the match.

Glamorgan eked out another waterlogged draw with Surrey at the Oval, Wilf Wooller taking 4-47 with his right-arm seam before the heavens opened at teatime on the first afternoon and washed out any further play in the match. Looking back on it, it sometimes seems remarkable that the polymathic Welshman ever found the time for cricket in his busy schedule. As we've seen, in mid 1939 Wooller was also playing competitive rugby, football and squash, as well as casually turning his hand to half a dozen other sports. He still held down a job with the Cardiff coal magnate Sir Herbert Merrett, which sometimes obliged him to spend extended amounts of time supervising the firm's shipping operations in cities like Algiers or Marseilles. That Wooller enjoyed life to the full had been established when a drunken undergraduate escapade involving the theft of a receiver from a phone box resulted in a £5 fine from magistrates and a headline in the daily press: NIGHT-TIME EXPLOITS OF CAMBRIDGE BLUE. As a rule Wooller was brave, headstrong, irreverent and not a martyr to false modesty. When he reported to Cardiff Arms Park for his county championship debut in 1938, a steward on the gate at first refused him entry, saying, 'I've never heard of a cricketer called Wilfred Wooller.' Wooller replied instantly, 'You will.' He was right.

Wooller was away on business when Glamorgan began their next championship match of the 1939 season, against Warwickshire at the Stradley Park ground, Llanelli, on 22 July. It produced another dramatic finish. Rain prevented any play on the opening Saturday, Sunday was a rest day, and Warwickshire finally went in to bat after tea on Monday. The visitors then closed their innings at 48-0, and Maurice Turnbull did the same for Glamorgan with the scores exactly equal. There was some later discussion about whether or not this arrangement was strictly in compliance with the spirit of Law 54 governing declarations, but it set up a thrilling conclusion to the game. Warwickshire closed their second innings at 197-6, leaving the home side 150 minutes in which to chase 198. Belying his nickname of 'The Rock', Glamorgan's 35-year-old opener Emrys Davies smashed 67 in forty-five minutes, while the wicketkeeper Haydn Davies (no relation) polished off all the last 27 runs in 2 overs, the Welshmen winning by 3 wickets with fifteen minutes to spare.

The weather again intruded that week in London, where Middlesex and Lancashire managed a total of just over four hours' play in the first two and a half days of their match at Lord's. Its sole redeeming feature was a characteristically gritty innings of 125 by Bill Edrich. Edrich was now averaging 45 for the season and was about to run into some of the best form of his life. Although ignored by England, there were compensations. He always cut a dash around town, appearing in suits which grew nattier and nattier as his various investments improved. One day Edrich went out to dinner with some of his Middlesex teammates at Kettner's in Soho and emerged later that night with two statuesque lady companions, both taller than he was, one on either arm. He had the key to a little-used room at Lord's, an exceptionally understanding wife, and life was good. A bit later in the summer a few of the Middlesex team were driving down the A23 to a match at Hove and Edrich, who was at the wheel, looked over, saw a pretty girl in the next lane, and waved at her. The girl waved back. Without a word Edrich then pulled over, and so did the girl. He calmly got in her car and that was the last any of his county colleagues saw of him until a few minutes before the start of play the following morning, when, after a quick cigarette and a cup of coffee, he went out to bat and scored 161.

'Old Trafford carried on its tradition for bad weather,' *Wisden* was forced to admit, as Saturday's play in the second Test between England and the West Indies was restricted to thirty-three minutes, and the home side finished at 11 without loss. Another storm flooded the ground on Sunday, leaving the outfield unfit for play when the teams returned on Monday morning. This was the signal for one of those peculiarly English feats of mass improvisation (preceding in miniature the definitive 'Dunkirk spirit' of just ten months later) when the official Old Trafford groundsmen were joined by scores of ordinary spectators who took off their shoes and helped to mop up the playing area with blankets and towels. As a result of their efforts, the match resumed a few minutes after midday, Hammond eventually declaring with the score at 164-7 to leave the West Indies to bat for seventy-five minutes at the end of a grimly overcast day. Despite the conditions, there were over 11,000 spectators present to see the 64 deliveries, including four no-balls, sent down on the Saturday, and nearly as many again paid for admission on both Monday and Tuesday. No ticket refunds were offered in those days, and no one appears to have complained about having spent what in some cases amounted to the equivalent of two days' wages to watch half an hour's cricket. The *Manchester Evening News* reported 'well-deported crowds' who walked home on Saturday evening among the 'intermittent showers', findings that were somewhat belied by the headline on an immediately adjacent page: 'Gales, Rain, Hail Lash Town.'

The England selectors, pursuing their recurrent twentieth-century policy of including a number of personally affable and technically sound county cricketers who ideally should never have been asked to play in a Test match, had earlier made two changes to the side that had acquitted itself well at Lord's. Arthur Fagg of Kent replaced the mercurial Harold Gimblett at the top of the order, and Gloucestershire's veteran offspinner Tom Goddard came in for Hedley Verity, who, as it turned out, would not represent his country again. Although this latest apparent foible on the selectors' part failed to make much of an impact on the match at Old Trafford, it dramatically affected at least one of the players involved. 'A lot of people have been nice to me since I joined [England] and Mr Hammond is not one of them,' Harold Gimblett wrote in a letter of September 1939, signifying his permanent breach from the cricket establishment. Elsewhere the Somerset player appeared to suggest that his sometime captain was personally envious of his own batting talent, although their then current Test averages of around 32 (Gimblett) and 65 (Hammond) would not seem to support this contention. It was a curious thing. For Gimblett, making contact with the ball was often as elusive as scientists seeking to determine if there was life elsewhere in the solar system. At other times, he cut and drove and hooked bowlers right and left, playing like a singularly uninhibited father toying with the opposition in a prep school match.

While Arthur Fagg was opening the England innings at Old Trafford, Gimblett went out to bat for Somerset in front of a sparse Monday morning crowd at Derby and flayed an even-time 71 off a home attack that included both the Pope brothers and the former Test player Les Townsend, widely regarded as one of the strongest seam-bowling line-ups in the championship. The other ten Somerset players managed exactly 100 runs between them. After that Gimblett went on to successive first-class scores of 7,15,46, 1,11, 17,5, 1, 19, 15 and 6 before launching a one-man blitz against Surrey at Weston-Super-Mare. Although the scorebook recorded only a relatively modest total of 79, his innings was said to have 'pulverised Gover, Watts, Parker et al, [following] which he strolled from the middle looking as cool and relaxed as if having just risen fresh from a favourite armchair'. Like Hedley Verity, Gimblett had also now played his last Test.

Back at Old Trafford, wrote *Wisden*, 'real fun began after lunch' on Monday.

> Suddenly, England collapsed before the accurately flighted off-breaks of Grant and the clever bowling of Clarke, who mixed leg spin with an occasional googly. Both men maintained an admirable length and the ball often jumped unexpectedly. In the field West Indies supported their bowlers magnificently; their agile picking up and swift returns kept runs down to a minimum.

The result of all this was Hammond's subsequent decision to insert the West Indies for what might have been an uncomfortable time for them between tea and the close. In fact it was the Englishmen who initially seemed to suffer worst. *Wisden* continued:

> With the pitch likely to become even more difficult, Grant set a fine example to his men by going in first and launching a severe attack on the bowling. He began by freely cutting Bowes and Copson and when Goddard came on at 22, Grant showed an utter disregard for the imposing array of short legs. Compton, standing within eight feet of the bat, received a fearful blow on the thigh.

The Tuesday, however, belonged to the English bowlers, and more particularly to Bill Bowes, who was celebrating his 31st birthday. Demonstrating both parsimony and penetration, the Yorkshire seamer took 6-33 in 17.4 8-ball overs, the last 7 West Indies wickets going down for 38 runs. As a result England had a first-innings lead of 31 but only four and a half more hours of play in which to exploit it.

The indefatigable 67-year-old social critic and philosopher Bertrand Russell happened to briefly be at Old Trafford that morning prior to lecturing at Manchester's Victoria University, and bravely spoke to several groups of spectators around the ground about his passionate opposition to Britain's rearmament, a stance of which they did not much approve. Before the cricket resumed, Walter Hammond's voice again echoed out over the pavilion loudspeakers with a contrary plea for military volunteers. The third-day atmosphere as a whole was said to have been 'dreary' and 'funereal', to which the England captain's sombre appeal no doubt in a small degree contributed. Certainly Hammond and his fellow batsmen did nothing further to release the ground from its pervasive air of wintry melancholy. England declared again at 128-6, which left the tourists the improbable task of scoring 160 in seventy minutes. Rolph Grant apparently meant to have another go at the English bowling because he launched an almighty swing at the first ball he faced from Bowes, only to be caught by Hardstaff on the deep-cover boundary. A few overs later Hammond recorded his own 100th catch in Test matches when he held a thin edge from Headley after the ball had bounced off the wicketkeeper's gloves. It was not everyone who could go on standing in the slips at the age of 36 and routinely bring off the sort of dismissals the England captain did. Learie Constantine remembered a moment elsewhere on the tour when he flung the bat at a ball from Verity and watched it 'shoot off like blue lightning somewhere behind me, and in the blur you could actually see people's heads turning to where they thought it would land somewhere far over the third-man boundary. But the ball was already in Hammond's pocket.' The West Indies batted out for the inevitable draw at Old Trafford, with some 10,000 spectators still there at the close. 'Rain considerably interfered with the game,' the *Manchester Evening News* was left to conclude, with some understatement.

At 11.30 the next morning the West Indies were in action 200 miles away at the Oval, where they beat Surrey by 7 wickets. The tourists batted first and scored 487, with a century by the Boston-born Bam Bam Weekes, whose innings, untypically cautious at first before accelerating away smoothly, reminded some of a sports car being run in. The future rogue doctor Bertie Clarke took 5-64 in the Surrey first innings and his fellow convict-to-be Leslie Hylton came on as twelfth man. Both these individuals were presented to the king during lunch on the first day. It was one of those English summer spells of alternating sun and showers. Constantine remembered playing one shot in a froth of grass and mud, the ball 'shooting straight up like a water-spout', although by the close the pitch had dried out sufficiently for Clarke, bowling in a floppy white sun hat, to take another 4 wickets with his leg-breaks and googlies.

While England played cricket, the country continued slowly to rearm. Godfrey Evans summed up the jumpiness of this waiting period when he recalled seeing two men carrying rolled-up posters and buckets of paste up and down Castle Street in central Canterbury early one Saturday morning.

They were slapping up civil-defence notices, and one thing I remember is that there was a lot of technical stuff about how to use your gas mask and then a line that said: 'You must not test your apparatus by putting your head inside a gas-oven as it is not designed for this purpose and may well prove harmful to your health.' No kidding. I later heard that a bloke near us in Faversham actually did that and bloody nearly asphyxiated himself.

Another warning note of a sort somehow peculiar to English cricket came in the minutes of the MCC committee meeting of 24 July:

It now appears that the Balloon section, RAF, might wish to apply for leave to erect huts at Lord's, and if the actual inflation of the balloon clashed with a match, the Car Park on certain occasions might be out of commission.

There was also a more benign glimpse of the future elsewhere in the same meeting:

The Secretary reported that, with the approval of the news reel companies, Messrs Metro-Goldwyn-Meyer and the Realist Film Unit Ltd had been given facilities for taking moving pictures at Lord's.

Like a stagnant pond, motionless to the naked eye, English youth cricket was also teeming with furious and important activity that summer. In late July an 8-year-old on his school holiday made a precocious debut for his local village side in Stainton, South Yorkshire, which his father captained. The older player's name was Alan Trueman and his young son answered to Freddie. One hundred and fifty miles due south, a 9-year-old called Peter May was already setting batting records at Leighton Park junior school near Reading, whose magazine for June 1939 notes: 'There are many cries of "Shot!" when May is at the crease.' That same summer a cricket-mad 10-year-old growing up around Bognor Regis became 'seriously obsessed' with Hedley Verity, 'standing around in a howling gale by the Lord's practice nets before play began in the first Test, desperate to get the great man's autograph.' Unhappily, when the moment came Verity politely but firmly declined, telling his young fan: 'Sorry, son. I've got a job to get to.' The disappointed boy grew up to become the bishop of Liverpool (and future England Test captain) David Sheppard.

Sometimes I'd stay on at the ground long after stumps, and if there wasn't a party to go to I'd just wander around there in the dusk. A lot of people want to get away from their work as fast as they possibly can, but I remember just liking the atmosphere of a cricket ground. Peering in windows, exploring the pavilion – I suppose it was just the peacefulness of the place and the thought that it could all soon be shot to hell.

Godfrey Evans, refuting his county secretary's memory of him having been the first into the pub each night, told me this fifty years after the fact, and even then somewhere inside this least nostalgic of old cricketers the slumbering wide-eyed teenager would sometimes wake with a start at the mention of a particular name. Evans once said of his first county captain:

Gerry Chalk? A very good player. A gentleman. You have to remember that nobody was making any money out of English cricket in 1939. At least none of the players were. I was just coming into the Kent team and still living out in the country, and I needed my own transport. My first motorcycle had just died on me. One morning there was a meeting about it with Messrs Chalk and Hough. Perhaps we could buy you another bike, Hough said, but it would have to be a used one. Out of the question, said Chalk, he needs a proper car. It went on like this a while, and the upshot was that the skipper lent me twenty quid out of his own pocket – a fortune in those days – and I put it down on a shiny blue Jensen S-type, a bloody gorgeous machine, convertible, the size of someone's living room. You should have seen Hough's face when I turned up in it at Canterbury and fucking nearly rammed the front gate trying to get in. Of course, I still had to keep up the payments on it, which proved a bit of a bother when they cancelled all our contracts when the war broke out.

This same point about the relative paucity of the professional cricketer's life was made in another note in the MCC minutes about the sum of £38 the committee had voted as a gratuity for a retiring member of the Lord's ground staff identified only as 'W. Smith'. Smith had repeatedly asked that they release this fund to him at the rate of £2 a week. There had been 'strong correspondence' on the subject, particularly when the MCC explained that some of their investments of Smith's capital had not done as well as expected. The final note on the matter reads: 'Smith has again asked to be paid £2 per week instead of the £1 we proposed, and we have reluctantly agreed.'

The Kent side Godfrey Evans joined continued its generally good form in late July and early August 1939. They beat Derbyshire at Gravesend by 171 runs after declaring at 377-4 in the second innings. Ames and Todd made centuries and Harding took 8 wickets in the match. Evans brought off a smart catch to dismiss the Derby captain Robin Buckston. It was another of those summer weeks when bright sunshine alternated with violent thunderstorms. There was a small but revealing incident in the final session of play when the visitors were chasing 403 to win and Alf Pope hit the amateur off-spinner (and future MCC president) Jack Davies high in the air towards the square-leg boundary. Ames caught the ball but fell backwards among the specta-tors sitting in their shirtsleeves immediately outside the rope as he did so. In something of a role reversal from modern practice, the fielder promptly signalled a six but the umpires insisted that the batsman was out. For a moment all three individuals were in sharp dispute as to whose will should prevail. At that stage, the *Dartford Chronicle* reported, 'Pope departed without cavil, pausing to shake the hand of the fields-man as he passed by him en route.' Jack Davies believed that Ames's behaviour was that of 'a mature individual who had passed beyond the realm of any preoccupation with self, or with unlimited success, power or brilliance', which may seem an unusual analysis on the part of a county cricketer, but perhaps less so coming from a wartime intelligence officer and enemy interrogator, and a future Fellow of the British Psychological Society.

Gerry Chalk was back again from his now increasingly frequent army training duties to captain Kent in their next match, against Essex at Chelmsford. The home team batted under ink-black skies and made 172. Several of the fielders slipped and fell while chasing the ball in the steady rain. 'The most nervous man on the field was our masseur,' Chalk remembered in a note on the 1939 season. 'He kept pacing up and down in front of the pavilion carrying his little black bag – ready for someone to fall and break their leg, I suppose. Finally, it got so bad I walked over and said to him, "Take a seat and let everyone concentrate on the game. You're making me as nervous as you are."' Kent got to 51-1 in reply, and after that it rained non-stop for the next two days.

'The talk around Canterbury was all about Hitler and the bloody war,' Godfrey Evans allowed, but as late as the middle of August there was still plenty of more congenial discussion in the local pubs about the prospect of the county's cricket team winning the championship for the first time since 1913. 'If there was another topic on people's minds, once inside the ground it was swiftly superseded by "If we could just find a couple of good batsmen,"' said Gerry Chalk. It was a point underscored by Kent's next home game, against Hampshire, in which they managed completed innings of just 161 and 83. The visitors won by 7 wickets.

Evans himself missed the Hampshire match, but characteristically remembered coming back from a second XI fixture in Norfolk to join in a 31st birthday party for Kent's left-arm spinner Claude Lewis. Lewis's first county captain Geoffrey Legge also looked in, 'a very refined chap with a tweed jacket and a tie, who told us he flew his own plane'. In Evans's view, Legge's attitude was 'somewhat condescending'. This may have been true, but it hardly did justice to the former Kent skipper's activities in the summer of 1939. Right up until the last days of August Legge continued to fly his Percival Q6 on company business to places like Hamburg and Munich, and then to pass on his observations of local troop movements and civil defence installations to British intelligence.

There is some evidence that he may also have brought a number of Jewish contacts out of Germany by concealing them in the hold of his plane. Legge was typically generous at Lewis's birthday dinner, where he paid for the wine to accompany a fine meal of wild cherry soup, roast beef, salad and pudding served by what Evans called 'two frilly-bloomered girls' in a mock-Tudor hotel or inn of some sort on the outskirts of Canterbury. An anonymous correspondent later wrote of Legge in *The Times*:

> He never revealed so much of his inner self that you wanted to know more. He never wore his heart on his sleeve. He did not make friends easily or lightly, but I doubt whether he ever lost a friend once he had made one. Loyalty was the keynote of his character.

At the other end of the British Isles, a strong MCC side led by the sometime Lancashire, Middlesex and Devon Dumplings all-rounder Sandy Baxter took on Scotland in a two-day match at Raeburn Place, Edinburgh. The years may have enlarged the local stature of this particular contest, but it was clearly a sterling effort by the home team. Scotland led on first innings by 290 against 133, of which just 4 – a first ball heave to the midwicket boundary – came from the bat of the bibulous ex-England Test captain Percy Chapman. Following on, MCC at least made a game of it by scoring 224. The Scottish target of 68 to win in three hours seemed a formality, but the rain again intervened with the home side still 24 short and all their second innings wickets intact. Chapman remembered 'waking up two days later in bed at the Adelphi hotel, Liverpool, covered in blood; my own, luckily'. A young Edinburgh accountant and occasional leg-break bowler named Bill Laidlaw had earlier taken 4 wickets in 5 balls, including a hat trick, in the MCC first innings. Known as 'Billy the Kid', he made an unlikely candidate as a Western gunslinger: tall, thin and bespectacled, he was also afflicted with terrible nerves. Sandy Paris, a fellow member of the Scottish team, recalled that when the fifth or sixth wicket fell and it was time for Laidlaw to go out to bat, 'the Kid rushed to a bathroom and vomited. He had a horror of being the focus of anyone's attention.'

Scotland also recorded a famous 162-run win over Ireland at Dublin that season. Laidlaw took 4-28 in 17 overs in the first innings. The acclaim he received that day 'nearly killed him', Paris said.

There was further drama for Scottish cricket later in July when the Bermuda-born Alma 'Champ' Hunt took 7 wickets for 11 runs in 13 overs of right-arm seam for Aberdeenshire against West Lothian at Linlithgow, as West Lothian were dismissed for just 48. In reply, Hunt opened the batting and personally scored all 49 runs needed to win, hitting 2 sixes and 8 other boundaries in twenty-four minutes. There may be no single greater all-round performance in the history of organised cricket. Hunt asked for a piper to play a lament at his funeral, which occurred in March 1999, to honour the Scottish connection.

The weather was so wretched in Swansea around the end of July 1939 that play between Glamorgan and Leicestershire was restricted to the first day and the match did not count in the championship. Glamorgan's next fixture, against Worcestershire at Stourbridge, at least came to a finish, if not the one the Welshmen would have hoped for. In a low-scoring contest where no individual batsman managed more than 31, the last-wicket home pair came together with 9 runs still needed for victory. Three hours earlier, the Worcestershire batsmen hadn't wanted to go out on the field in the bad light. In the end, they didn't want to leave it. The crowd chaired 20-year-old Roly Jenkins from the crease after he made the winning shot, and the whole Worcester team then took a protracted, if by today's standards notably decorous victory lap, some of the players strolling around in their buttoned-up dark suits and hats. Crusoe Robertson-Glasgow was there and watched as Glamorgan's captain Maurice Turnbull strode across in his flannels and blazer to congratulate his opposite number Allan White. 'One was reminded of two boxers politely touching gloves after having assaulted one another in the ring,' Crusoe said.

Yorkshire had fallen off of late from their flying start to the 1939 season. They could hardly have done otherwise, with a record that had seen them win seven of their first eight championship fixtures, most of them by an innings. Their match against Nottinghamshire at Sheffield in late July, at least from the perspective of providing entertainment for the paying customer, was a disaster. *Wisden* was unsparing in its review:

> For once Yorkshire players were barracked for play of the kind likely to ruin cricket. With victory out of the question, they descended to negative batting in order to prevent any first innings result … This happened on a lovely day after the loss of Saturday and further delays owing to the soaked pitch. When play proceeded at half-past-two only 26 runs came in an hour and three-quarters before tea. No one attempted to score and Mitchell stayed all the four hours over which this cricket travesty extended.

The catcalls of the mob did not faze the Yorkshire batsmen. Between lunch and the close they poked their way to 94-3 off 79 overs among growing uproar from those members of the crowd seated at the northern end of the ground, where what Jim Kilburn called the 'proletariat thirst' was catered to in a maze of open booths and refreshment stalls. In time one elderly spectator looked around, rose slowly to his feet, and then lodged a protest at what he considered the over-deliberate pace of the Yorkshire batting. 'Get it off the fucking square, Ticker,' he urged, referring to the home batsman Arthur Mitchell by his generally affectionate nickname. Several more dot balls ensued, and the spectator rose again. 'What followed then,' recalled Kilburn, 'was an oratorical masterpiece, which any actor might well envy.' The man made it clear that Mitchell's parents had at one time made a grave error in their conjugal bed, that the mysterious lump of wood presently residing in Arthur's hands was called a bat, and that if he turned it over he might find the manufacturer's instructions for it printed on the back. Kilburn was not alone in finding the repartee from the north bank 'entirely more creative' than the moribund spectacle of the cricket. 'Between the wars the Bramall Lane crowd was a legendary place of sharp wit and shrewd comment,' he wrote. 'It was partisan, yet gave a memorable ovation to "foreigners". It could be mercilessly critical, yet in the next breath warmly appreciative.' Ruing the 'lax post-war culture' that had followed, Kilburn concluded:

It was only later, when a period of sport disenchantment set in, that the crowd quality changed. Witticism became vulgar banality, loyalties became myopic and the huge crowd became an empty and echoing shell, a sounding board for the portable radio.

Yorkshire's next match, against Worcestershire at Stourbridge, elicited altogether better reviews. A drying wicket helped both pace and spin bowlers, and no batsman scored more than 39 runs. Worcestershire were all out for 102 before the first lunchtime; Yorkshire had been dismissed for 91 by tea. In their second innings Worcester recovered from 41-7 to 118 all out, and at lunch on the second day Yorkshire, needing 130, were 77-7.

At this stage the visitors' hopes rested squarely on their number four batsman Maurice Leyland, who was 15 not out. Despite the match situation he continued to play his normal game, which involved a generally positive and free-flowing approach to strokeplay, sustained by his remarkably agile footwork and reflexes apparently impervious to the fact that the batsman had just celebrated his 39th birthday. Leyland swung one straight ball from the South African seamer Sid Martin, an all-rounder good enough to be on his way to the double for the second time in three seasons, high over the bowler's head. They eventually fetched it back from under the wooden benches of the football stand. A few minutes later, with Yorkshire 113-9, Leyland hit a fierce, skimming shot towards long-off, where the fielder sank to his knees as if in gratitude and held it. Worcestershire had won.

Like all the other bowlers, Hedley Verity had enjoyed the conditions at Stourbridge, where he returned figures of 4-33 and 4-40. In an interview later that week with the *Yorkshire Post* he still managed to sound imperturbable and calm, responding coolly to any suggestions about 'the European crisis' interfering with cricket by saying, 'We play on.' In private Verity was sometimes less sanguine, telling a colleague as he left the War Memorial ground, Stourbridge: 'I wonder if I will ever bowl here again.'

Jim Kilburn thought 'Verity's face in repose look[ed] thin, and about the jaw somewhat sunken. This is a man who has just been omitted by

England after eight years' service.' That sunken look, Kilburn supposed, 'accounts for some of the dour photographs of him of late', but it was offset by a voice that remained 'powerful, positive and resonant' even when talking about the 'bleakest of events'. Verity was not a man given to emoting or complaining, but in private he admitted how worried he sometimes was, both about his wife Kathleen's health, and now, too, the rapidly fading prospect of a much-needed winter's break for her and the family in South Africa. In a later interview, Len Hutton remembered sharing a room with Verity during their next county match, against Surrey at the Oval, and staying up talking far into the night. 'Hitler scared the hell out of both of us,' Hutton acknowledged.

It was the sadly familiar story again when Lancashire played Northamptonshire at Blackpool in late July. Instead of breathing in the heady aroma of Stanley Park and promenading in the sunshine up and down the Golden Mile, local holidaymakers encountered only what the press called 'rain, wind and muck' that week. Northants batted first and scored 368, with a captain's innings of 76 not out by Robert Nelson, the man who not long before had led his team out on to the Northampton pavilion balcony to celebrate their first championship win in 100 starts. Lancashire could manage only 198-9 in reply. That concluded the proceedings, because not a ball could be bowled on the last day.

Grim as all this was, it seethed with sun-kissed excitement compared to the county's next home match, against Gloucestershire at Old Trafford. The ground was so saturated that play was limited to twenty-eight minutes on the second day. Following that Lancashire took the unusual step of preparing a wicket on their practice field for the visit of Warwickshire on 2 August. At the last moment the club secretary, Rupert Howard, decided that the main ground was 'just firm enough' for cricket, though offering 'no guarantee as to its future state of repair'. His caution was as well, because no play was possible on the second day, the *Evening News* referred to a 'mudbath', and the match failed to produce a result.

Derbyshire meanwhile played Somerset in the match where Harold Gimblett, freshly dropped by England, opened his shoulders for an even-time 71 out of a total of 171. The northern side were on their way to finishing outside the top half of the table for the first time in seven years. Middlesex trounced them at Lord's, where Denis Compton scored an unbeaten 214 that included a six and 26 fours. The batsman repeatedly found the gap between cover and third man, and Bill Copson genially recalled: 'Compo made a monkey of me by hitting one ball a yard or two to my left and the next ball a yard or two to my right. He could do that, just to needle you.' Similar indignity befell Derbyshire's next away fixture, against Kent at Gravesend, where they lost by 171 runs. This was the match where Les Ames's self-denying behaviour in the field won the plaudits of his teammate Jack Davies, the future wartime spymaster.

The wettest high-summer weather in recent memory finally broke just in time for the arrival of the West Indies to play Somerset in a three-day game at the County Ground, Taunton, beginning on 2 August. There was a curious-looking crowd on hand for the start. Many of the spectators already carried bulky gas mask cases around their necks, and special constables walked among them to distribute notices about matters such as petrol rationing and the suitability or otherwise of home-built air-raid shelters. Once again, the home captain appealed over the loudspeakers during the lunch interval for men to volunteer for military duty, and lest anyone have missed it large hoardings at the River Stand end reinforced the message. Set against this sombre backdrop a degree of the rich and agreeable vein of eccentricity that seems to run through West Country cricket shone through the gloom. The Somerset *County Gazette* reported that there had been an increasingly carnival-like atmosphere as play proceeded, with rock cake and lemonade stalls catering to a large second-day crowd in their shirtsleeves, 'not a few of them accompanied by their pets, or even livestock … One rosy-cheeked gentleman strode the boundary in a smock decorated with stray tufts of straw and a rubber mouse attached to his waistband as a further spur to merriment.'

Although the weather had finally warmed up, the Taunton wicket was still wet enough to ensure that the crowd seated around the boundary rope would be safe from undue disturbance. Batting first, the tourists managed a total of just 84, more than half of the runs coming from Jeff Stollmeyer. The pitch, though damp, and with the hot sun beating on it, 'never became truly adhesive,' the *Gazette* wrote, before adding, 'From a West Indian point of view it was a day of abject misery.'

Some of the Somerset batsmen acquitted themselves better than others in their eventual reply of 345. Harold Gimblett, though in the midst of a purple patch in the county championship, looked pitiably unsure of himself, a trait perhaps over-egged in the myths surrounding his life, but his relative diffidence here stood out all the more in contrast to the free hitting of his colleagues Jack Meyer and the wicketkeeper Wally Luckes. After forty tortuous minutes at the crease Gimblett at long last looked like emerging from total seizure with a clipped on-drive for four, but was then immediately LBW to the part-time seamer Foffie Williams for a score of 11. Bam Bam Weekes flogged 12 fours in his second innings of 54, but clever bowling by the slow left-armer Horace Hazell brought proceedings to an end late on the second afternoon. Somerset won by an innings and 72 runs. It proved to be the last-ever match played by the county's young amateur Mike Bennett, who signed off with an innings of 56. Bennett went into the army the following week, served with distinction in the war, surviving the D-Day landings, and later emigrated to Canada, where he died, aged 72, in July 1982. 'He was loved for a basic warmth of character, a total benevolence which no amount of gentle mocking of later English cricket standards could disguise,' *The Times* wrote.

In the same week that Somerset entertained the West Indies at Taunton there was a seemingly inconsequential and, under other circumstances, almost comic episode of bureaucratic turmoil some 1,200 miles away that dramatically lessened the chances of the Polish question being settled without bloodshed. This followed the apparent announcement by Germany's sock-puppet district administrator, Albert Forster, that Danzig customs officials could no longer carry out their normal duties.

The Warsaw government responded with an irate demand that he withdraw the order within twenty-four hours, whereupon Forster furiously denied that any such directive had been issued, charging instead that it was all part of a plot to undermine German interests in the area. Four days later, on a note of near-farcical indignation, Berlin warned Warsaw that any repetition of the Danzig ultimatum 'would lead to greater tension in the relationship between Germany and Poland'. Warsaw replied that she would consider any possible German intervention an act of aggression, and that this would require a 'full retaliatory response'.

A second tragicomic set of circumstances soon followed, when an Anglo-French delegation, urgently invited to Moscow to discuss a possible non-aggression pact with the Soviet Union, took a week to arrive by slow cargo-ship and train when they could have made it in a single day. The deputation's senior officer had come without proper credentials, and when the talks finally got under way it seemed that the British were not all that serious: a Soviet offer to provide 137 divisions for a common defence against the Nazis was matched by a British proposal to supply one mechanised and four infantry divisions, with some repurposed Great War lorries thrown in.

Assessing all this in a letter just over a week later, Learie Constantine wrote: 'There is such terrible news from Poland. The war is now inevitable. We go out to play the final Test tomorrow.'

6

THROWING THE BAT

August 1939, which would prove to be one of the most tumultuous and ultimately calamitous months in British history, began with the superbly nonchalant announcement of the names of the sixteen English cricketers due to tour India that winter. It was either an impressive show of detachment, or one of stunning myopia, on the MCC selectors' part. By then there had already been weeks of press speculation that the tour might be scrapped, and on the very day the names were read out *The Times* carried a front-page story about plans to evacuate British children out of the range of the Luftwaffe. E.W. Swanton remembered it all as a 'queer' bit of timing, 'starkly at odds with the mood of the nation … [By then] the frivolities were all but over: the west-end lights were soon to give way to the long blackout.'

One way or another, it was a curious list that Lord's released to the press that Wednesday morning. The tour party was to be led by 40-year-old Flt Lt Jack Holmes, a popular amateur batsman who had turned out for Sussex on and off since 1923 without ever quite threatening to fully impose himself on the county scene. Only two of the squad – 33-year-old Jim Langridge of Sussex, and Stan Nichols of Essex, who was turning 39 – had been on the previous MCC tour of the subcontinent in 1933–34, and the Sussex batsman Hugh Bartlett, who had learned his craft as a boy growing up in India, was the sole survivor of the team that had finally staggered on to their homeward boat at

Cape Town following the protracted ordeal of the Durban Test just five months earlier. Three of the party – the veteran Surrey batsman-wicketkeeper Gerald Mobey, Worcestershire's long-serving amateur Roger Human, and, representing youth, Lancashire's 23-year-old leg-spinner (and future chairman of Cunard) John Brocklebank – had not even appeared regularly in championship cricket in 1939. For his part, Warwickshire's Bob Wyatt, having made his first-class debut as long ago as 1922, provided a link back to the world of bushy grocers' moustaches, skeleton pads and starched shirt fronts, if not conspicuously advancing the cause of any youth policy on the selectors' part.

Perhaps just as striking as the names of some of those chosen for the tour were those who were left out. Hammond had declined to go; Verity, as we've seen, still pined for a winter's rest with his wife and family in Cape Town; and Yorkshire were reportedly not keen for their professionals Hutton, Bowes and Wood to participate. Denis Compton again preferred to spend his off-season playing on the left wing for Arsenal. It's unclear if Bill Edrich, Ken Farnes and Doug Wright had elected not to tour, or if the decision was made for them, although Wright's county colleague Godfrey Evans later remembered him as 'relaxed' about missing a four-month, 28-match trek through pre-partition India. In his absence the selectors chose Essex's 30-year-old spinner Peter Smith, the man who had once been the victim of a cruel hoax summoning him to play for England. When the India tour in turn was scrapped he must have wondered if he would ever represent his country. Harold Gimblett was in the squad but in the event never won another Test cap. He was called up to play for England against the West Indies at Trent Bridge in 1950 but pulled out of the team either because of a large boil on the back of his neck or due to a nervous breakdown, depending on which account you read.

Hampshire, meanwhile, played Surrey at Portsmouth, suddenly a bustling scene of 'convoy[s] of army lorries, ambulances, wagons, commandeered bakers' vans, horse boxes and even farm carts rattling in and out of the docks', while a bulbous observation balloon swayed precariously aloft above the active gunwharf installation (today a shopping centre) immediately adjoining the ground.

Hampshire won the toss, batted, and made 301. Don Walker hit an unbeaten 108, an innings the *Cricketer* described as 'delightful … possessing all the classical virtues of a relaxed stance, a long, straight back-lift, and with the overall impression of a man unhurriedly assessing a menu of available shots before making his selection'. Freddie Brown's knock of 61 was the bright jewel of Surrey's reply and followed on bowling figures of 7–86 by the same player. He must have been a strong candidate to add to his existing six Test caps on the winter tour of India. Unfortunately, the sunshine that had broken out over the south coast on the morning of 1 August soon gave way to more familiar periods of wind and drizzle – enough to 'raise apprehension about the large dirigible tethered overhead', the *Evening News* reported – and the match was abandoned as a draw.

Along the coast at Hove, Sussex had to delay the start of their match with Middlesex, but when it finally got underway the ground was said to be 'looking its green and lovely best, basking in seaside sun'. Bill Edrich soon made up for lost time with his hungover innings of 161, including a fourth-wicket stand of 223 in just over two hours. Jack Holmes celebrated his recent appointment as de facto England Test captain by top-scoring with 79 for Sussex. He hooked one six off Compton to long leg, another to midwicket, and drove a third one straight back over the bowler's head, hit full into the sea breeze and landing on a mobile bookstall. This match, too, ended in a draw.

From time to time, more so eighty years ago than now, county cricketers enjoy fraternising together after a match, and there was a small intermural party that night at the Regency Tavern in Brighton. By this stage the spectacle of Bill Edrich walking into a pub was a bit like Cary Grant walking into a tailor's shop, or Winston Churchill into a wine merchant's. He was happy to be there, and on the whole they were glad to accommodate him. Fifty years later Les Ames remembered that 'Bill arrived at Canterbury [next] morning looking distinctly green around the gills, still wearing his clothes from the night before, downed some evil-smelling muck with about a pint of marmite in it, and tottered out to bat first wicket down.' He scored 91.

The Middlesex bowler Jim Smith added an unbeaten 101 coming in at number ten in the order, and the visitors won by an innings. Despite the fickle weather, 21,000 spectators paid for admission to the St Lawrence ground during the week.

The sun at least peeked through the clouds at Worcester for the home team's match that week against Essex, although the wicket was still wet enough to raise what Swanton called 'trepidation or worse in several of the batsmen'. Peter Smith, the perennial nearly-man of English Test cricket, took 7-85 in 21 overs with his leg-breaks and googlies. 'On soft turf he kept a good length, varied his pace and spun the ball with real skill,' *Wisden* reported. 'They were quite right to select him for the tour of India,' Bob Wyatt later reflected, 'and he might have found conditions there very much to his taste. By September 1939 I should call Smith by some distance the unluckiest cricketer in England.'

Worcestershire gave a first outing of the season to their dark-haired and compact all-rounder Roger Human, known for the slight suggestion of bandiness to his gait, who emphasised the aptness of his surname by comprehensively failing with both bat and ball. A master at nearby Bromsgrove School, Human's first-class appearances were necessarily limited, like those of Ken Farnes, to coincide with half-terms and holidays. He had made his county debut in June 1934, when he hit 75 against Cambridge, his old university, but after that promising start had remained a 'thoroughly unspectacular, conscientious and amiable performer who always made the team, rather than himself, the main focus of attention'. Rather surprisingly, Human had been selected for the winter tour of India, after arranging to take a two-term sabbatical from Bromsgrove. *The Times* correspondent prematurely wrote: 'He will surely be an asset on the dusty turf of Karachi and Bombay, and whatever the final tally of his runs and wickets will be as popular an England cricketer as has ever set forth abroad. India may be the making of this versatile and likeable player.'

'The arrival of the West Indies was a great adornment to the arena whose pavilion might more properly have been called Valhalla for the number and variety of the deities now passing through it,' wrote the *Herald of Wales* correspondent, in an unusually fulsome passage to describe the St Helen's ground, Swansea. Even without the hyperbole, it was an undeniably good game of cricket. 'The dismissal of 25 men for 273 runs on Saturday seemed to have ruined the match but 7,000 people saw a grand finish on the Bank Holiday,' *Wisden* reported. Facing a target of 191 to win in front of a vocally partisan crowd, the tourists scraped home by 2 wickets, Constantine finishing proceedings with a six and a four. Ivan Barrow, the West Indian wicketkeeper-batsman, had earlier told a reporter that he was worried about playing cricket on the Jewish *shabbat*, traditionally the period of rest observed from a few minutes before sunset on Friday until nightfall on Saturday. The headline duly appeared: 'Windies' Hebrew Holiday – To Play or Pray?' Barrow himself said, 'I'm hoping for rain', and added that he would consult the local rabbis to discuss an exemption.

Perhaps Barrow was only joking with the Welsh press, because he had already played several times before on a Saturday, including representing his country in the Lord's Test. He eventually scored 0 and 12 at Swansea and stumped the Glamorgan tail-ender 'Closs' Jones off Constantine's slower ball. The young Anglo-Irish club batsman Louis Jacobson later recalled the scene outside one south London synagogue when Barrow showed up for services there dressed in his West Indies tour blazer, dark flannels and a close-fitting yarmulke skullcap. Jacobson remembered people cheering and rumours spreading that other famous cricketers were also in the congregation. When they met in Australia in the 1960s, Barrow told him it had never happened.

On Wednesday 9 August, as the West Indies arrived by train to play Warwickshire in a stormy Birmingham, Britons all over the Midlands and home counties looked up to see a startling sight in the skies: 1,400 warplanes of all varieties flew in patterns at intervals throughout the day, some leaving wispy vapour trails, others swooping low enough so that those on the ground could hear the insistent drone and distinctive whistling supercharger of one of the RAF's 350 new elliptical-winged Spitfire fighters. It was only a defence test, but many of those who had not heard or read about it in advance rushed instinctively for shelters and cellars. This was what the popular fear of bombing, and more particularly of a gas attack, had led people to expect in the last jittery days of peace.

That same damp Wednesday morning, the king arrived in his yacht to take a review of 133 Royal Navy ships assembled at Weymouth. The official Admiralty report notes drily that, following these manoeuvres, 'The ships of the Fleet began to disperse to their war stations' and that, shortly afterwards, 'It was decided that Polish destroyers should sail for Britain in "Operation Pekin" rather than have them seized by the Germans.' Forlornly watching the rain spatter the window of the visitors' dressing room at Edgbaston, Ivan Barrow wrote in his diary: 'The end is near, and I feel a curious wave of relief. People stand silently listening on the radio to the news. Some are worried, but they accept the inevitable.'

As the West Indies eked out a draw with Warwickshire, an Army XI met the Public Schools at Lord's. Heavy rain also ruined this match. The cricket itself was forgettable (both sides 'exercised much caution' in *Wisden*'s measured view, although 'Pawson made two grand catches, particularly the one off his own bowling'), with only eighty minutes' play possible on the final day. But there was a dreadful, retrospective symmetry to the fact that each side lost an opening batsman of strikingly similar name in the war. The Public Schools' Lancelot Hingley soon joined the RAF, once going out to bat for MCC against Rugby, his old school, within six hours of his return from a bombing raid on Dusseldorf – arriving at the ground late, he was listed merely as 'Absent' in the team photograph reproduced in *Wisden* – and was lost in action in February 1943, aged 21. Lancelot Grove of the Army was killed in a military transport plane crash in Newfoundland, also in February 1943. He had played three matches alongside the likes of Godfrey Evans in the pre-war Kent seconds, and was 37 at the time of his death.

In that same week in August, Lancashire drew with Essex at Old Trafford, marking the home side's seventh experience in eight consecutive games of rain preventing a result; Surrey drew with Hampshire at the Oval, where only forty-seven minutes' play was possible on the last two days; and Northamptonshire similarly failed to reach a definite conclusion with Derbyshire.

About the one exception to the rule of flooded grounds and tiny, diehard crowds huddled under umbrellas came at Ashley Down, Bristol, where the rain finally allowed a delayed start in the game between top-of-the-table contenders Gloucestershire and lowly Glamorgan, who were without the services of both Closs Davies and Wilf Wooller. Hammond declared Gloucester's first innings at 223-7 at the start of the last day, but his strategy backfired when the visitors then ran up a fast 235-7, with 41-year-old Cyril Smart hitting the only century by a visiting batsman against Gloucestershire of the season. When Maurice Turnbull in turn declared, Hammond himself then scored 73 in forty-five minutes and, with the third declaration of the day, set Glamorgan to make 117 in just over an hour. Smart was again the hero with an unbeaten 67, flogging his last 2 balls for a six and four to bring off the win with just four minutes to spare. It had been a 'jewel of a match', Turnbull remarked, 'not only wildly thrilling, but impeccably played. Say what you like about Wally Hammond, he was the first one to stand us drinks in the bar afterwards.'

By the time of the Roses Match at Headingley in early August, it was clear that Lancashire were not about to challenge the likes of Yorkshire, Middlesex or Gloucestershire for the county title. The visitors ground their way to 217 in the first innings, but defied form by dismissing Yorkshire for 163. Lancashire then collapsed to 92 all out, Ellis Robinson taking 8-35 in 21 overs of immaculate round-the-wicket off-spin. There was just time for Yorkshire to knock off the 147 runs needed to win,

Len Hutton supplying 105 of them, before the ground was flooded by a thunderstorm. Neville Cardus called Hutton's century 'one of the greatest innings I have seen in my 30 years as a student of the game'. Another critic thought the blameless Bill Bowes's bowling in the match 'little more than a joke', but if so it was a singularly practical one – the 31-year-old with the gawky wire glasses took only 1 wicket but sent down 28 8-ball overs for just 32 runs in the Lancashire first innings, and 2 overs for 4 runs in the second.

It speaks to the spirit in which English first-class cricket was generally played in 1939 that Lancashire's young stand-in captain Tom Higson, deputising for Lionel Lister while the latter was away on Territorial duty, declined the umpires' offer to leave the field as the rain began to fall on the final afternoon. 'The visitors' chivalry in getting wet while their rivals were winning received full appreciation,' *Wisden* wrote.

At Canterbury, Kent and Middlesex at least managed to stay on the field long enough in between showers for the visitors to win by an innings and 64 runs. Bill Edrich hit a brisk 91, and then picked up three sharp catches while standing provocatively close in at short leg. The increasingly flustered home batsmen were reduced to 'sudden protective lunges, like a self-conscious lady minding her skirts on a windy day', Robertson-Glasgow wrote, in a simile Edrich himself would have approved. In something of a veterans' parade, 37-year-old Gubby Allen took 6-46 when opening the Middlesex bowling, and Les Ames, in his fourteenth consecutive year as a county professional, hit 89 out of a Kent total of 156. Though damp, the St Lawrence ground was at its loveliest, with a brass band, striped deckchairs and what *The Times* called 'many fetching raiments, some of them cast off sufficiently to draw appreciative male eyes away from the cricket', if also with fewer off-duty military personnel than usual.

Reading the spectators' diaries and published accounts of the opening day's play at Canterbury is a bit like looking through the pinhole of a scenic souvenir charm at some late Edwardian garden party. There's an innocence about the newspaper reports as dated as some of the facilities on the ground itself. The *Empire News* said there were 'marching bands and decorous applause … parasols and fans, and vendors selling straw boaters to strolling Kentish vicars – a halcyon scene'. Or at least that was the case during one of the match's sunny intervals on the first day. The dark clouds returned overnight, and to Keir Webbe, a local bank clerk who sat on a 'splintered wet bench' awaiting the start, 'the place was so quiet you could hear the umpires' footsteps as they walked over the grass to inspect the wicket.' Despite the erratic weather, some 13,000 customers paid at the gate to watch the top-of-the-table clash with Middlesex.

From there, Bill Edrich went on to score 54 and 62 against Surrey at the Oval, 26 against Essex at Southend, 17 against Gloucestershire at Cheltenham, 36 against Somerset at Lord's, 110 not out and 79 in the return match with Surrey, and a final flurry of 101 at home to Warwickshire. That concluded his first-class cricket for nearly six years. Since Edrich also managed to conduct several brief if not uncomplicated affairs, start a small fire in his spare bedroom, sign a book contract and join the RAF Physical Training Branch at Uxbridge during the same thirty-day period, it's tempting to conclude that he simply elected to throw the bat at life while he could. Other than the fire, about the one serious mishap during this eventful month came when the Middlesex team alighted at Victoria station late in the evening of 11 August following their win that afternoon at Canterbury. Apparently Edrich had failed to read the recently-issued Public Information Leaflet No. 2, or had forgotten about it in all the excitement, because this had warned of an overnight test of the London blackout. It might also be noted that the champagne had flowed freely in the Middlesex professionals' train compartment on their return journey to London. Anyway, Edrich lost his footing when stepping down on to the platform, and duly reported for duty next morning at the Oval with a multitude of bruises along with what he called 'the most tremendous shiner – all the colours of the rainbow', accompanied by some 'pretty offensive' comments from the crowd.

'Of course,' Edrich acknowledged, 'you couldn't blame them. You know what it is when you've got a reputation for having a few. Very easy to give a wrong impression. On top of that I had to go out to bat half an hour after the start on an absolute pig of a wicket.' He top-scored with 54 in the Middlesex first innings.

Ken Farnes, meanwhile, continued his own late-summer form with Essex. The philosophising strike bowler had returned to his county side in time to capture the only Kent wicket to fall in the rain-shortened draw at Chelmsford. According to those who saw it (and to the batsman, Gerry Chalk, who didn't) it was a ball of electric pace and of such raw power that the ground physically shook as Farnes's left foot pounded it in his follow-through. He remained the most enigmatic of all cricket's speed merchants. Once reduced to tears after returning figures of 2-135 against Yorkshire at Scarborough in 1932, and not known for his brimming self-confidence in general – at one time thin, and standing 6ft 6in, he unflatteringly described himself as 'like toothpaste squeezed out of a tube' – he became a physical-cultural devotee whose party piece was to strip off his shirt and ripple first one half, then the other, of his impressively sculpted torso. In his diary, Farnes wrote not so much about runs and wickets as about matters such as having seen some children in the east end of London, 'monstrous in their lack of realisation', whose appearance seemed to him a 'horrible reflection on the state of civilisation or education'. Later on in the same entry, he confessed to feeling 'detached' and 'somewhat disgruntled with myself', and craving a 'subjugation of self' that he felt might induce 'the required metaphysical state'. These are not words that one readily associates with Farnes's England fast-bowling successors such as Fred Trueman or Ian Botham.

On 9 August, Essex went on to the familiar soggy draw with Lancashire at Old Trafford. Farnes took 1-20 in the only home innings possible. He had better luck the following week against Derbyshire at Southend, where he returned figures of 0-34 and 5-52. Farnes added another six victims during Middlesex's visit to the same ground, and four more in his county's crushing win against his old nemesis Yorkshire at Sheffield. He won respect and a reputation for durability and toughness. 'Ken played when 90 per cent of bowlers couldn't,' said John Stephenson, the professional army officer who was one of Essex's three rotating captains that season. 'He would come off the field and sit in the dressing room with his feet all bloody and blistered, look mournfully down at them, close his eyes in apparent contemplation, then hobble off somewhere in his dark suit, and return the next morning to bowl flat-out again.' A schoolteaching colleague would add of Farnes in *The Worksopian* magazine: 'Despite his well-deserved success and popularity, he never became swollen-headed; his innate modesty – almost shyness – prevented him from the usual fault of the outstanding athlete.'

For all that, Farnes's ruggedness in defending his turf became legendary. 'Where most bowlers just deliver the ball, Ken would keep going, massive paw outstretched, ready to act as his own fielder,' Stephenson added. 'It put the fear of God into the batsman, I can tell you from experience, because it was like looking up to see a runaway London bus bearing down on you.'

There was a curious and poignant interlude in the late English summer when a team representing the Netherlands played MCC at Lord's from 14 to 15 August. Percy Chapman captained the home side, which also included the sometime Northamptonshire batsman Geoff Cuthbertson, the Middlesex fast bowler John Nevison, and 47-year-old Reg Scorer, late of Warwickshire, who illustrated the fitness of his surname with a whirlwind innings of 26 struck in just fourteen minutes. It was an uneven contest from the start, although the visitors' Leen Sodderland – author of the definitive Dutch technical manual *Het Bowlen* – took 2-60 in 27 overs of tidy medium pace, and the all-rounder Willem Gallois showed what the official tour history called 'gross immobility' in reaching an unbeaten 72 out of a total of 165 all out. MCC won the match by an innings and 56 runs.

Just nine months after playing cricket in the sunshine at Lord's, the Dutch players would see their homeland under armed occupation, its largest port bombed into submission and consumed by a massive firestorm, and the majority of the country's Jews deported to Nazi death camps. The tourists' young Willem Gallois, who lived nearby, was one of thousands of civilians pressed into service gathering up bodies and parts of bodies from among the rubble of the destroyed city centre of Rotterdam. The conscripts were directed to collect as many corpses as they could, and then to carry the remains to a communal pit conveniently blasted into the earth when a bomb had ignited nearby vegetable-oil tanks to create what Gallois called 'an infernal crater which bubbled and stank like a vision of hell.' He would later say that the biggest shock was that most of the bodies were of children, recognisable by the small limbs he picked up. Gallois himself was then aged 22, and many years later wrote that he never quite recovered from the experience. He played competitive cricket until 1954 but found that 'I could never again take it quite as seriously as before.'

The Dutchmen weren't the only unfamiliar visitors to be seen on English cricket fields in 1939. There were also tours by Scottish, Canadian and Egyptian teams, and from 18 to 19 August an Irish representative side took on Sir Julien Cahn's XI at West Bridgford. The Cambridge blue Tom MacDonald scored a century for the visitors and remembered that he had been invited at around this same time to sign papers for Middlesex. He was tempted by the financial terms, but not by the prospect of 'play[ing] cricket six days a week every week for four months, finishing a match one evening and travelling through the night to start another the next morning'. More immediately, MacDonald enjoyed the prolonged dinner and party games later that warm August night at Stanford Hall.

> Everyone dressed up. Cahn, rather curiously, marched up and down in a belted trench coat jerking his right arm aloft, possibly an allusion to certain continental dignitaries. One big Irish lad who shall remain nameless wiggled around in a tight black shift and a ratty silver-fox fur. He looked like Marlene Dietrich.

Essex took on Middlesex that week at Southend, in the home batsman Laurie Eastman's benefit match. Born in 1897, Eastman had fought with gallantry in the Great War before making his county debut in 1920. His reward for his twenty years' service to Essex was a total of just over

£1000, including a collection of £68 taken from among the crowd at Southend. He pulled up with an injured knee during the course of the match and in the second innings batted with a runner at number eleven. Eastman was last man out as Essex lost a tight game by 5 runs. It proved to be the last first-class appearance of his long career.

Laurie Eastman died in April 1941, aged 43. He had been serving as an air-raid warden, and most accounts put his death down to severe shock after a bomb had exploded nearby. Eastman's family have said that he was also suffering from lung cancer. Like many sportsmen of the day he was a heavy smoker, the Essex dressing room, he once noted, 'often look[ing] like a thick pea-souper had settled in' thanks to all the free cigarettes handed round by a local firm. A reporter went to the veteran player's bedside at Harefield Hospital to get some quotes from him not long before the end. Eastman was remote and wistful. 'Funny world ... lovely game,' was all he said.

When Sussex played Leicestershire at Hastings that week, the visitors included four teenagers in their ranks, a first-class record that would stand until matched by Surrey in 2017. In marked contrast to this extreme youth policy, Leicester's batsman Norman Armstrong had made his debut in 1919, and was then approaching his 47th birthday. He lived for another fifty-one years. None of the four juveniles particularly distinguished himself. John Langridge scored his second century on successive days for Sussex, who declared at 501-5. The visitors managed just 114 and 281, losing with a day to spare. Crusoe Robertson-Glasgow was covering proceedings for the *Daily Telegraph*, characteristically throwing a party for several of the players and their friends on the final evening. Norman Armstrong thought Crusoe:

> A difficult man to read, [who] showed a certain amount of what would now be called manic behaviour. He was naturally high-spirited and vital, always bustling around at one's elbow, and seemed to pretty well do without sleep. I never saw the other side, but people said he could darken a room when he walked into it.

Several years later, E.W. Swanton said of his journalistic colleague: 'A writer with a touch of genius, without an enemy in the world but himself.'

In an even tighter finish than the one that week at Southend, Derbyshire beat Gloucestershire by 1 run at Cheltenham, where *Wisden* noted 'the last [session] was packed with thrills'. Walter Hammond had claimed the extra half hour on the second day and Gloucester were left needing 14 to win with 3 wickets in hand on the final morning. Twelve more of the runs had been knocked off, for the loss of 2 wickets, when the last man in skied a catch to the fielder just inside the cover boundary. Hammond was not pleased. He had scored a rapid 87 when his team were chasing runs on the second afternoon. Gloucester's Tom Goddard remembered: 'The skipper, who'd arrived on the ground so full of vim just two days earlier, left it again to the sound of mutual insults and slammed doors.' Signs of the dark mood swings and serious manic episodes of Hammond's later life were already present in these earlier years.

The next morning, Rupert Howard, the genial, 50-year-old secretary of Lancashire, opened a crumpled brown envelope from the Lord Privy Seal's Office in Whitehall. It contained a single typed sheet of paper folded double, with a two-page addendum attached to it by a rusty clip. The text of the letter announced that the county should take note of their obligations under the terms of the recent Civil Defence Act to ensure their place of business or domicile [Old Trafford] was 'ready for the eventuality of War'. This included the duty for Howard to provide air-raid shelters for those living or working on the premises, whose construction the local authority might, on request, subsidise; the training of a suitable number of such individuals to give first aid, deal with the effects of gas and fight fires; and to be aware generally of the 'imminent possibility' that facilities such as his own might be acquired or requisitioned to accommodate military personnel, or be put to other unspecified use in the event of an emergency involving the threat of enemy invasion or attack.

'This does not mean that war is expected now,' the note concluded, reassuringly. 'But it is everyone's duty to be prepared for the prospect of such an occurrence.'

One way or another, the cricket season was fast being overtaken by the pace of outside events. Howard himself could at least see the mordant humour of the situation. He and Hitler had been born within a few days of each other. 'You'd think that would count for something,' Howard told a group at dinner on the night of 18 August, and when one of them remarked that Hitler had always been a good friend of Britain, added 'That's possible, but he's no friend of mine.'

While Rupert Howard dined with friends, Godfrey Evans was a few miles away at the bar of the Britannia Hotel in Manchester. It happened to be the new Kent wicketkeeper's 19th birthday. Although still based at his family's home in Faversham, Evans was spending an increasing amount of his time on the road with the county team, who began a match at Old Trafford the following morning. Seldom needing an excuse for a party, the young stumper later insisted that he had downed nineteen tots of gin that night to properly celebrate the occasion. He never much cared for the north, he further admitted, although this policy did not extend to the area's women. Fifty years later, Evans still fondly remembered that the party had ended in a convivial ménage with two prostitutes engaged for the evening by his county colleagues. He said that he was deeply touched by this supreme gesture on the part of his teammates, and that it would have been churlish of him to refuse it. The women had apparently made unusual use of some toothpaste. It may or not be so, but it's a tale characteristic enough of Evans to be true.

In the county match starting the next morning, Les Ames made 108 (and Evans himself just 2) out of a Kent total of 215. Old Trafford was *en fete*, Howard, possibly in a gesture of defiance, ordering Union flags to be flown above every stand. After some early rain the weather was fine and fresh throughout. Lancashire eventually needed 218 for victory and crossed the finish line for the loss of 6 wickets. Cyril Washbrook and Winston Place made runs for the home team, and their all-rounder Eddie Phillipson took 12 wickets in the match. There would be only one more first-class fixture on the venerable ground during the next six years.

Later that week yet another directive went out from Whitehall to the managers of thousands of factories, offices and sports facilities around Britain. It reminded them that 'any premises or vehicles may be taken possession of by any Government department or any persons acting on behalf of the Crown during the present exigency'. The urge to control in those who aspire to dictate what is good for us arguably first took root in British life in 1939. Evans again caught the anxiety and tension of this stop-start period:

> I woke up on a Sunday morning [27 August] and it seemed that bombs had been dropped on Faversham station, or so people were saying out in the street. Many rumours were flying about and streams of cars clogged up the road, some going in to town to see what had happened and others busy getting the hell out. It turned out it was a gas explosion in a house somewhere down by the Recreation Ground. An old man and his wife had gone to bed the night before and left the cooker on. I heard they survived, although the blast knocked all the windows in, and they picked glass out of the old boy's beard for a week afterwards.

The West Indies tourists spent the night of 18 August in somewhat more decorous circumstances than Godfrey Evans, tucked up early in bed, two to a room, in London's Strand Palace Hotel, before the start of the third Test with England at the Oval the next morning. They had warmed up for the match in a manner that might strike us as unusual today, with a two-day game against part-timers Wiltshire, which they nearly lost. Learie Constantine always remembered the newspaper headlines that greeted him at the team breakfast table on the 19th – '"War Peril Imminent, But I Still Hope" – Mr Chamberlain.' And, below the fold: 'School Evacuation Plans Mulled – Gas Masks For Babies.' Lest anyone miss the point, another nearby story was splashed simply: 'Drama Week'.

Somehow, Constantine couldn't shake the feeling that it was faintly ludicrous for them to be playing cricket at that particular moment in man's destiny. Surely someone would even now cancel the match? Yet, when the West Indies' tour bus pulled up outside the hotel, and two uniformed porters helped carry out all the equipment, before the players themselves climbed on for the short journey across the river to Kennington, Constantine knew that he could not turn back. The bus sped past men going by in uniform and women queuing up outside a butcher's shop behind Waterloo station. Then it turned to the south and slowed on reaching the crowds already milling around outside the gates of the Oval. The tourists got out of the bus and filed through the pavilion to the visitors' dressing room, where some mugs of tea and a rather basic flower arrangement awaited them.

Constantine changed into his whites. It was eleven o'clock.

Hammond won the toss and England went out to bat thirty minutes later. The sun was for once shining, and there were some 20,000 seemingly carefree spectators on the ground. Paynter, Fagg, Bowes and Copson were replaced from the England team that had drawn at Manchester by 'Buddy' Oldfield of Lancashire, Stan Nichols of Essex and Reg Perks of Worcestershire, alongside that perennial man of promise Walter Keeton, now being rewarded for his consistent batting at the top of the Nottinghamshire order with a second England cap five years after his first one. The 38-year-old Nichols was the only member of the England side who was also in the MCC party still scheduled to tour India that winter.

The West Indies dropped Cameron, Williams and Hylton, and brought in Vic Stollmeyer, Bam Bam Weekes and Tyrell Johnson. It was the first and only Test to be played by both Stollmeyer and Johnson, and the second and last one for Weekes. There was something of a sunset mood to the match in general, which also proved to be the last Test appearance by England's Keeton, Oldfield, Nichols, Goddard, Wood and Perks, as well as by Grant, Sealy, Martindale, Constantine and Clarke for the tourists.

E. W. Swanton again commentated on the Test – his own last for seven years – and later wrote that 'premonitions of war led many to a sort of "last fling" attitude.' He was speaking of social affairs, but it could have applied just as well to the cricket. Over the three days 1,216 runs were scored while only 23 wickets fell. There were three individual centuries, as well as two other scores in the mid 90s. Constantine, coming in at 389-6 in the West Indies first innings, thumped 79, with 11 fours and a six, in a stay of an hour at the crease. *Wisden* said that he 'surpassed even Bradman in his amazing strokeplay', and Swanton long remembered an 'almost belief-defying shot off the back foot at the expense of Perks that cleared the sightscreen at the Vauxhall End'. Constantine was out only after hitting a ball from the same bowler so high in the air that England's 40-year-old wicketkeeper, Arthur Wood, had time to run most of the way back to the pavilion to catch it.

In terms of raw figures, England scored 352 in their first innings, with 80 from the debutant Oldfield and a robust 94 by Joe Hardstaff. Hardstaff and Stan Nichols put on 89 in sixty-five minutes for the sixth wicket before Nichols was run out. To again quote *Wisden*:

> Constantine, the bowler, fielded the ball at cover and threw down the stumps in amazing style … This incident led the way for the West Indies to dismiss the tail cheaply, for the last four wickets went down for 19. Hardstaff made a great effort to reach a hundred but, with his colleagues falling so quickly, he abandoned all caution and was last out, done middle stump.

Constantine returned figures of 5-75 and following the Nichols incident there were frequent sharp cries of 'No!' from one or both batsmen whenever the 37-year-old West Indian patrolling the off-side field was anywhere near hailing distance of the ball. Denis Compton later remembered the moment when he'd stepped out to drive Martindale through the covers, only to see Constantine 'take about six giant strides to his right, scoop the ball up and throw it back in one blurred movement, both feet off the ground, with yours truly doing a swift U-turn to just get home. He was like one of those buggers who throw knives around in the circus.'

West Indies replied with 498. There were runs throughout the order, but it was only when Bam Bam Weekes joined Vic Stollmeyer at the crease that the batting went beyond mere display and became actively destructive. Between them these two put on 163 for the fifth wicket in ninety-nine minutes. Stollmeyer fell for 96 but Weekes raced to his century in even time, departing for 137 only to a brilliant one-handed catch taken high above his head by Hammond at first slip. This brought the twelfth men out, each neatly blazered and bearing a silver tray in the attitude of some comic stage butler. A drink, far from cooling the West Indian batsmen down, only fuelled them to a renewed frenzy. Next came Constantine's flailed cameo of an innings – a knock, said *Wisden*, for once abandoning its air of critical reserve, that 'revolutionised all the recognised features of cricket … He was absolutely impudent in his aggressive treatment of the bowling.' In fairness, a new-ball attack consisting of the balding Stan Nichols with the strictly military-medium Reg Perks in support wasn't, perhaps, the most kinetically hostile in English Test history, and real indignity later befell Hutton's 7 overs of somewhat eccentric leg-spin. But Constantine still did what it took to turn the game on its head and see the West Indies to a first-innings lead of 146 in the process.

That same morning, a British agent in Berlin, Group Captain Malcolm Christie, a former air attaché, reported to the Foreign Office in London that Germany's invasion of Poland was scheduled to begin on any day between 27–31 August. The press, too, now openly speculated on the date. Swanton remembered that there was suddenly 'a certain amount of drive to the previously rather ad hoc and British preparations' for war. Over the weekend of 19–20 August, military personnel on leave were recalled to their units, the band of the Royal Scots Greys received its immediate mobilisation orders while in the middle of a concert at Southend, and even Neville Chamberlain came back to London from a fishing holiday at Lairg in Scotland, in turn prompting George VI to cut short a shooting party at Balmoral. The king was not pleased at the intrusion. 'It was utterly damnable that the villain Hitler had upset everything,' he complained.

In cricket, everything changed and everything stayed the same. On the Monday morning of 21 August, there was a crowd of 23,500 at the Oval to watch the West Indies run riot. Beginning the day on 27-1, they finished it at 395-6. The scoring rate was all the more impressive when you allow for the fact that a sudden thunderstorm held up play for over an hour after tea. England matched the pace in their second innings, declaring at 366-3 after just 310 minutes' batting. Cricket has a way of finding the truth about people, and the evidence at the Oval was that most of the spectators were quite self-possessed and resilient enough to simply shrug off the presence of the sausage-shaped barrage balloons tethered on masts behind the pavilion, or that of the anti-aircraft gun mounted on a tractor parked immediately outside the gate on Harleyford Road, and that for the most part the players followed in the same positive vein. 'The gaiety of the match was not perceptibly diminished by the war,' Swanton remembered.

Hutton, as if determined to leave warm memories behind, scored what by his standards was an almost dissolute unbeaten 165, and Hammond recorded his own twenty-second and final Test century. The last rites of English international cricket for the next seven years were thus played out by two of the greatest batsmen of their respective generations. They put on a record stand of 264 for the third wicket. There was something poignant and perhaps only fitting about all this, although at least Hutton and Hammond, if arguably never quite the same players again, returned to top-flight cricket after the war. In contrast, there was the case of the West Indies' young seamer Tyrell Johnson. As we've seen, Johnson had taken a wicket with his first delivery of the tour at Worcester but appeared in only eight more of the West Indies' scheduled thirty-six matches. Drafted in to the side at the Oval, he repeated his instant success by bowling Walter Keeton with his first ball. He finished with figures of 2-53 and 1-76 in the match, which was drawn. This single Test was Johnson's last ever first-class cricket appearance. Forty-seven years later, *Wisden* wrote:

JOHNSON, Tyreli [*sic*] Francis, who died in Trinidad on April 5, 1985, played one Test match for West Indies against England at The Oval in 1939, when with his first ball he caused Keeton to play on. Very tall and thin, he bowled left-arm at a brisk medium pace and with appreciable in-swing. Of the 16 first-class wickets he took on his one tour, those of Hutton and Oldfield also came at The Oval.

That was all. No sooner did Johnson come, it seemed, than he went, with only that small, typo-marred obituary to honour him. It wasn't much to show for a man universally described by colleagues and opponents as a shrewd sportsman on the field and a supremely generous and affable host at home in Trinidad. But by that one flash of inspiration at the Oval Johnson at least had the satisfaction of becoming only the eleventh man in sixty-two years of organised international competition to take a wicket with his first ball in Test match cricket. By doing so he joined the ranks of England's George Macaulay and Maurice Tate, and his name would be indelibly stamped in the record books as a result.

'Nobody can take that from me,' Johnson had remarked, surrounded by friends and family, shortly before he succumbed to cancer while living only a few miles from the village where he had been born sixty-eight years earlier. He told a reporter who came to interview him at his bedside of his regrets, disappointments and mistakes on the cricket field. In the end, however, Johnson had only smiled when recalling the events of August 1939:

> It was really a joke, because we had three leg slips posted and still Keeton tried to leg-glance that first ball and instead clipped it straight onto his stumps. Bertie Clarke had to stuff a handkerchief in his mouth to stop from laughing. Walter himself saw the funny side of it later. We had a couple of drinks together after the match. He never played another Test, either.

Just as the England and West Indies teams met at the Oval, a week of county cricket was being played in blazing sunshine at the Saffrons ground in Eastbourne. Sussex beat Worcestershire by 8 wickets in the first of two back-to-back fixtures, and then disposed of Derbyshire by an innings and 39 runs in the second. The Worcester match produced a thrilling finish, with Sussex scoring 200-2 in just an hour and a half to get home with nine minutes to spare. Hugh Bartlett, the England batsman who had once fallen foul of his captain over a woman, hit up 59 of the last 76 in half an hour. Impressive as this was, it was almost dilatory compared to Bartlett's first-innings score of 89 in forty-three minutes, an effort that ended only when he was caught at deep midwicket off a tennis shot that would have gone for six had the fielder missed it.

The Sussex Ladies' player and loyal county supporter Laetitia Stapleton later wrote of the Saturday afternoon of 19 August at Eastbourne:

> It was a lovely, scorching summer's day. Even those in the pavilion were shedding as many garments as was comfortable with the times. I went back to our hotel with friends for lunch and there was a sudden decision to bathe. We lay on the beach looking out to sea and saying that it was quite, quite impossible for there to be a war. What a dream world we all lived in that August.

The West Indies were due to begin a three-day match with Sussex at Hove on 26 August, but by then 'the European situation [had] not necessarily developed in a way conducive to prolonging our presence in the United Kingdom', in the guarded phrase of the tour manager Jack Kidney. Kidney's public statement tactfully failed to mention certain other factors that had possibly played into his team's decision to leave Britain prematurely. There had been an 'unhelpful' wire from Gerald Hough at Kent, for instance, questioning whether the tourists' match scheduled to begin at Canterbury on 30 August should now go ahead. One or two of the West Indies players had already begun to wonder whether their continued presence was entirely welcome. On the Sunday of the Oval Test, the two Stollmeyer brothers had walked from their team hotel down the Strand to a small Baptist church located in a narrow lane off Fleet Street, where they sat in a front-row pew, joined the congregation in praying for peace, and heard the officiating minister offer a special prayer for the safe onward travels of the two cricketers and their colleagues. That would not have been easy on an ordinary day; the priest in question regarded cricket as 'a frivolous joke' according to his son, and sportsmen in general as 'pampered children paid to play silly games' at a time of national crisis. The Stollmeyers smiled for the cameras outside the church, but it was not the usual broad calypso grin. Both brothers voted to cut the tour short when the matter later came up for discussion.

Ivan Barrow, Gerry Gomez and Jack Sealy were all in the Stollmeyers' corner, although what could be called the anglophiles of the party – Manny Martindale and Learie Constantine, both of whom had homes in England, and Bertie Clarke, who planned to practise medicine there – lobbied to stay. Leslie Hylton was worried about his being fully paid. Jack Kidney was also concerned with finances, reasoning that the British public would be in no mood to attend festival cricket matches in late August and early September, meaning the tourists would be hard pressed to cover their expenses for those games. The result of all this was a decision to cancel not only the West Indies' remaining county fixtures, but also such 'late-season flummery', to quote Kidney, as a planned limited overs clash with Billy Butlin's XI at Skegness, and instead to leave Britain at the first available opportunity. Most of the players duly caught the night train from Euston to Glasgow on 25 August, and the following morning, when they were scheduled to have met Sussex, boarded the SS *Montrose*, bound for Canada.

Back at Hove, Laetitia Stapleton was not impressed by the defection:

When the day came never have I seen such a deserted cricket ground. The general opinion was that West Indies had done a cowardly and unsporting thing in returning immediately; Jim Parks said, 'It's breaking their contract.' He was the one to suffer as the collection for his benefit would have been at least £50.

A hurriedly arranged replacement match billed as President's XI v Captain's XI failed to attract wide support, and the Mayor of Brighton, Talbot Nansen, later took the opportunity to remark at an official lunch meant to welcome the tourists, 'The failure of the West Indies to keep their agreement will clearly give the impression that we are not putting up a united front.' Nonetheless, prayers and other messages of support were again offered for the players' safe passage home. These were not entirely fanciful, because at one time the West Indians had planned to set sail on the *Montrose*'s sister ship SS *Athenia*, which subsequently left Liverpool, bound for Montreal, on 2 September. A day later, the *Athenia* was torpedoed by a German U-boat and sank in the icy Atlantic waters 300 miles off the coast of Scotland with the loss of 128 lives, fifty-two of them when one of her lifeboats was crushed in the propeller of the Norwegian tanker coming to rescue it.

Following their narrow loss to Middlesex in Laurie Eastman's benefit match, and an away win over Yorkshire, Essex hosted Nottinghamshire at the small but well-kept Vista Road ground in Clacton. As at Lord's, the pitch at Clacton sloped perceptibly from one side to the other, and the local joke was that the more genteel spectators in the upper tea-tent area were thus able to look down on the masses who gathered around the tin-roofed tavern and mobile whelk stalls that operated at the seaside end. Walter Keeton, coming straight to the match from the Oval Test, soon had two of the fingers of his right hand broken by a short ball from Ken Farnes. Farnes took 3-90 in the Notts total of 271, but really turned up the heat in the second innings. Tom Wade, the Essex wicketkeeper, remembered being knocked flat on his back when collecting some of his teammate's deliveries – 'it was like catching a shell.' The sight of the classically built strike bowler with the shock of jet-black hair tearing in with a stiff sea breeze behind him was one that few of those who saw it would forget, nor that of Stan Nichols plugging away gamely for figures of 5-34 and 3-38 at the other end. 'It was not possible for Nichols to be disturbed, whatever the circumstance,' Swanton wrote admiringly.

Nottinghamshire, from 30 without loss, collapsed in just over an hour to 74 all out. Farnes soon had the visitors' George Heane and Joe Hardstaff caught off successive deliveries, bringing 34-year-old George Gunn Jr, a batsman good enough to score 1,300 first-class runs that season, to the wicket. Gunn played a number of unruffled air-strokes into the covers as he walked out and took a leisurely guard, before cupping his right hand over his eyes to closely inspect the furthest reaches of the legside field. Taking no risks, he then repeated the performance on the off side. Following these preliminaries, Gunn indicated his willingness to proceed. He lost his middle stump first ball. It was Farnes's first ever hat-trick, and he was also the first into the visitors' dressing room after the match, which Essex won by 7 wickets, to offer his condolences. 'I didn't mean to hurt you,' he repeatedly assured Walter Keeton, who had already changed back into his civvies, his right hand heavily bandaged. It was as though Farnes himself was the one who craved sympathy. Two days later, he tore into the Northamptonshire batsmen on the same ground, with match figures of 8-126.

'My own opinion is that sportsmen can be professionally ambitious if they so desire without necessarily becoming personal antagonists,' Farnes wrote on the last night of the Northants match, which resulted in another convincing Essex win. He added: 'How sad it is when cricketers get too self-confident – they have so many problems.' It was his final first-class appearance.

Surrey crushed Warwickshire at Edgbaston that week, largely thanks to the visitors' seamer Eddie Watts taking all 10 wickets in the second innings. 'He made the ball swing in heavy atmosphere,' *Wisden* commented. No other Surrey bowler had achieved this feat since 1921. Even so, Watts was almost matched in the first innings by his teammate Freddie Brown, who took 6-46 and had 3 seemingly simple catches dropped.

From there, Surrey went on to comfortably beat Glamorgan at Swansea. Watts was wicketless for once, but Brown took 8-112 in the match. Surrey were left 82 to win and got home for the loss of 4 wickets.

Brown himself finished the match by hitting 3 fours and a six off consecutive balls. Since it was a Thursday night and they had nothing much to do until Saturday morning, Glamorgan's captain Maurice Turnbull took some of the players from both sides out to an extended dinner. 'Buggered if I know *how* I got home,' Freddie Brown told Bill Edrich, when they met at Lord's forty-eight hours later. Brown went out to bat before lunch that day and scored 38 in a brief innings which was said to have combined 'grandeur of style with a palpable sense of impatience' to return to the dressing room.

By now more and more English cricket grounds had erected signs about air-raid provisions, and scorecards bore the advice not to loiter in the street, nor to ignore the 'invisible but toxic' effects of a poison gas attack. On the morning of 23 August, the sandbags were piled waist-high on Wantage Road, outside the county ground where Northamptonshire began a match with Lancashire. Robert Nelson won the toss for the home team and sent in his opponents on a flat track. 'He was not one disposed to shirk a risk, even if the occasional decision appeared arbitrary or whimsical,' Robertson-Glasgow later wrote. Nelson had apparently thought that his seamers might make something of the overcast conditions, but in the event it was the leg-spinner Bill Merritt who took 7-83 in the Lancashire total of 195. Northants managed just 156 in reply. Frank O'Brien – like Merritt, a New Zealander – scored 51 of these runs, again proving the wisdom of the county's progressive overseas recruitment policy.

Shortly before lunch on the second day, a teenaged messenger on a bicycle appeared at the back door of the Northampton pavilion and asked for the visitors' young captain, Lionel Lister. Lister was found, already padded up, and the boy handed him a War Office telegram. It was a summons for him to immediately rejoin his Territorial unit. Just as Lister was reading it the players and spectators heard a distant humming in the sky. The hum turned into a rumble, the sound of heavy aircraft, coming closer. Soon people were pointing and shouting, and, in some cases, diving headlong under their benches. The old wooden stands shook violently with the noise, and Frank O'Brien remembered that he had held his breath while awaiting what seemed like the inevitable rain of bombs. 'But the planes just turned away, and we realised they must have been our boys out on some training exercise. I didn't know what they might do to the Germans, but they bloody well terrified us.' Lister later shook everyone's hand during the lunch interval, saying an unflustered 'Cheerio' several times, and went off in a taxi. He was listed as 'Absent, 0' on the scorecard, thus recording his eighth duck of the season in 22 innings. Lancashire won the match at Northampton by 95 runs.

Many English county cricketers of the day particularly welcomed the chance to play at Old Trafford, and not just because of the superb ground facilities or the warmth of the partisan but knowledgeable Manchester crowd. There were also the charms of the newly opened Mere Country Club, some 30 miles away in rural Cheshire, where Godfrey Evans had gone with some of his young Kent colleagues following his 19th birthday bender at the Britannia Hotel. Built as a Victorian manor house, the Mere was already fabled on the county circuit for its championship golf course, elegant dining room, and a notably convivial bar open at all hours for residents and their guests. 'The first thing you did when you got the season's fixture list was to look for Lancashire, away,' said Evans.

People were queuing up for that match. The lame could miraculously walk again when it came to getting fit for Old Trafford. Gerry Chalk went up there lying down in the back of a car for five hours with a 102° temperature just so he could have a couple of nights at the Mere. That's what he thought of the place.

Evans himself liked the Mere well enough to rave about it in a rare letter home to his brother Jack, who was then working in the motor trade in West London. On 23 August the young Kent stumper wrote that he and the team had done some 'A1 boozing'. Five or six of them, he reported, on a Saturday 'killed' several bottles of champagne and then enjoyed the local 'crumpet'. The teenager may have been showing off for his older brother, both his capacity for drink and for women, but even with that in mind it seems reasonably clear that a good time was had by all, and that a professional cricketer of the era, while notoriously ill paid, still enjoyed certain social compensations which the exclusively male sports press overlooked in a way it would be difficult to carry off today.

Later that week, Kent lost by an innings to Yorkshire after being caught on a damp wicket at Dover. Even before then, it appeared all but certain that the northern side would again be county champions. They had two of England's most statistically consistent batsmen in 23-year-old Hutton, with a first-class average for the season of 62, and 44-year-old Sutcliffe with one of nearly 55. When you add in Hedley Verity's 191 wickets at just over 13 apiece it's easy to see why Jim Kilburn, the doyen of Yorkshire cricket writers, called the county one of the 'best rounded teams of all time, with two men of true genius in Hutton and Verity ... Some of the side's performances were no less than magnificent, and they suggested increasing rather than diminishing power as the younger players developed and the older retained enviable ability.'

Kilburn added this of the final round of championship matches:

> Remarkable cricket was played and scarcely roused remark because even for spectators it was only at the back of the mind, and communications spreading sports news were in confusion. Telephoned reports were often hours delayed; telegraphed reports were handed to Post Office messengers to find delivery without mishap or to disappear completely in the process of transmission.

'At Dover, the outbreak of war had seemed imminent every minute,' Kilburn added of the match that finished on the afternoon of 24 August. Several telegraph messengers appeared at the ground with more cables like the one that had recently summoned Lionel Lister to military duty. There seemed nowhere to escape from the government's passionate anxiety to advertise the need to conserve food and fuel supplies, or to bathe only when strictly necessary, and all the other seemingly ineluc-table burdens of war. It says something of the English genius for simply carrying on that people still went out to support their local county cricket team, and that lengthy reports of the matches themselves, despite the challenges of transmission, continued to appear in the pages of the morning papers.

Kilburn's two great Yorkshiremen again demoralised the opposition in the championship game at Dover. Hutton scored exactly 100, with 13 fours, passing 2,000 runs for the season as he did so, and Verity returned figures of 4-32 and 5-48 on a drying pitch. Gerry Chalk rose to the occasion in the second innings with an unbeaten 115, also including 13 fours, but this was only to delay the inevitable. Godfrey Evans was twelfth man for the day, and his poignant recollection was of Verity wheeling away to Chalk, 'one great player bowling to a very good one, and both of them stubborn buggers who hated to lose but knew how to enjoy themselves once stumps were drawn'.

In fact, Verity seemed to some unusually subdued during the Kent match, making no obvious show of pleasure on the departure of any of his nine victims. By then the 34-year-old bowler had abandoned any remaining plans he may have had to take his wife and their two young sons to South Africa for the winter. Instead, Verity spent his time when not in the field obsessively reading infantry manuals and training pamphlets supplied by his friend Arnold Shaw, an army officer who went on to command the Green Howards, as the former Yorkshire Regiment was now known. Les Ames remembered:

Hedley always had his head in a book. When you went in the dressing-room for a chat, he wasn't the happy-go-lucky character of old. I walked out of the ground with him one night and he had the gait of a 20-year-old. Very brisk. If I didn't keep pace, he would just keep walking. I remember he admonished some teenaged girls in the street because they weren't carrying their gas masks with them. He had that natural air of authority. The kids responded to him with respect and reverence, even if they didn't have a clue who he was in the cricket world.

As late summer settled in, the Women's Cricket Association staged a keenly fought tournament in and around the village of Colwall on the Herefordshire–Worcestershire borders. The first match began in the relative international calm of 21 August, and by the time the last one finished six days later Britain had given its guarantee to Poland and the wheels of war turned with unstoppable momentum. The now 40-year-old Marjorie Pollard showed why she was still regarded by so many good judges as the best female player in the world, with scores of 45, 28 and 73 in three successive games in which the ball dominated the bat. There was a mildly amused – if not patronising – note to much of the press coverage, such as it was, where the *Daily Herald* applauded 'the girls' for managing to perform 'while each clad in a trim white skirt and stockings, and perhaps just a dab of makeup', with the inevitable plays on someone getting a tickle or bowling a maiden over. In general, the female cricketers were still viewed as having less athletic skill and less commitment to their sport than the male players. However, the women were more interesting than the men for what we would now call their 'journey' to the top – 'Mrs Pates had a dazed look as she approached the wicket, perhaps the result of a late night spent nursing a sneezing child, and kissing goodbye to a husband hurrying off to his regiment departing in the morning' – as opposed to the dry facts of scores and results. To much of Fleet Street it was really more like a prototype reality show or a television miniseries than a proper sports contest, although there was at least guarded praise in *The Times* for 'Mrs Pollard, a woman of great natural dignity who strode to the wicket with a composure Mr Walter Hammond might not have disowned.'

In a two-day match that week at the New College ground in Oxford, 27-year-old Roger Winlaw hit a 'thundering' 66 for Bedfordshire against Oxfordshire in the minor counties championship. He was the former Cambridge blue who had played sixteen times for Surrey, latterly going in at number four or five in a batting order still opened by Jack Hobbs and Andrew Sandham. Winlaw took a determined but also refreshingly positive approach to cricket. 'One would dearly love to see him batting in tandem with George Headley,' Robertson-Glasgow wrote. 'It would be a spectacle to bring casual pedestrians breezing in from the street.'

Winlaw, a vicar's elder son, had recently left a teaching job at Harrow School to join the RAF. He was married to the former Marsali Mary Seal of Cookham Dean in Berkshire, and in time they had a son, Anthony, and a daughter, Juliet. Robertson-Glasgow later remembered Winlaw's 'Colgate smile', along with the conviction which he seems to have held right from the start that 'fate had destined or ordained him for service in a great moral struggle, which he acknowledged quite airily he might not survive'.

Thirty-eight-year-old Claude Ashton had played the last of his 127 first-class matches just a year before, when he scored 8 and 17 for Essex against the touring Australians. It was not quite the end of his cricket career, however. Like Roger Winlaw, Ashton, a stockbroker in civilian life, went on to join the RAF, and appeared for them in a series of services matches between 1939 and 1942. The youngest of four sports-mad brothers, he had also played top-level football, possessing the opportune facility for turning out anywhere on the field from goalkeeper to centre forward, winning a single cap for England in their international against Northern Ireland at Belfast in October 1925. Ashton had been educated at Winchester and Cambridge, also like Winlaw. He won a triple blue while at university at hockey, cricket and football. It was said of him that 'he was a shy person by nature, and intensely aware of the oddness of life'. In early middle age, Ashton was still a boyish-looking figure with a curl of dark hair habitually tumbling over his right eye and a 'hint of a dry smile generally on his lips'. He was married to the former Isabel Norman-Butler of Blofield in Norfolk, with whom he had three children.

In August 1940, Ashton picked up a cricket bat for the first time in over twelve months, when he went out to represent the air force against a British Empire XI, which included Ken Farnes in its ranks, at Mill Hill. He scored 26 off 8 balls before being caught on the mid-wicket boundary off the bowling of the West Indies' Bertie Clarke. After that Ashton declined any more invitations to play cricket in 1940, and instead put his name down for flight training with the General Duties branch of the RAF.

The future commentator Brian Johnston was 27 years old in the summer of 1939, and on the reserve list for the Grenadier Guards. He lived in a flat in Central London and went to the local cricket on a regular basis. Through his roommate William Douglas-Home, Johnston became friendly with the fun-loving Kathleen 'Kick' Kennedy, daughter of the American ambassador, and her older brother Jack, who was 22 and now acquainted with Crusoe Robertson-Glasgow. 'There were a lot of laughs, and white ties and dynamite martinis and ebony cigarette-holders,' a diary note recalls of their circle. Jack Kennedy himself fondly remembered the dying days of that 'golden summer' in London as 'bustling with marchers, [and] flags fluttering everywhere from buildings and cars, and pretty young girls kissing soldiers in the street'.

Sometime in August, all four friends had gone to watch a cricket match in the sunshine at Lord's, where Johnston remembered that Paul Brooks of Middlesex had scored a century. If so, it must have been a two-day game between the Young Amateurs and Young Professionals, and also present in the modest Saturday afternoon crowd on 12 August, he later told me, was a cricket-obsessed 8-year-old from Hackney named Harold Pinter. *Wisden* fails even to mention the match, and the MCC archives note only that 'the Amateurs won a good contest by two runs'. That's all we know of the event. But it surely stands as one of the few English amateur sports fixtures of that or any other era to have been attended by a future president of the United States; a future Nobel Prize winner; and, in William Douglas-Home, a future dramatist and politician later to be cashiered by the army for refusing to participate in an attack on the enemy-held port of Le Havre without first allowing its civilian population to be safely evacuated, and whose eldest brother, Alec, was also a distinguished cricketer and, briefly, prime minister.

The spark needed to ignite the powder-keg of European rivalries and distrust into full-blown war came in Moscow on the Wednesday night of 23 August, when the Soviet Union concluded a non-aggression pact with Germany. Negotiations for a similar treaty between Britain and Russia had seemingly broken down only at the twelfth hour. Neville Chamberlain's own private assessment of the affair long rang in the ears of his friend Ambassador Kennedy. The 70-year-old premier was as a rule not one for vulgarity, but he permitted himself an exception in reporting to Kennedy about the way he thought he had done his job: 'I fucked it up, Joe.'

The news that a deal had been struck between the avowed ideological foes in Moscow and Berlin came as a bombshell to almost all outside parties. So swiftly had events moved that the swastika flags lining the route taken to the Kremlin by the German delegation had been rushed up from a local propaganda unit until that morning busy producing anti-Nazi newsreels. It was the equivalent moment to Gavrilo Princip's assassination of Archduke Franz Ferdinand at Sarajevo in July 1914; not, perhaps, in itself a *casus belli*, but sufficient to start a vicious circle of diplomatic turmoil and intensified military preparations. Although the front page of the *Daily Worker,* patchily available outside English cricket grounds on the morning of 24 August, heralded 'Soviet's Dramatic Peace Move To Halt Aggressors', a more representative headline was that in the *Guardian*: 'War of Threats Deepens'. In those pre-internet days few in Britain could have been aware of the leader in that same day's *Frankfurter Zeitung*, which read: 'No one need be surprised if Germany, contrary to earlier possibilities, takes the only possible course, which is to demand full reparation of the wrong of Versailles.'

At noon on 24 August, while Hedley Verity was on his way to devastating Kent with second-innings figures of 5-48, and Gerry Chalk to scoring a defiant 115 out in the middle at Dover, with Godfrey Evans nursing his hangover somewhere in the back of the pavilion, the British cabinet met in emergency session in Downing Street. There was an almost surreal note to some of the proceedings. Neville Chamberlain announced, for instance:

> I [can] report that the Polish Ambassador to Germany, M. Lipski, has now returned to Berlin and has accepted an invitation to shoot a stag in September with Field Marshal Goering. It has been suggested that, now that M. Lipski has returned to Berlin, it might be possible for negotiations to be started between Germany and Poland in regard to minority questions, which may well ease the tension.

This was truly a remote contingency, since advance German army formations were even then moving towards the Polish frontier and a further 1.5 million men waited in depots and barracks with their weapons primed for the order to attack. Hitler was puzzled by the low-key official response in Britain to the Soviet pact and openly amazed, apparently, that Chamberlain's government remained in office. War would be all Britain's fault, he announced on the 25th, since she was 'determined to destroy and exterminate Germany'. He had recently celebrated his 50th birthday, he reminded the British ambassador, and he preferred to fight now rather than in five or ten years' time. When the ambassador left him, Hitler then spent some time in poring over the press photographs taken of that week's treaty-signing ceremony in Moscow. In particular, he requested a close-up of Stalin, which he studied at length through a magnifying glass, in order to see if the Soviet leader's earlobes were 'ingrown and Jewish, or separate and Aryan'. The results were apparently reassuring. His new brother-in-arms, according to the earlobe test, was no Jew.

Godfrey Evans was back behind the stumps for Kent in their last county fixture of the season, against Lancashire at Dover. The 19-year-old had reacted to the signing of the Soviet-Nazi pact by another prolonged visit to the pub, and had probably escaped official censure only thanks to the quick thinking of Doug Wright in hurriedly slapping a hand over his young teammate's mouth when, on returning together to the team's bed and breakfast hotel late on the night of 25 August, Evans had broken into a lusty rendition of 'Nessun Dorma' in the corridor immediately outside the room occupied by the club president Major H.S. Hatfield and his wife. The teenager evidently bounced back with his usual resilience, because *Wisden* reported: 'Evans, seventeen [*sic*] years of age, kept wicket specially well on the first day.'

There was to be a dramatic finish to the match when Kent, after being 80 behind on first innings, were set 382 to win on the last day. They knocked off the runs in just over four hours. Arthur Fagg (138) and Gerry Chalk (94) put on 181 for the first wicket, the latter, according to *The Times*, batting with 'a felicity that displayed savagery to the bowler but made no demands on the spectator, whom he charmed and beguiled.' It was Chalk's last ever first-class innings. He turned 29 the following week, which also saw him report for an advanced three-month training course with the Royal Artillery. The county secretary Gerald Hough expressed a widely held view when he later wrote:

> Apart from his ability as a batsman and fielder, Chalk was an excellent leader in the field. The way in which he nursed the bowling in 1939 was outstanding. He nearly always managed to keep one bowler fresh for use at a pinch, and I think it is fair to say that our [success] was largely due to this, and his example in, and placing of, the field.

The 36-year-old former Kent and England batsman Geoffrey Legge was present in the modest committee room at Dover to watch his old county colleagues score the winning runs against Lancashire shortly after tea on 29 August. As we've seen, he now regularly flew around Europe in his own plane, housing it at his airfield near his family home in Cornwall. Whenever his business commitments allowed, Legge touched down on a convenient runway like that at Lympne, a dozen miles from Dover, to watch the local cricket. Married with four children, he still promptly volunteered for service in September 1939. The Fleet Air Arm judged Legge too old for operational flying but sent him to a training unit at Lee-on-Solent, near Portsmouth, while requisitioning his private airfield and converting it into the Royal Navy shore base

HMS *Vulture*. Remembered as a 'lean, neat, undemonstrative sort of fellow' who 'knew his mind', Legge spent most of his weekdays from September 1939 in the spartan wooden hut that served as his office at Lee-on-Solent, working with his usual thoroughness, writing elaborate technical manuals for the young recruits of 752 Squadron. At week-ends he liked to fly himself to a friend's country estate near Colchester for a morning's pheasant shooting, before continuing on his four-hour cross-country flight home to Cornwall. Sixty-seven-year-old Sir Roger Keyes, the former navy commander who orchestrated the April 1918 assault on the German-held ports of Zeebrugge and Ostend – and soon to become Britain's first director of commando operations – met Legge at one of the shoots. He told the younger officer that he not only had the 'strength and ability, but also the imagination and idealism which are prerequisites for a man of destiny'.

Yorkshire effectively finished their championship season by completely outplaying Hampshire to win by an innings and 11 runs in a match at the Dean Park ground in Bournemouth. This was the second in a three-legged southern victory lap for the new county champions, who also managed to fit in crushing wins at Dover and Hove over the same ten-day period. Verity was again the man of the match, taking 7 Hampshire wickets for 51 runs. Yorkshire could not now be caught at the top of the table. The small but increasingly vocal Monday afternoon crowd stayed on to sing 'Land of Hope and Glory' and 'Auld Lang Syne' at Bournemouth. Many years later, Len Hutton, not a man given to excessive public emotion, remembered that he and his teammates had been 'quite struck' by this performance, and that considering the international situation 'no one in our car spoke for about an hour after we left the ground, and it was bloody quiet even then. We all knew what was coming.'

As play began on the Saturday morning of 26 August, the ground at Aylestone Road, Leicester, swelled with people and patriotic enthusiasm. The home county remained anchored firmly at the foot of the championship table, and Glamorgan, their guests, stood only three places higher. Nonetheless, there was an atmosphere that morning that 'combined celebration with a very becoming martial display', *Sporting Life* reported. Brass bands and military units were on hand during the lunch interval, and the day's festivities would later include speeches from the two county presidents, fireworks, local hotel receptions and general civic excitement. Glamorgan's captain Maurice Turnbull had risen earlier than usual that morning and walked to the ground to discover opaque skies threatening rain. Even so, having won the toss, he batted. Turnbull himself went out to the crease an hour later, with his team's score on 43-2. When he left again shortly before tea, they stood at 294-7, and their indefatigable captain-secretary had hit 2 sixes and 18 fours in his run-a-minute innings of 156. Things calmed down a bit after that, and the match was already drifting towards a draw before a thunderstorm flooded the ground on the third morning.

Ten days later, Turnbull, who was 33, married 23-year-old Elizabeth Brooke at Holy Souls Roman Catholic Church in Scunthorpe. The couple set up home in a modest semi-detached house at Rhydypenau Road in Cardiff, conveniently located near the city's golf club, and in time had three children. Turnbull, who was already in training with the Welsh Guards, would not play competitive cricket again.

That same week in August 1939, Gloucestershire trounced Nottinghamshire at Trent Bridge with the help of a century by Hammond; Derbyshire disposed of Somerset at Taunton; and Middlesex, abandoning any remaining hopes of winning the title, drew with Surrey at Lord's. Bill Edrich continued his late-season form with a personal total of 189 for once out, attracting notice for the way he 'fairly hared' between the wickets in each innings. The young all-rounder was another one of those surprisingly numerous English cricketers of the day to show a degree of what might now seem to be manic behaviour, classic symptoms of which include excessive energy and grandiosity, racing thoughts and sexual or other intemperance, along with occasional depressions and self-destructive tendencies.

Despite his recent run of form, Edrich was not a happy man when he drove home in the steady rain following the close of play at Lord's on 29 August. He had just heard that the annual Scarborough Festival had been cancelled due to the European crisis, and he was bitterly disappointed by the news. The Middlesex professional had had a high time of it while representing the MCC against Yorkshire at the equivalent stage in 1938. Edrich had appeared for breakfast one morning still wearing his dinner jacket but missing his false teeth. The local pubs opened at 10.30 a.m., and play typically began at noon, so there was usually ample time for the cricketers to slake their thirst on the way to the North Marine ground. According to Freddie Brown, Edrich once did so to the extent that 'he was soon lying down underneath the table, from which vantage point he occasionally joined in the conversation'. 'The sun shone and there was the usual large and appreciative crowd spilling over the mound near the main gate,' the *Cricketer* wrote of the late-summer scene at Scarborough. 'The Town Band played the "Eton Boating Song" and selections from *Rose Marie* with the brio and that reckless disregard for their conductor which had made them famous.'

After reading the crushing letter informing him of the festival's cancellation for 1939, Edrich had only one question when he walked up the pavilion stairs at Lord's to the room set aside for his young county captain George Mann, who was just down from Cambridge, before play began in Middlesex's final match on the morning of Wednesday 30 August. Mann later thought that there had been both a 'narrow and a more general component' to the sometime England Test player's enquiry.

'What the fuck happens now, skipper?' Edrich had asked him.

THE DEAD CAT

Whatever his inner thoughts about the darkening world crisis, Bill Edrich showed no apparent sign of stress when he went out to bat for Middlesex against Warwickshire at Lord's shortly after lunch on 30 August 1939. His innings of 101 contained 15 fours and lasted just over two hours. He and Denis Compton shared a third-wicket stand of 137. It proved to be Edrich's last fully organised cricket match until he came to represent England against Australian Services on the same ground in May 1945. He finished the 1939 season with 2,186 first-class runs at an average just below 50. Roughly half of the runs had come in a five-week rush that began with his whirlwind century against Lancashire near the end of July. Despite all this – and the fact that Len Hutton had gone out to bat with three different opening partners in the short series against the West Indies – the England selectors ignored Edrich until the final home Test of 1946. Middlesex beat Warwickshire at Lord's by an innings and 200 runs.

Thirty-two-year-old E.W. Swanton was now in active training with the Bedfordshire Yeomanry, a role that involved him 'promenading up and down the Godforsaken beaches of East Anglia' while still permitting his distinctive 'fruity' voice to be heard commentating on the season's final county cricket matches. Swanton later wrote that he 'remembered nothing of covering the game at Bournemouth where Yorkshire finally clinched the championship, [but] very well recall standing with George

Mann on the Middlesex balcony, after they had with equal emphasis disposed of Warwickshire, and as the Lord's crowd dispersed wondering when we should see them next assemble.'

The journalist Roy Peskett captured some of the same wistful tone when he wrote of meeting the veteran stage and film actor Huntley Wright that week at Lord's.

> We watched from the Long Room the gallant Edrich innings ... At the close, the dapper, immaculately dressed Wright turned to me, and with his face expressing tragedy that gained nothing from his seventy years of service on the stage, said, 'When, Oh when, shall we see the like again?'

Something curious happens when reading the vivid account Neville Cardus gives in his autobiography of sitting in that same Long Room watching the cricket on the Friday morning of 1 September, 'the day', he specifies, 'Hitler invaded Poland'. Although it's certainly possible that members of the MCC ground staff elected to play an impromptu game of some sort in the middle that morning, the Middlesex and Warwickshire teams had in fact both gone home the night before, bringing first-class cricket at Lord's to a halt for the next six years. Perhaps Cardus, a writer of undoubted narrative gifts not always matched by his attention to prosaic detail, simply confused the sequence of affairs. If so, he wasn't the only person confounded by the fast-breaking events of that week.

He writes:

> As I watched the ghostly movements of the players outside, a beauti-fully preserved member of Lord's, spats and rolled umbrella, stood near me inspecting the game. We did not speak of course; we had not been introduced. Suddenly two workmen entered the Long Room in green aprons and carrying a bag. They took down the bust of W.G. Grace, put it into the bag, and departed with it. The noble lord at my side watched their every movement; then he turned to me. 'Did you see, sir?' he asked. I told him I had seen. 'That means war,' he said.

THE DEAD CAT

Surrey were scheduled to host Lancashire in the championship that week, but by then the military authorities had already requisitioned the Oval and begun to erect anti-aircraft searchlights on the pavilion roof. This was a similar fate to the one suffered by the ground in August 1914, when several hundred Territorial soldiers and their horses had appeared overnight and been billeted at the Vauxhall end, with disastrous consequences for Jack Hobbs's benefit match. The Surrey team now agreed to hurriedly travel to Manchester, where they managed to get through two days' cricket with Lancashire. In *Wisden*'s stark report, there was 'no play on third day, owing to Crisis'. Old Trafford itself was soon occupied by the army, and in the winter of 1940–41 the ground took several direct hits from the Luftwaffe. The surrounding area was so badly damaged that in time the authorities built a mock-up version of their city in the Burnley moors out of plywood and oil drums, which were lit at night to make it look as if 'Manchester' had already been bombed.

In a strained effort to reconcile themselves to the prospect of war, England's county cricket authorities had begun to review what Derbyshire called their 'future requisites', or players' contracts, for 1940. At Hampshire, a special meeting was called on 26 August 'to discuss the re-engagement of the Professionals ... It was decided to grant each of the capped men a salary of £3 per week for one month in the form of a gratuity. In the event of the international situation becoming settled by the end of September,' the county chairman wrote, 'this arrangement will be cancelled and such Professionals as are required will receive their wages according to the decision of the Committee.' At Kent, Gerald Hough wasted no time in writing to each of his fourteen salaried players on 30 August to tell them, 'Owing to external events, the prospect of your re-engagement [for 1940] is now remote.' Bill Edrich later remembered a 'great crisis confab' at Lord's where the Middlesex players had been addressed by an 'old boy on the committee with his bushy eyebrows twitching [and] his face jumping around with a tic – not exactly a performance designed to spread calm through the dressing room'. By 1 September, most of the seventeen county secretaries had either met or written to their contracted players with much the same message.

Some would be paid a nominal monthly retainer, but most were simply let go. On the evening Britain declared war, Yorkshire's Hedley Verity saw his chairman Sir Stanley Jackson in the dining room of the Queens Hotel in Leeds and went across to shake his hand. Neither said anything. It was the last time they met.

There was something almost comically unreal about the few remaining matches of the 1939 season. On 28 August the British War Office had ordered the mobilisation of 40,000 Territorial Army soldiers, and other steps were taken that reflected the gravity of the situation, including the evacuation of London's major art treasures to locations in the west of England. Yet the county cricket championship continued. It was as if the players were like so many Merrie Melody cartoon characters, still frantically pumping their legs after running headlong over the side of a cliff. At Taunton from 30 to 31 August, Somerset beat Northamptonshire by an innings and 92 runs. Arthur Wellard took 7 wickets in the match, and Harold Gimblett finished his season with an innings of 67 that included 10 fours and a glorious drive that sailed back over the bowler's head for a six into the pavilion. Needing 242 to avoid an innings defeat, Northants found themselves at 33-5 shortly before tea on the second afternoon. Their captain Robert Nelson 'tried hard to make a fight of it,' *Wisden* reported, 'but the collapse could not be checked'. Nelson, who top-scored with 42, was by then travelling the country in between matches to raise funds for the Red Cross and other relief organisations. He joined the Royal Marines later in October 1939. Having taken the county from a disorganised rabble to the slopes of respectability, his committee were understandably keen for him to return for at least one season after the war. Nelson wrote back to tell them that he hoped to do so, but that Nazism represented the 'barbaric underside of European civilisation', and that this first needed to be 'thoroughly erased'. In the event he would not play organised cricket again.

Leicestershire finished their season with a draw against Derbyshire that, somehow aptly for 1939, ended when a thunderstorm washed out the last day's play. Worcestershire won by an innings at home to Nottinghamshire, thanks largely to a maiden first-class century by their

25-year-old amateur 'Sandy' Singleton, playing his last match before joining the RAF. He returned to briefly captain the county side in 1946. During that same period Glamorgan and Somerset also played out a rain-soaked draw in the Second XI championship at a sparsely attended Cardiff Arms Park, a match notable only because 16-year-old Graham Woods on the home side and 17-year-old Peter Pearn on the visitors' would each go on to join the air force the moment they were old enough to do so, and both would later die in action.

When the final figures were added up – the table was determined on an average points basis because not all the teams played the same number of matches – Yorkshire and Middlesex occupied the top two places in the championship for the third consecutive year. Gloucestershire, who had managed to beat the champions both home and away, were third. Leicestershire ended one of the worst seasons in their modern forty-four-year history in last place, with a dismal 16 points at an average of 0.80 compared to Yorkshire's tally of 260 and 9.28 respectively. Essex, Kent and Glamorgan could all congratulate themselves on a small improvement on their previous year's form, while Northamptonshire at least avoided the ignominy of enduring a fourth successive season without a single win. Modest as their final record was, it showed a marked step up from 1938, when they lost 17 of their 24 matches and drew the rest.

There was something only fitting about the season's first-class batting averages, which were led, in descending order, by Hammond, Hutton, Compton, Hardstaff, Sutcliffe and Keeton. All of these players except the 44-year-old Sutcliffe had represented England in the series against the West Indies. Verity led the bowlers with his 191 wickets, closely followed by the likes of Bowes, Goddard, Copson, Wright and Farnes. Six out of the top ten names on the list were spinners. Fred Price of Middlesex and Arthur Wood of Yorkshire each accounted for 83 victims behind the stumps. Hutton took 40 catches in the field. Of course, statistics alone are absurd when it comes to describing the summer of 1939 in the light of what followed it. Crusoe Robertson-Glasgow later reviewed the season in *Wisden* and wrote that it was 'like peeping through the wrong end of a telescope at a very small but happy world'.

The cabinet meeting of 30 August – the day the final round of county cricket matches got underway – displayed both optimism and uncertainty. In giving 'consideration to Herr Hitler's position', the foreign secretary remarked:

> Although the matter is open to several interpretations, nevertheless the line we should now take is fairly clear. The terms of Herr Hitler's latest message are somewhat bombastic, but stripped of its verbiage it reveals a man who is trying to extricate himself from a difficult position … Reports have been received from various sources of anti-Government demonstrations up and down Germany. It is difficult to assess the value of these reports, but everything points to the line which we take being at once firm yet unprovocative.

The mood in the country as a whole also swung uneasily from expectation of war and hope of compromise. In Yorkshire, Bill Bowes recalled that his county and Test colleague Hedley Verity had long harboured no illusions about the crisis. 'As early as 1937 he was certain that the war was coming, and he said it would last six years.' In short order Bowes and Verity, neither of them a young man, reported to the recruiting office in Bradford. Although they had wanted to serve together, in the end Verity took an infantry commission and Bowes went on to train as a gunnery officer. In Kent, Godfrey Evans was now 'absolutely bloody positive' about what was coming. He wrote in his new diary on 31 August: 'All Peace-War-Peace in the papers. [I] don't believe it. The Germans are playing us for fools.' At Middlesex, Denis Compton, one of life's blithe spirits, remembered:

> Everything we heard from on high was to not panic. The general feeling was still good. We all believed Mr Chamberlain wanted peace as much as we did, and that all these telegrams flying back and forth to Berlin about

us standing with Poland, etc., would fool Hitler into submission. We all thought he was a bully who would back down.

Compton was not alone. As late as the afternoon of 31 August, with half a dozen county championship matches being played out around Britain in a mixture of showers and sunshine, the view still flourished that Hitler really was bluffing and would be deterred by a show of firmness. But, as Godfrey Evans remembered, there was also a 'very odd' and 'somehow very English' reaction to the prospect of war.

> I was back down in Faversham. The season was just over. The spinster woman who lived next to us came out of her front door about eight in the morning crying her eyes out. We went out to see what had happened. She showed us a shopping bag she was carrying. There was a stiff dead cat in it. Not a pretty sight. She told us she'd tried to kill it with poison, and when that didn't work she'd tied a bit of string round its neck and strangled it. She loved that cat. Now she was going off to bury it in a pit the council had dug somewhere on the edge of town. Later we heard that people all around there were destroying their pets. They were worried that food supplies would run dry and there would be nothing to feed them on.

This mass euthanasia of Britain's household animals was perhaps the strangest thing that happened during that week when the mood in the nation as a whole swung almost hourly from the wildest flights of optimism to the deepest despair. On 8 September, *The Times* reported that 'millions' of pets had been put down over the previous fortnight. In Greater London alone, an estimated 400,000 cats and dogs were destroyed in the period between 31 August and 3 September. Although there was no government edict telling people to do this, an official pamphlet issued earlier in August had suggested it was kinder to act now than wait for the worst: 'During an emergency there might be large numbers of animals wounded, gassed or driven frantic with fear, and destruction would then have to be enforced by the responsible authority for the protection of the public.' Within two years, some 30 per cent of all the dogs and cats in the south-east had been put down. Godfrey Evans was no shrinking violet, but to the end of his life he remembered the sight of his neighbour's dead pet 'with its eyes popping out and a bright red scar round its neck where she'd throttled it ... That really made the coming of war real for me'.

In London that same evening the foreign secretary sent a note to the Polish government. It read: 'While we here can not take the responsibility of advising you not to carry out full mobilisation, we hope that your measures will receive as little publicity as possible, [so as] not to provoke Herr Hitler.'

Hitler himself was beyond such niceties by then. At midday on 31 August he published 'Directive No. 1 for the Conduct of the War' and at 4 p.m. gave the armed forces the order to attack. He told his army chief of staff, Franz Halder, 'France and England will not march.' To Hitler the invasion of Poland was not war, only a coup to seize what was rightfully Germany's. It was a localised action, and Halder repeatedly heard him say: 'The English will leave the Poles in the lurch as they did the Czechs.'

It is for others to judge to what extent the outbreak of war can be blamed on the deteriorating European order during the 1930s, or to apportion responsibility between such factors as the rise of totalitarian dictatorships, the unresolved administrative and economic dislocation brought about by the Paris peace treaty of 1919, or the deficiencies of Anglo-French diplomacy during the period. But there is one curious historical incident that may go at least part of the way to explaining Hitler's fundamental misjudgement of the British character, and of the British will to fight. This took place not in the chancellery in Berlin, but in a dressing station situated in a field south of Wervick, part of the Western Front near Ypres, in the autumn of 1918. Mustard gas was by then in extensive use by all the belligerents, and was deployed during a

British attack, undertaken in shifting wind, launched in the early hours of 14 October. In the ensuing chaos, both German and Allied victims were taken back to a communal area for first-aid treatment before ultimately being evacuated behind their respective lines. According to a sitting Conservative MP and Machine Gun Corps officer named Oliver Locker-Lampson, one of the enemy combatants in the dressing station was none other than 29-year-old Corporal Adolf Hitler.

'While he was recovering,' Locker-Lampson wrote, 'he came to us and asked whether he might watch an eleven of cricket at play, so as to become initiated into the mysteries of our summer game. We welcomed him, of course.' But when himself invited to play in a friendly match, 'the corporal proposed altering the laws of cricket, which he considered good enough for the pleasure-loving English, but not for the serious-minded Teuton'.

Among other innovations, says Locker-Lampson, Hitler 'advocated the withdrawal of the use of pads. These artificial "bolsters" he dismissed as unmanly and un-German. He also commented adversely on the need for batting gloves, and recommended a bigger and harder ball.' In a final critique, the future dictator summarised the overall tempo of play as '*Ohne hast*', or sluggish, proposing that instead of each team bowling the other one out in its entirety, some sort of truncated version be considered to achieve a result 'within less than a week', which if true was to anticipate the pioneering work of the Gillette Cup by some forty-five years.

A day or two later, Hitler was sent on to a military hospital near Stettin, thus ending his active involvement in England's national sport. It remains an intriguing possibility that his core assessment of his primary opponent in 1939 as being both 'civilised' but 'weak and effete … always stopping their artillery barrages at tea time so that I, a messenger, could run my errands safely at that hour', owed as much to his fleeting exposure to cricket as to any more narrowly political factor.

The news of the German action in Poland reached London at around breakfast time on Friday 1 September. The British War Minister, Leslie Hore-Belisha, was rung up at home at 6.30 a.m. to be told 'Germans were over'. He rolled over in bed, cursing the enemy's thoughtlessness. A day of mutual diplomatic ultimatums and crisis cabinet meetings ended with Neville Chamberlain telling the House of Commons that, should Germany withdraw the troops now ravaging western Poland, 'the way would yet be open to discussions between the Berlin and Warsaw governments of the matters at issue before them, on the understanding that the settlement arrived at was one that safeguarded all vital interests and was secured by an international guarantee'. In other words, Chamberlain still hesitated. The blackout that descended all over Britain that evening was nevertheless a grim omen. At home in Faversham, Godfrey Evans wrote in his diary: 'Nailed up sheets over the windows. Father in tears. Nothing to do now but join the army.'

Germany's rape of Poland did not quite complete the English county cricket season. Of the six matches that began on Wednesday, 30 August, three were brought to an end with a result on the second day, and two more were abandoned as draws by mutual consent early on the Friday morning after news of the German offensive was reported. But in what Len Hutton later described as a show of 'British defiance [and] good Northern stubbornness' play continued uninterrupted through the sunny early afternoon of 1 September at Hove, where Sussex hosted Yorkshire in Jim Parks's benefit match. It was the last county cricket fixture in England for almost seven years, and the same two sides had also faced each other on the same ground at the equivalent moment in September 1914. When the lights had finally gone out at the end of that earlier match, nearly a month after the outbreak of the Great War, they did so in a torrential thunderstorm. The weather had had the last sardonic laugh on that occasion.

There had been some discussion about whether or not the Yorkshire team would continue on to Hove following their crushing victory over

Hampshire at Bournemouth on 28 August 1939, but in an interview published in the *Argus* on the afternoon of the 29th the visitors' captain Brian Sellers remarked: 'We are public entertainers and until we have instructions to the contrary we will carry on as usual.' Besides, the Yorkshiremen always enjoyed a trip to the south coast. At stumps the players would generally head off for 'one of those enormous bars [in] the great seafront hotels and stay there until chucking-out time,' Hutton remembered half a century later. 'I seem to recall pushing Arthur Wood up the road to our digs one night slung over a porter's trolley borrowed from the station.' Belying their reputation as the circuit's famously unsentimental and hard-nosed professionals, the newly crowned county champions may also have been moved to fulfil their commitment to appear at Hove out of a sense of goodwill for the popular Sussex all-rounder Jim Parks. Parks's benefit fund had already lost out when the West Indian tourists had cancelled their highly anticipated match scheduled earlier that week. Hutton told me that the team had wanted to show that 'life went on, and also to stretch our legs for a few days on the coast', where the players awoke in their bed and breakfast each morning to the sight and sound of 'hundreds of trumpeting seagulls' strung out in the blue sky 'like a long, flapping clothes line of white linen'.

When the time came, Sussex won the toss on a flat pitch and 28-year-old George Cox scored 198 out of 387, the highest team total of the season against the champion county. Cox's father, also named George, had been the Sussex bowler who took the last wicket to wrap up the game against Yorkshire twenty-five years earlier. The journalist Dudley Carew later wrote of the scene at Hove in 1939:

> It was crowded, but nothing like so crowded had there been no threat to Poland. Groups of people were gathered around cars parked on the boundary listening to the wireless as it spoke of the hopeless, last-minute efforts to save a peace that was beyond aid … Concentration on the cricket was fitful and disjointed. Yet Cox's strokes through the covers insisted on drawing attention to themselves. They were played in the grand manner, and again and again the ball came rattling up against the pavilion rails.

In truth there were probably only about 1,500 spectators scattered around the ground on the first morning. Laetitia Stapleton was one of those seated in a canvas deckchair in front of the Tamplin's tea pavilion and remembered that 'you could hear the players in the middle clapping their hands together and sometimes joking with each other in between overs'. There was a faintly damp, leafy, end-of-season smell in the air. An elderly man known only as 'Cushions' rented out what appeared to be thin, embroidered hassocks used for kneeling on in church, and two small boys in shorts sold scorecards for twopence each. On the front of the card there was a slightly erratically typed list of the players' names, and on the back there were advertisements for 'Flinn & Son Ltd, the Dyers & Dry Cleaners of the South – Men's Soft Felt Hats Cleaned & Reblocked (1sh.)', and 'Cold Luncheons in Chalet Hotel, with vegetables, salad and sweets, 2/6d (or 1/6d sans veg and pud)', among other displays for cold remedies and tinned beef, and the stark notice, also reprinted on signs hung around the ground, from the Ministry of Home Security:

If the INVADER comes,

What to do – And how to do it

If the Germans come, by parachute, aeroplane or ship, you must remain where you are. The order is 'Stay Put'. It is no good fleeing from your homes. If you keep your heads, you can also tell whether a military officer is really British, or only pretending to be. If in doubt, ask the Police Man or the A.R.P. Warden. Stay calm and use your common sense.

The light deteriorated steadily during the final session on 30 August, but the two teams still got through a full day's play. Yorkshire finished on 112-1, meaning that a total of 499 runs had been scored in six hours of cricket. Both sides went out to dinner together at the nearby Old Ship Hotel. Something between a heavy downpour and a monsoon flooded the ground overnight, and play was delayed until teatime on the Thursday afternoon. Yorkshire then reached 330-3, a scoring rate of around 90 an hour, by the close. It was suddenly a warm late August evening, and Hutton remembered that several of the visitors, himself included, had walked down to the front after stumps, rolled up their trousers, and 'behaved like schoolkids, splashing gaily around in the sea', an indelible image of professional cricketers staying calm and using their common sense, even as, 1,000 miles away, German special forces were staging a mock Polish attack on the small border town of Gleiwitz, and the German training ship *Schleswig Holstein* 'retaliated' by opening fire on the Polish fort at Westerplatte, launching the Second World War.

At 9 a.m. on Friday, the Yorkshire committee wired their captain Brian Sellers to suggest that the match at Hove should be abandoned. Sellers took a straw poll among his team and announced that they preferred to continue. Yorkshire then went out to bat under a cloudless blue sky and lost their last 7 wickets for 62 runs. Jim Langridge took 4–84 off 20.4 8-ball overs. The pitch was still drying out and Hutton, who had just scored 103, remembered that the ball left dark bruises on the surface as it skidded through. These were conditions tailor-made for Hedley Verity. Incredibly, the Sussex second innings lasted for less than 12 overs as they were dismissed for 33. Bowling unchanged, Verity, playing what proved to be his 378th and final first-class match, took 7 wickets for 9 runs, and after that the visitors briefly went in again to score the 30 needed to win, which they did to the accompaniment of patriotic songs issuing from the stands.

At that the Yorkshire team gathered in the picture-lined committee room to say goodbye to members and friends, shook the hands of their opponents, then boarded a dark green Southdown coach and headed north through ominously quiet, boarded-up Sussex villages. Reaching the outskirts of London, Hutton remembered, 'hundreds of cars passed by in all directions, a lot of them with suitcases and even bits of furniture strapped to their roofs'. The players spent that night in a roadside establishment somewhere near Leicester, not even bothering to unpack, and finally reached home around noon on Saturday 2 September. The Sussex club had collected £734–10s–6d in gate money during the three-day match, and a whip-round raised £75 for Jim Parks's benefit. Parks's 7-year-old son, also named Jim, remembered walking home that warm Friday afternoon hand-in-hand with his 'very quiet' father:

I think he clearly knew what was coming. By then it was a question of when, not if, the war broke out. That was the ghastly truth that hung in the air as we walked slowly along, clutching each other's hands, while people drove past us in lorries or in cars with everything they had piled up on top of them.

The younger Parks added that this had been one of those 'really immortal' experiences in a life that also saw him play 739 first-class matches for Sussex and 46 Tests for England.

Back in Yorkshire, Hedley Verity and his friend Bill Bowes enjoyed a last, well-lubricated night on the town with members of the Harrogate Rugby Club and then reported to their respective units. Early the next spring, Verity, by then a captain in the First Battalion, Green Howards, found himself accompanied by some of his old county colleagues changing trains at Brighton while on their way to a training camp nearby. The station master spotted them and asked if he could take their photo. It still exists. All five cricketers stand there proudly in uniform, posing for the camera. Their whole demeanour is good-humoured, breezy and confident. Verity has a wide smile. Across the top of the picture, he later wrote: 'Dear Jimmy, Our regards to Beautiful Sussex from Yorkshire County Cricket Club.'

Six years later, Yorkshire's captain Brian Sellers put on his county blazer again for the first time since his side had beaten Sussex on that long-ago Friday afternoon at Hove. When he reached in the pocket he pulled out a faded slip of paper. It was the scorecard from 1 September 1939, and Sellers admitted that a shiver had run down his spine when his eye suddenly fell on the name 'H. Verity', reminding him with a jolt of his friend's 'grand achievement' that day.

It is often said that English cricket stopped dead in its tracks on the day the Wehrmacht invaded Poland, with none of the regrettable tendency to linger, merely delaying the inevitable, of August 1914. This account needs correction. It's quite true that the first-class season ended with Yorkshire's defeat of Sussex on the afternoon of 1 September, but the sport survived for several more weeks at the grassroots level. There was a full round of Lancashire League matches on the weekend of 2–3 September, for example, with Learie Constantine returning to play for Nelson in their 4-wicket win over Rawtenstall. The great West Indian scored 35 in a couple of overs before making a weak attempt to play a plumb half-volley and being caught at slip. The impression among some, if not all, the Rawtenstall team was that Constantine, having seen his side to the brink of victory, deliberately allowed himself to be dismissed by edging the ball to the fielder. This is a quite difficult thing to do without clearly betraying the fact to the opposition. That was to prove Constantine's last appearance for Nelson until September 1940, when, now aged 39, he took 5-43 in 14 lively overs against Rishton. According to the *Liverpool Post*, when he came to bat, 'the West Indian seemed to simply miss a straight one from Hacking, and departed with a warm smile and a handshake of congratulation for the jubilant bowler'.

At Woodhall Spa in Lincolnshire, where the town's two main hotels had already been requisitioned by the RAF, the local Gentlemen and Colts sides played a series of matches during the week of 4 September, while at Wallasey on Merseyside a team raised by Cheshire's George McEntyre took on one led by his minor counties colleague Arthur Crooke, playing to a large crowd serviced by a 'school marching band, [with] fruit and cake vendors, pie stalls, tea tents and various bars estimated at holding a fortnight's supply of ale' on the day the Red Army entered Poland from the east. There was another match between the two sides with substitutes allowed on Saturday 23 September, played for the benefit of the Wallasey Education Committee's clothing fund for displaced children. Slightly under £10 was raised. Seventeen of the twenty-six players who took part saw active service at some stage during the war, and all of them survived.

Cricket seems to have flourished in the north-west as a whole, with E. W. Swanton regularly travelling across the country from his beach-guarding duties in East Anglia for a weekend game. 'In 1939,' he wrote:

Liverpool boasted three recent University bowlers of distinction, John Brocklebank, Alan Barlow and A.R. Legard, a Winchester and Oxford scientist of much erudition who was therefore known as 'Loopy'. Thus I gravitated to Aigburth and on the Friday evening before the first match took a net before being hastened back to our quarters by the air-raid sirens.

Swanton also remembered appearing at the ground in Liverpool later in 1940 and finding 'the field spattered by shrapnel, and a hole in the face of the pavilion clock made by an ack-ack shell'.

English village cricket, the pure and original manifestation of the game, sputtered on in different parts of the country for more than a month after the first-class season wound up. A local teenager named David Blake, later to play 73 first-class matches for MCC and Hampshire, remembered turning out for Wickham against Botley on a field in nearby Southampton:

> And at the end of the match everyone trooped off for the evening to the Bald Faced Stag in Edward Road and our skipper stood up and made an emotional speech about the brave people of Poland and the evil Reds, and someone else started a fight on the subject, and I woke up the next morning in Wickham with the first major hangover of my life.

After that the autumn increasingly began to assert itself on the game at all levels, and the journalist Home Gordon found a suitable metaphor when he wrote in the *Cricketer*: 'England has now begun the grim Test match against Germany.'

At 11.30 on the sultry Sunday morning of 3 September 1939, Bill Edrich had just passed through the Grace Gates at Lord's after listening to the prime minister's declaration of war on the radio and was strolling in the sunshine towards Baker Street tube station.

Suddenly there was a horde of people rushing past me, and wholesale panic as many of them poured down into the station. The air-raid sirens had just gone off. Men and women fought for seats on trains. All the platforms were jammed. A minute or two later, a guard managed to climb up onto some steps and shouted out that it had been a false alarm. People broke out into loud applause. The guard jumped down and as I walked past I heard a man in a dark suit mutter 'Bloody fools! If they only knew what they're cheering.'

Godfrey Evans was at home in Kent and remembered that his elderly father had snapped out an unsatirical salute towards the radio set after listening to Chamberlain's announcement. Following the broadcast, Arthur Evans and his two sons had walked down the lane to the village pub. 'As we marched along in the lovely late-summer sunshine it was hard to believe we were really all about to start killing each other.'

The 33-year-old British author Mollie Panter-Downes wrote of her experience that Sunday:

> Squadrons of bombers bustled overhead, [and] on the ground motor buses full of troops in bursting good humour tore through the villages, the men waving at the girls and howling 'Tipperary' and other ominously dated ditties … The English were a peace loving nation up to two days ago, but now it is pretty widely felt that the sooner we really get down to the job, the better.

Bill Edrich had abandoned Baker Street after the excitement of the morning's air-raid siren and, somehow characteristically, now found himself wandering around with a pretty girl he had met only minutes earlier, 'longing to make love but unable to afford a decent room'. Like many other people's, Edrich's basic courtship technique, impressively brisk at the best of times, was charged with new urgency once the possibility of death stalked the scene. In the end, he improvised with his new friend: 'There were fireworks up against a tree in Regent's Park.'

Typically, Edrich had no intention of moving home in order to be further away from the likely path of German bombing raids. In fact just the opposite. In one of those coincidences shunned in fiction but quite prevalent in the cricket world, Edrich found that one of his instructors at RAF Uxbridge was none other than his Middlesex captain Walter Robins. Robins asked the new recruit if there was any small favour he could do for him. Edrich said yes, there was: he wanted to train as a pilot, and to fly what he cheerfully allowed might be 'rather hairy' sorties over enemy territory. Robins granted the request. Just over a year later, Edrich was duly at the controls of a twin-engine Bristol Blenheim engaged in successive low-level daylight bombing raids on the German industrial heartland, a target from which about a third of all British crews ultimately never returned. Many historians have since competed to write more dramatic descriptions than each other of the obvious perils of such missions. Edrich himself was more succinct. 'It was the bollocks,' he said simply. 'Flattened low on the water, tucked in as close as I dared to the leader, I felt an exhilaration that swamped all other emotions. Low flying did not bother me. I loved it.'

But while Edrich headed jauntily into harm's way, many other Britons either chose to move, or did so involuntarily, in the other direction. The Yorkshire-born author Storm Jameson later wrote of her experiences of touring London neighbourhoods that had once teemed with children playing, but now seemed to be so many wastelands as they sat silent and deserted in anticipation of a disaster.

Half a million children were hurried out of the city, and some further hundreds of thousands went independently, packed off to relatives and boarding schools in the country. On Wednesday, September 6, London looked as it would if some fantastic death pinched off the heads under fifteen. It was an exquisite day, the wind mild and fitful, the sky clear. In this light, London is extremely handsome. Very early in the morning the balloon barrage looks unreal and very frail. As the light strengthens, the balloons become clear and hard, oversize stars in a perfectly blue sky. A pity there are no children to point at them.

On Monday, 11 September, Godfrey Evans took the train up to Victoria in order to offer his services to an army recruiting office housed in a temporary hut near the National Gallery. As he walked up Whitehall towards Trafalgar Square he paused to watch:

A huge gang of 8- or 9-year-old boys and girls march past in the opposite direction. Each of them had a gas-mask, and a label with their name pinned to their coat. Some of them were clutching little teddy-bears. They were heading off to the station. All very quiet and brave, although that wasn't the case with some of the worried-looking mothers bringing up the rear. I saw one of them sobbing uncontrollably. It was awful. As one of the older kids passed by me I heard him complaining to his chum that his parents had taken him up to the zoo as a treat before he left home, but all the poisonous snakes and insects had already been destroyed. Apparently their keepers didn't want them to escape if they got bombed. Very glum about it he was.

When Evans got to the recruiting station, they took down his name and particulars and then told him that, at 19, he was still too young to join up just at present, but that they would let him know if and when the situation changed, which was how he came to spend the winter of 1939–40 working alongside his cricketing friend John Pocock driving a baker's delivery van around Kent. Still not having heard anything official, the young wicketkeeper went back to the recruitment office the following spring. He got another frosty reception. 'The buggers still thought they could win the war without me,' Evans said. 'At least they did until I slipped the recruiting sergeant a fiver. From then on, after all that farting around, the papers went through like lightning.'

Evans was formally inducted into the Royal Army Service Corps on 1 June 1940. As at other critical times of his life, he celebrated by buying a large car.

Unfortunately, France then chose to surrender and I had to abandon the motor in Maidstone and head off post-haste to a training depot in

Chesterfield. All the talk there was about us being urgently needed to repel the invasion that was expected at any minute, but in the event I spent most of the rest of the summer playing battalion cricket and getting acquainted with the local talent. Not a disagreeable life in its way.

Among those hurriedly leaving their homes in England on the outbreak of war were 33-year-old William Joyce and his wife Margaret. Joyce had spent the previous twelve months in a sadly forlorn attempt to whip up fascist activity in and around Worthing in West Sussex, while often unwinding after a hard day's propaganda work by looking in at the county cricket ground. Over time he made friends of several of the team's players. Hugh Bartlett came to know Joyce, whom he later described as:

> An inveterate schemer; intelligent, olive-skinned and leering ... morally just this side of an oil-slick. He was always full of these great plans for making cricketers rich, none of which ever materialised. I suppose there was a touch of Kerry Packer but without the actual money to him.

When the authorities came for Joyce at his Sussex farmhouse in late August 1939, they found that he had just eluded them. There was still a warm kettle on the stove, as well as high-powered radio transmitting equipment hidden under the floorboards. Joyce became the best-known German propaganda broadcaster during the war. When he was captured in May 1945, his old Sussex membership card was found among his possessions. Still insisting that war had been forced upon Germany, he was executed the following January at Wandsworth Prison aged 39; the last person to be hanged in Britain for treason.

Despite – or because of – the national emergency, many English crick-eters took the opportunity to put down roots in the autumn of 1939.

We've seen that the swashbuckling captain of Glamorgan, Maurice Turnbull, married as soon as the county season ended. Len Hutton did the same thing, hurriedly bringing forward his wedding to his fiancée Dorothy, planned for November, to Saturday 16 September. Later that month, the Yorkshire club paid each of its players a £30 bonus (roughly £800 today) for winning the title. Hutton put the money towards a down payment on a new semi-detached home in Pudsey where he and Dorothy would live for the next sixteen years. Meanwhile, the England captain Walter Hammond apparently resolved to leave his wife, also named Dorothy, on the occasion of his joining the RAF reserve in September 1939 and to marry his long-time mistress instead. This plan was shelved only when Hammond was sent overseas in 1940, a time when the military authorities still considered it 'inimical to good order and discipline' for an officer on active duty to divorce his spouse.

William Joyce's theory that a peace-loving Reich had been provoked beyond reason by bellicose factions in Westminster and elsewhere perhaps fails the test of objective historical scrutiny. But Joyce was right in so far as observing that Britain for the most part rallied swiftly behind Chamberlain's announcement of 3 September. The scale of mobilisation was at its peak between 4 September and 9 October 1939 and 6 May–16 June 1940, the 'phony war' intervening, with an additional 1.6 million civil defence volunteers in place by the first Christmas of the war. Taken as a share of national population, the British response to the events of autumn 1939 surpassed that of all other belligerents. Within nine months, military costs accounted for 55.3 per cent of national expenditure. By 3 September 1940, 48 per cent of the UK labour force was in the armed forces or in war-related employment; the comparable figure for Germany was 29 per cent

English cricketers played their full part. To give just some of the many examples available of those who immediately answered the call to arms: Somerset's veteran all-rounder Jack Lee, despite approaching his 40th birthday, promptly enlisted as a private in the army's Pioneer Corps. He died in June 1944 in the wake of the Normandy landings. Cyril Washbrook, the up-and-coming Lancashire and sometime England batsman, similarly joined the RAF. Washbrook's Test opening partner Len Hutton in turn volunteered and was called up to serve in the Army Physical Training corps. At Canterbury, the fun-loving Hopper Levett at once went into the Royal West Kent Regiment, telling his successor as county wicketkeeper, Godfrey Evans, that he meant to 'hit this bugger in Berlin [Hitler] like a bloody cannon ball.' Thirty-year-old Peter Smith of Essex, the man who had once been on the receiving end of a hoax Test call-up, joined the army on the day that Germany invaded Poland. Having recently been selected for the cancelled MCC winter tour of India, this was the second time that Smith had seen his hopes of international recognition dashed in unusual fashion. Later commissioned as a second lieutenant in the Essex Regiment and posted to Egypt, he rose to become director of Allied troop movements at Alexandria and captain of the Alamein cricket club.

At 28, Smith's county teammate Ken Farnes was already past the age of compulsory call-up and returned to his teaching job at Worksop College for the 1939–40 academic year. He went into the RAF reserve in June 1940, coming top of his group in flight school. Like others, at the time he signed up Farnes made the distinction between his desire to obliterate what he called 'the stench of perverted National Socialism' and his reluctance to harm innocent German civilians. He had also just become romantically involved with the 30-year-old (and married) Catherine 'Aeron' Narracott, who escaped the London blitz that September in order to move to Devon with her 7-year-old daughter Diana. Some of those close to Farnes believed that Catherine was the first serious love of his life. Bill Edrich met his fellow pilot later in 1940 in a canteen at the RAF operational base at Upwood in Cambridgeshire; although not particularly notable for its exchange of technical detail about flying, it was an encounter that both parties would later recall fondly. By that stage Edrich, although still just 24, already had wide experience of affairs of the heart. 'Ken loved her,' he said, 'and he was devoted to the little girl, but after talking about them in the sweetest manner suddenly cut himself off with: "Well, that's that. There's a war on. And there's nothing you or I can do about it except to get it over with as fast as possible."'

Farnes was as good as his word and soon volunteered as a night flier, an elite and uniquely hazardous world where young pilots not only ran the gamut of enemy flak and searchlights but also faced the distinct risk of collision with one of the vast stream of 'friendly' bombers looming up all around them in the dark. Over the course of the war fully 60 per cent of Bomber Command aircrews were killed, wounded or taken prisoner. Nor was Farnes indifferent to the ethical considerations of attacking enemy civilian centres. 'Really,' he told Edrich, 'sometimes we can protect life only if we fight and kill.'

The autumn of 1939 was a transitional time for many people, but few of them can have been as affected by the outbreak of war as the small but distinguished group who had assembled at Lord's to watch the cricket on the warm Saturday afternoon of 12 August. Within thirty days of what he called that 'last idyllic fling', 27-year-old Brian Johnston had resigned from the family's coffee business, and was in training at the Royal Military College, Sandhurst. He would eventually be in the thick of the Allied breakthrough following the D-Day landings. Having made clear his opposition to the war on political grounds, Johnston's best friend William Douglas-Home had gone on to join the fire service; conscripted into the army in June 1940, he was court-martialled for his subsequent refusal to join in an attack and served eight months in Wormwood Scrubs as a result. Meanwhile, 9-year-old Harold Pinter had been uprooted from his parents' home in the east end of London and sent as an evacuee to a mock-Gothic castle near St Austell in Cornwall. Sixty years later, Pinter told me that this experience had played a 'not insignificant part' in helping shape the themes of 'loneliness, isolation and loss' that informed his adult work.

It was an even stranger time for 22-year-old John F. Kennedy. On 3 September 1939, the American ambassador's high-spirited son had been present with his family in the strangers' gallery of the House of Commons to watch Neville Chamberlain issue the formal announcement of hostilities, and Winston Churchill respond to it from the back benches. While walking home, the Kennedys had been caught up in the panic of the war's first air-raid alarm and forced to take shelter with thirty or forty other 'thoroughly frightened' ordinary British citizens in the cellar of a ladies' dress shop. Just four days later the young Harvard undergraduate was sent post-haste to Glasgow to meet with the traumatised American survivors of the torpedoed SS *Athenia*, the liner that the West Indian cricket tourists had at one time considered taking home. Kennedy was 'there to represent his father because the Embassy staff in London was so rushed with work that no regular member could be spared', the *Boston Globe* reported. Other papers approvingly dubbed him the 'schoolboy diplomat'. Although Kennedy met with a mixed response from some of the bruised and bloodied victims of the *Athenia* disaster, the days around 7–9 September effectively mark the beginning of a political career that ended twenty-four years later with an assassin's bullet in Dallas.

On 11 September, an emergency committee of the MCC met at Lord's under the chairmanship of their president Stanley Christopherson. Christopherson, who was 77, had appeared as an occasional amateur for Kent and England at around the time of Queen Victoria's golden jubilee. The minutes acknowledge the existence of what were called 'the troubles' currently afflicting Europe, but also reflect the essentially imperturbable old spirit of the club:

> The President reported that [MCC secretary] Lt-Col R.S. Rait Kerr had already left Lord's for military duty … It was agreed to keep club employees on at full pay for two weeks, then at half-pay for eight weeks, and then to further review the situation in Europe … C. Almond, senior clerk in the Ticket Office, had some experience in the Great War as a wages clerk, and would like now to apply for similar employment if tickets were to be sold at Lord's on a more select basis in 1940.
>
> Precautions have now been taken at Lord's against Air Raids, including the blacking out of lights, the removal of seats, and the provision of suitable shelters … Permission has been granted to troops at present stationed on the ground to use the baths on the top floor of the Tennis Court building,

the coke used to be paid for by the units concerned. Members of the permanent staff are taking their holidays as usual, with the exception of W. Webber, plumber, whose services are essential. All work in connection with the new bakery has been temporarily suspended.

Neville Cardus's account of the two overalled workmen removing the bust of W.G. Grace from the Lord's Long Room on the morning that Hitler invaded Poland may owe something to that writer's undoubted gift for imagery and metaphor rather than factual reporting, but the minutes of 11 September also record: 'All pictures of historical value [have] been taken from the walls in the pavilion and stored in the basement.' The subsequent details are unclear, but it seems fairly certain that at least some of the ground's treasures were quietly moved to various temporary locations around Wales, including an anonymous-looking stone cottage near Aberystwyth and the extensive wine cellar of Caernarfon Castle. A later MCC meeting proposed evacuating unnamed 'special goods' by sea to Canada. But the vulnerability of ships to U-boat attack – as well as the bad impression the plan, if discovered, might give of the state of British defences – seems to have killed the scheme. In the end some of the club's valuables remained behind below stairs in the Lord's pavilion, while others, such as the original scorebook of the 1882 Oval Test that marked the birth of the Ashes, joined all the Turners and Constables and other heirlooms salvaged from the National Gallery in a cave system just outside Blaenau Ffestiniog, a small slate-mining community in Merionethshire.

With first-class cricket and most concert performances both suspended, Cardus himself was unemployed, 'imprisoned in Manchester, useless to anybody'. At 51 he was too old to fight, although there were those who felt he might conceivably have served his country in other ways than promptly join the staff of the *Melbourne Herald*, as he now did. His books on cricket were already well known in Australia; one critic had commented in 1929, 'Mr. Cardus mingles fancy with fact. The latter is preferable.'

Meanwhile the new editor of *Wisden*, Haddon Whitaker, wrote: 'Future issues must [reflect] both the reduced amount of play and the urgent necessity for conserving paper supplies, but I hope that the time will not be far distant when we can recover all our sturdy bulk.' Of the game's other foremost correspondents, Harry Altham, author of the magisterial *History of Cricket*, served on the wartime MCC committee and continued tirelessly to coach the sport at all levels. With train and bus services disrupted, Jim Kilburn, the austere senior cricket writer of the *Yorkshire Post*, had been forced to sleep overnight on the floor of a Midlands pub while on his way home from covering his county's last match of the 1939 season at Hove, but despite this indignity continued producing a semi-regular column (the only bylined one in the paper) until 1976, when he retired. Their young broadcasting colleague E. W. Swanton eventually left his billet in East Anglia and repaired with his Territorial unit to the north of England, where the arrival of the king one day to inspect the troops signified an overseas deployment, Swanton's ship briefly looking in at Durban, the scene of his marathon Test commentary of two years earlier, before peeling off east to Singapore.

Crusoe Robertson-Glasgow happened to be in Worthing during a German air raid early in the first summer of the war, and perhaps fittingly took refuge in the lounge bar of the nearby George and Dragon hotel. A young man named Herbert Repard, who played regular club cricket around West Sussex, remembered the scene when, on hearing the sirens, he ran pell-mell through the door of the pub and found a frightened crowd there, most of them huddled together in a corner and a few lying flat on the ground under the billiard table.

'Bombs were falling ominously close by, somewhere in the direction of the pier,' Repard said:

One of them blew all the glass out of the front windows, sending jagged splinters shooting across the room. By that time *I* was under the table. And amidst all this terror and mayhem there sat Crusoe alone at the bar with a large scotch, wearing an old raincoat and gym shoes, looking completely unruffled. 'Ah, Bert,' he said as I stumbled to my feet, blood pouring from a deep gash on my cheek, 'What will you have?'

8

'NOW YOU BUGGERS WILL BELIEVE YOU'RE IN A WAR'

'The British middle classes were not scared, whereas the French bourgeoisie was gibbering with fright.' That was the scathing verdict on the years 1939–40 of General Sir Edward Spears, who served as a liaison officer between the two nations in successive world wars. It's possible he exaggerated for effect, but it seems fair to say that morale in England, at least as measured by its cricket authorities, remained commendably firm even after the miracle-disaster of Dunkirk and the subsequent tragicomic events of August 1940, when a lone German pilot accidentally dropped his bombs on London, and the RAF, assuming it had been done on purpose, promptly retaliated by striking Berlin, thus bringing about the reflexive steps that led to the Blitz.

'A visit to Lord's on a dark December [1939] day was a sobering experience,' Harry Altham admitted in the following spring's *Wisden*:

> There were sandbags everywhere, and the Long Room was stripped and bare, [but] the turf was a wondrous green, old Father Time on the Grand Stand was gazing serenely at the nearest balloon, and one felt that somehow it would take more than totalitarian war to put an end to cricket.

Even in the depth of winter, Altham already anticipated the annual act of renewal:

> Today the horizon is dark, and it is idle to try to look far ahead. But I believe there is a general feeling that cricket can and should be kept going wherever possible. Where the game can be played without interfering with the national effort it can only be good for morale ... The MCC have already arranged one or two big charity matches at Lord's with a number of minor matches, and undertaken a long programme against the schools.

This is the kind of talk that every true cricket-lover knows in their marrow. Admitting that opinion varied widely on the prospect of any organised play resuming in 1940, Crusoe Robertson-Glasgow added:

> The idea of having anything remotely resembling the ordinary championship is certainly not only improper but wildly impossible. But I can see no reason or gain in wearing mental sackcloth in advance ... The only solution is the improvising of one-day matches, and be d----d to the score and the points and the cup! Many would delight to see again a few early-Edwardian drives and a late-Victorian pull or two. And if most of the pence taken at the gate should go to help a greater cause than cricket, so much the better.

Some of the same never-surrender spirit imbued the MCC emergency meeting of 13 November 1939, which reported:

> There was a decrease in cash takings from 1 January to date, as compared with the same period in 1938, of £3,465-1sh-11d, [but] it was decided to make the usual Christmas gifts to the members of the MCC staff who were working at Lord's, and a further donation of 300 guineas to the Red Cross.

Individual cricket clubs struggled in their own ways to adjust to the trying circumstances. By the first Christmas of hostilities all seventeen first-class counties could proudly report that most, if not all, of their eligible playing staff were in uniform. Every one of the twenty-four contracted players at Derbyshire was involved in the war effort, both big and small. The side's 26-year-old batsman Gilbert Hodgkinson, serving with the Highland Division, was badly wounded in the head while taking part in the desperate fighting around Calais in May 1940. The 1941 edition of *Wisden* reported his death, but in fact he was repatriated by the Germans in a prisoner exchange in 1943 and had recovered sufficiently to captain his county in 1946. Several other Derby players elected to work in the coal mines. Yorkshiremen made a similarly stout response, and their president Sir Stanley Jackson launched a county-wide appeal 'to keep our club in its present efficiency ready for the happier times I pray I will see when the troubled world has returned to normal conditions'. Jackson at least got his wish, surviving the war before dying in March 1947 of complications following a road accident.

The Lancashire secretary Rupert Howard wrote to the MCC to propose a system of regional tournaments in 1940, each group including a proportion of the minor counties. A five-page letter he later sent them on the subject, insisting that 'no one in these parts wishes to see a blank summer', touchingly suggests the dedication of a lifelong cricket addict. Lionel Lister, the popular county captain called up by army telegram, survived his subsequent service as a brigade major in the Normandy landings. 'I've gotten more out of cricket than most men ever do because of the cards sometimes turning up the wrong way for them,' Lister said after the war. 'For me, they've invariably been in my favour.'

In Kent there was some amusement at a report in the daily German newspaper *Der Angriff* suggesting that cricketing and non-cricketing factions in the county were locked in a heated debate about whether to plough up all the local pitches for agricultural use. The civilians, said the paper, 'in a fury of rage, decided to reduce [*sic*] the cricket club by means of arms. As a result, club members, armed to the teeth, patrol the field nightly, not for parachutists but for the advance guard of Sixth Column yokels'. (Gerald Hough's meticulous notes somehow fail to mention this state of affairs, and not long afterwards, aged 46, he felt able to write

to the War Office offering his services for active duty.) The Kent committee issued a statement in December 1939 'to express our gratitude
to those supporters who have continued their subscriptions' of a guinea
apiece, and to note that new members would be warmly welcomed.
'There are no formalities about joining the club,' they added. Twenty-
one of Kent's staff were variously serving their country. The county
would lose a total of thirteen current or former players, and one senior
committee member, during the war.

The same carry-on spirit prevailed at Hampshire, where, it was
noted evenly in the minutes of the 1940 annual meeting, 'conditions
[were] trying on the south coast, especially in those cities subject to
the attentions of German aircraft'. There was an attempt made to keep
cricket going locally, although the county ground at Southampton took
a pounding from repeated air raids. The army took over the field at
Dean Park in Bournemouth, and in time there was a display there of a
downed German bomber.

The experience of the Leeds-based Romany Club perhaps speaks
for many of the amateur sides up and down England that struggled
with all the privations of the next few years. An entry in the club's
logbook for 1939 reads: 'Written up from notes 24 March '46. At war,
'39–'45.' The minutes end with a September 1939 vote of thanks to the
chairman, 'and wishes for our future health and success, proposed by
A.A. Haslam'. Captain Arthur Haslam of the Royal Artillery fell while
fighting in the final phase of the North African campaign, at Tabarka in
Tunisia, on 29 March 1943. He was 34 at the time of his death and left
a young family behind in Yorkshire.

Well before then, so many cricketers had been lost that Robertson-
Glasgow remarked that the whole sorry series of events seemed to him
'like a divine jest of unfathomable cruelty'. Not every loss was war-
related. Robert Bush, a contemporary of W.G. Grace and a mainstay of
Gloucestershire cricket in the 1870s, died in December 1939, aged 84.
After his playing days, Bush had emigrated to Western Australia, where
he managed a sheep farm and helped to raise the funds to build the
WACA ground in Perth. In his 60s he retired to a large estate at Bishop's

Knoll, near Bristol, which he converted into a hospital for Allied troops wounded in the Great War. Bush himself served there as an orderly. On the day war was declared in 1939, Gloucestershire's president Sir Stanley Tubbs was invited to Sunday lunch at Bishop's Knoll. He sat in the ornate drawing room for some time, with only a loudly clucking goose for company, before his host was ushered in, wearing a 'red silk coat with a clown's tassels and comic trousers' while himself looking 'as pale as paper'. 'The damn fool doctor says I'm dying,' Bush shouted, by way of introduction. The two men had gone on to listen to the terrible news on the radio and then, Tubbs recalled:

> To eat an extravagant meal, [Bush] seeming to revive greatly with each successive course … Even then, you felt he was someone you could completely rely on. He seemed to disregard himself entirely, always giving his full attention to those he was with, and fixing them with his bright gaze as steadily as when he glared down the Bristol wicket at the oncoming bowler more than fifty years earlier.

Bush's death was another sign that the last remnants of cricket's Victorian golden age, with its sense both of display and individuality, was giving way to one of comparative egalitarianism and uniformity.

Another depressing symbol of the times was the introduction of food rationing beginning on 8 January 1940. The quantity and quality of almost all British meals declined drastically during the early war years as production fell and imports evaporated in the face of an Atlantic blockade. The increasing shortages soon extended to other commodities. At work in Maidstone before joining the army, Godfrey Evans remembered rising before dawn on freezing winter mornings to breakfast on 'crusty bread and a smear of lard', with no lunch and a dinner of 'rubbery pink meat oiled by cold gravy' with 'a handful of gritty spuds pulled out of the back allotment'. After joining the Service Corps that spring, Evans was at least guaranteed the luxury of three basic meals a day, although he always remembered a 'distinct lack of fresh fruit and veg', and consequently joining in a lusty rendition of 'Yes! We Have No

Bananas' while on a route march between Chesterfield and Derby – 'twenty bloody miles in the pouring rain, which for some reason we did in tropical kit. It was about then that the rumour went round the camp that we were being shipped out to the Middle East.'

When it was suggested to Evans years later that he must have been apprehensive at the news, he said matter-of-factly that he 'didn't scare easily. None of us did.' In the end his unit wasn't sent overseas, and instead the young wicketkeeper found himself back square-bashing at a different army camp in Ossett, West Yorkshire, where in time he turned out for a local club side that evidently had no idea of his civilian occupation. He scored '80 in about ten overs', he remembered, 'and fielded somewhere out among the cow-pats in the long grass'. For all that 'it was a cushy enough number,' Evans later agreed, and a significant improvement on events such as the twenty-four-hour exercise under 'actual battlefield conditions' which involved spending the night in a waterlogged ditch, or the moonlit evening of 16 September 1940 when a stricken German aircraft dropped ten high-explosive bombs on a poultry farm just outside Ossett, killing some chickens, before crashing a few miles to the east. Evans and his platoon were hurriedly deployed to the scene, where they found the enemy pilot still strapped in to his cockpit, 'burned to a complete crisp … The flesh was bubbling on what remained of his face.' The young Kent cricketer would remember how quiet the other men in his unit had become at the sight, and the sergeant who then spoke up: 'Now you buggers will believe you're in a war.'

Just over 100 miles away in Cambridgeshire, Evans's kindred spirit Bill Edrich successfully completed his flight training on Blenheim bombers before joining 107 Squadron based at Little Massingham in his native Norfolk. He spent much of the spring and early summer of 1941 practising for a planned daylight attack on the Knapsack power station near Cologne. The fifty-four bombers to take part in the raid would fly 400 miles to their target at a height of only 50ft to avoid enemy radar. Edrich never forgot the strangeness of those 'lovely May and June days' when he filled the downtime in between training runs by playing cricket at Massingham Hall. 'Every now and then would come the old accustomed cry: "Owzatt?"' Edrich wrote. 'And then one's mind would flicker off from [the game], and joking with a pal … and one imagined his machine cartwheeling down, flaming from nose to tail.'

Forty years later, Edrich added the detail that he had also had vivid dreams in the summer of 1941 about which of his friends would live or die, and that in almost every case the premonition had proved correct. Even more disquietingly, he'd climbed into the cockpit of his aircraft before a live mission one morning and looked across to see another pilot strapped into his own plane waiting to take off nearby. 'For a split second the man's face was a skull,' he remembered. 'And then it changed back again, and he took off. He didn't make it.'

Edrich had several more material concerns too, including everything from the 'pigswill food' up to the moment he was told by an infantry instructor attached to 107 Squadron: 'If the Germans do ever land, there are just two possible choices for a position about to be overrun. One is "Direct fire", which means facing the advancing enemy and standing by your guns to die or be captured, and the other is to abandon your position and fall back.' 'Well, sir,' Edrich had said at length, 'Under the circumstances, there's really only one option, and that's to stand firm and shoot the shit out of them,' a formula that found 'wide support' among his fellow airmen.

Like a number of other county professionals, Len Hutton was able to combine his military duties in the early months of the war with playing regular weekend cricket. The averages for the Bradford League in 1940 show Hutton top of the batting and his Yorkshire colleague Bill Bowes top of the bowling. By that stage, many critics already surveyed the remnants of organised cricket with a warm, nostalgic eye. 'It was a truly great day for Pudsey St Lawrence and us all when Hutton turned out for his old club and scored 133,' *Wisden* reported. Later that summer there was a well-subscribed single-innings match between Pelham Warner's XI and the West Indies at Lord's. Hutton scored 44 and Denis Compton a run-a-minute 73, although to widespread disappointment the West Indies' Learie Constantine was run out for just 5. The following week Hutton opened the batting for Catterick Garrison in a one-day tie against Durham at Darlington. He scored a relatively modest 19, while his regimental colleague Hedley Verity went on to take 3-42 in the Catterick win. The Lancashire League also kept up a full list of matches in 1940. Even on the day France fell, effectively leaving Britain to fight alone against the Axis powers, Burnley went ahead with its scheduled 40-over contest against Rawtenstall, while Enfield took on East Lancashire, Nelson faced Colne and Haslingden hosted Lowerhouse in a game described as 'wholly pleasurable for players and spectators alike'. Here, surely, was the British genius for simply carrying on.

Elsewhere, of course, casualties among cricket-playing members of the armed services were already distressingly high. Twenty-three-year-old Michael Anderson, a hard-hitting batsman for Cambridge University and Free Foresters, fell in the Rotterdam blitz of May 1940. The Oxford blue Patrick Rucker, latterly of the Royal Sussex Regiment, died the following week in the fighting around Amiens. On 21 May, Reginald Butterworth, who had played in the prestigious MCC v champion county fixture at Lord's just twelve months earlier, was killed while serving as an air gunner over northern France. He was aged 33, and his older brother John, who had opened the batting for Oxford University and Middlesex, also fell in action. The Australian-born William Welch, who was 28, was killed in the fighting around Calais less than a year after scoring 104 for the Free Foresters at Fenners. Michael Matthews of Oxford University and Robert Philpot-Brookes of the Army both gave their lives on the same day during the chaotic retreat from Dunkirk, aged 26 and 27 respectively.

Later in the summer, the former Lancashire captain Peter Eckersley died in a plane crash near Southampton while serving with the Fleet Air Arm. He had been popularly known as the 'cricketing airman' during his playing days, when he had often flown himself to matches. Eckersley, who had gone on to sit as Conservative MP for Manchester Exchange before signing up to fight in September 1939, was 36 at the time of his death.

Almost everyone who continued to comment or write about English cricket increasingly seemed to agree that the game that eventually emerged from the war should be what they called 'modern'. It should share in what contemporaries perceived to be general worldwide technological improvements and cultural advances. There was even once-unthinkable talk in the MCC winter meeting of 1939 of some form of 'prospective review' of the longstanding distinction between the amateur gentleman and the professional player. For now, this particular convention remained sufficiently potent for the young Hampshire part-timer David Blake to remember having been 'well and truly bollocked' by his county secretary when found to be innocently changing his clothes alongside his paid teammates in the professionals' room at Southampton, simply because there were only two amateurs in the side that day and it seemed to him to be the logical thing to do. The same player later recalled having chased the last ball of the morning session down to the end of the ground farthest from the pavilion, and then experiencing the 'distinct embarrassment of jogging all the way back across the park to the pavilion gate, where eight or nine of the professionals were patiently lined up waiting for me so that they could go in to lunch. They weren't allowed to leave the field before an amateur.'

Of course, none of this potential revolution in the social fabric of English cricket would happen while the nation itself was at war. The game as it lay abandoned in September 1939 still glanced fondly backward to a time when male players instinctively knew in which dressing area they belonged, and any female spectators on the ground were essentially objects for decorative and conversational use. Most of the sport's critics and correspondents remained stout established pillars of respectability. Writing in the *Cricketer*, for example, the Eton-educated Sir Home Seton Montagu Gordon, 12th Baronet Gordon of Embo, Sutherland, to give him his full due, seemed to react to the steadily encroaching backdrop of national austerity with a well-nigh fantastical evocation of the spangled palisades of his youth. Gordon had first gone to Lord's as an 8-year-old boy in 1880, when he met W.G. Grace, an event he revisited frequently in print. In that same season he watched the Australian Test at the Oval and saw the future cabinet minister Alfred Lyttelton keep wicket for Middlesex wearing a monocle and a hard straw hat. Gordon himself favoured a classic ensemble of striped blazer with a red carnation in the buttonhole, adorned by the honorary Sussex cap voted to him by the county committee, his pride in which was certainly not untainted by an implied, though unjustified, aspiration to first-class status. No one denied Gordon's deep affection for cricket – during his long life he was said to have seen no fewer than seventy annual university matches – but he was not a man conspicuously likely to rattle the guardrails defining the limits of acceptable social or literary etiquette. Instead of writing that a particular team had lost a match, for instance, he would remark that they had 'suffered a discomfiture', while to him Walter Hammond exuded 'a stoicism and good breeding and an evident overall courtesy and comity that entirely qualified him' as captain of England. Next to Gordon, his colleague E.W. Swanton seemed like a hopeless subversive.

Swanton wrote of the straitened circumstances at the *Cricketer* in 1939:

> When war came, the office was moved complete to a house at Surbiton, and despite all the difficulties, the magazine, albeit in smaller format, continued to appear. A.C.L. Bennett, who made many thousands of runs for the BBC both before the war and after, and E.L. Roberts, the well-known statistician, nobly braved the Blitz and all the hazards of wartime travel to see the paper to bed, the printers being now – of all places – in Bermondsey.

The self-exiled Neville Cardus continued to write on cricket and music for the *Melbourne Herald*, most notably in a lengthy review of a concert series conducted by his friend Sir Thomas Beecham. At the end of his tour, Beecham tried to persuade Cardus to join him in sailing to America, asking, 'Do you propose to stay in this barbarous country all your life?' Cardus did stay but moved from Melbourne to a small flat in Sydney, where he wrote his autobiography. In time he befriended a young jockey turned footballer-cricketer and later Royal Australian Air Force pilot named Keith Miller. When in 1942 Cardus's wife Edith announced her intention of sailing from England to join him in Sydney, he rented her a separate flat a mile away from his own. According to the author Christopher Brookes, the couple 'dined together once a week, but otherwise continued to lead largely separate lives'.

Crusoe Robertson-Glasgow reacted to the coming of war by writing an enjoyably burlesque treatment of recent political events to which he gave the title *I Was Himmler's Aunt*. He (Crusoe, not Himmler) continued to contribute to *Wisden* and other outlets. A measure of the Robertson-Glasgow style and outlook on life as a whole was the way he preferred to report on a given match. His accounts were informative, yet often idiosyncratic and sometimes actively surreal. Once having recorded the necessary 'sporting accountancy, [to] me not much more enlivening than the financial sort', Crusoe was apt to veer off into felicitous descriptions of the particular ground in which he found himself, of the crowd, of the weather and the summer blooms. He began one essay: 'Success at games demands total freedom from care. I first learnt this truth at school when, soon after taking guard at the crease, I saw among the few spectators the unwelcome face of my schoolmaster, who had put me down for detention that sunny afternoon.' Writing of the charms of Victorian cricket, he concluded: 'What does it matter if it was all a legend? As the years lend enchantment to the days of youth, the runs and the wickets of the imagination are as good as any that illumine the pages of *Wisden*.'

Of course, he worked hard to make it all seem so effortless. Robertson-Glasgow always carried a small red journal which he referred to as 'the washing book' and in which he made copious notes. These would later form the basis of his seemingly facile reviews. Crusoe was by his own cheerful admission 'vastly disorganised in almost every other essential'. He never learned to drive a car and was notoriously cavalier about sartorial standards, once going out to bowl for Somerset in a pair of black, Sunday-best shoes that he confessed had hindered his run-up.

His despairing sub-editors sometimes complained that his liking for refreshment brought a noticeable change in the style and fluency of his copy later in the day. When in 1940 he went to dry out at St Andrew's Hospital in Northampton – where wartime treatment of what was still regarded as a self-inflicted ailment would have been at best rudimentary – he met a pretty, auburn-haired nurse named Elizabeth Hutton. They were married in 1943 and remained together for the next twenty-two years. Although contented domestically, Crusoe continued to struggle with the effects of a depression which he tried to keep out of sight from friends and colleagues. He made several further attempts to take his own life. For Robertson-Glasgow, his marriage to Elizabeth and his obvious affection for his young stepson Gordon were among the few positive things to emerge from the war.

In Cardiff, 27-year-old Wilf Wooller, another of cricket's renaissance figures, put the finishing touches to the 1939 Glamorgan county annual before enlisting as a gunner with the 77th Heavy Anti-Aircraft Regiment. During the winter he turned out for an Army rugby union side that beat France in Paris. He judged the team (to which he contributed three tries) 'not bad' and kept a tattered group photograph folded in his wallet when he was later posted to the Far East. The Peruvian-born Freddie Brown, Wooller's Cambridge contemporary, undertook some of the same journalistic chores at Surrey before taking a commission in the Royal Army Service Corps. We will return to these two individuals later. As well as being an accomplished seamer and an amateur magician, Bill Bowes of Yorkshire and England was also a practising journalist. He would go on to take a full-time job with the *Yorkshire Post* after the war. Tall and bespectacled, with a shock of wavy blond hair, he looked more like a gangling Nordic university professor (and, it was unkindly said, sometimes batted like one) than a professional sportsman. Bowes also possessed a famously relaxed bowling action, of which Robertson-Glasgow wrote: 'Bill's run-up is a leisurely business – I sometimes wonder whether he is going to get there at all. His whole approach to the supreme task in cricket suggests, quite falsely, indolence, negligence, almost reluctance. But he is just keeping it all in for the right moment.' Bowes, who was married with two small children, also swiftly rallied to the cause in 1939, becoming a Royal Artillery officer and eventually finding himself in the cauldron of the ferocious fighting at Tobruk, at around the usual time of the Lord's Test, in June 1942.

Many English cricket grounds were defaced in the first full year of the war, perhaps none more so than Old Trafford. The Lancashire secretary Captain Rupert Howard described its woeful state in the 1941 minutes. There was a large bomb crater at the front gate, while the grounds-man's hut, two of the stands and the tiles on the pavilion roof had also caught a packet. 'We have a water cart standing before Talbot Rd, and that is currently our only supply for daily use. The toilets are deplorable. Most of the playing area is in a distressed state.' Not surprisingly, there were no matches scheduled on the ground in 1940 or 1941, and like other county secretaries Howard was hard pushed to meet his club's basic expenses. A letter went out in May 1940 appealing to just over 5,000 members to continue their subscriptions at half the normal rate. About a third of them responded. Not long after that, the old ground was pressed into service as a transit camp for survivors of the Dunkirk operation, placing further strain on its already dilapidated facilities. Captain Howard eventually became Major Howard and increasingly left Lancashire's day-to-day administrative work to the former team captain Thomas Higson Sr, who had been born in 1873 and now practised as a Manchester solicitor. Higson would say, simply and dutifully, of the war years: 'We got through', which was the best any professional English cricket club could hope for.

There was a similar struggle for survival at Hampshire, whose dues-paying membership stood at just 1,093 in 1940. The figure would fall to 587 by the end of the war. It was the same bleak outlook for all the south-eastern clubs, lying as they did in the direct path of the 'knock-for-knock' German bombing raids, as Hitler referred to the aerial offensive unleashed against Britain from September 1940 to May 1941. Like his counterpart at Lancashire, the Sussex secretary Lance Knowles wrote to the membership asking them to pay at least half the previous season's subscription. The response was 'muted', Knowles was forced to admit, as just over £400 in dues came in for the year. Cricket nonetheless continued in piecemeal form at Hove. During a charity match on 14 September 1940 the players heard a series of explosions over nearby Brighton, then saw a lone German bomber, machine guns blazing, lumbering over the ground itself. The tenacious Sussex supporter Laetitia Stapleton was there:

> The pilot flew right above us … We all fled to the inside of the pavilion. The players fell flat on their faces on the grass, and someone yelled to us, 'Lie down!' and 'Keep away from the glass!' At length we were herded underneath the pavilion with the boilers, but later emerged to go look at the [bomb] crater in the south-east corner.

The cricket then continued.

A day or two later, Stapleton happened to be back on the ground to retrieve some personal effects left behind during the commotion of the air raid. It was about 6 p.m. on a grey early autumn evening, and the blackout was in effect. As she walked past the pavilion she glanced through a partly covered downstairs window, lit from within by a single candle. The elderly club secretary was standing on the other side of the glass with the distinctive figure of the ex-Sussex and England captain Arthur Gilligan, who was now in RAF uniform. Both men saw her and each nodded, smiling away, Gilligan adding a cheery thumbs-up. Not quite knowing what to do, the visitor waved quickly back and continued walking. Nothing had been said, the whole incident occupied only seconds, but to Stapleton it was a moment of encouragement worth recording in her diary. Something about the hearty way the two men had greeted her, and their very presence on the ground in those first terrible days of the Blitz, suggested to her that 'everything would be all right'.

Trent Bridge, for its part, managed to host roughly a dozen well-subscribed charity matches each year from 1940 to 1945 while serving successively as an army hospital and post office. It emerged relatively intact, although the Nottinghamshire president Major Tom Barber remembered that at one point air-raid alarms became so common that some of the spectators on the ground began to ignore them. It was a 'very English sight' to watch the unhurried progress of a cricket match while sirens wailed in the streets all around. Twenty miles away, Sir Julien Cahn's seat at Stanford Hall became a rehabilitation centre for wounded soldiers, the same role it performs today. There was some local drama when in the summer of 1941 a Blenheim bomber crash-landed on to the estate's cricket pitch in foggy conditions, fortunately without loss of life. Like Major Barber, Cahn was an exceptionally brave man with a healthy appreciation for prevailing civil defence regulations. During dinner on the night of the Blenheim's crash he delivered a lecture to his guests on the stupidity of their not taking shelter. 'Some of you are irreplaceable, and we simply have an obligation to survive,' he scolded. 'It is idiotic to prove your courage by placing yourself in danger of being struck by a bomb.'

In Kent Gerald Hough managed to keep the St Lawrence ground in playing condition, although there were unavoidable reminders of what he called 'the present world nonsense' in some of the surrounding buildings. An army unit took over the upstairs floors of the pavilion, there was a petrol store under one of the stands, and an explosives dump was established in the ladies' lavatory at the Nackington Gate. A total of 138 incendiary bombs fell on the Canterbury playing area during the war years, although one county history records that these caused little hardship: 'in fact their ingredients appeared to be good for the grass.'

The damage at both the main London grounds could perhaps be characterised as more self-inflicted than strictly hostile. As we've seen, Lord's was stripped bare but escaped any major enemy bombing, despite one or two near misses. The Oval was disfigured by a maze of wire cages and concrete blocks erected on the playing area in preparation for captured German parachutists who never came. Both venues preserved some of their essential social conventions when staging cricket matches. As the author Benny Green writes in *The Lord's Companion*: 'At all times officers in uniform in the British and Allied forces were allowed into the pavilion, the distinction between commissioned officers and Other Ranks being maintained as sternly in war as it had been in peace.'

Although professional cricket had stopped dead on the Friday after-noon of 1 September, and the government then announced the temporary closure of all places of entertainment and outdoor sports meetings, this did not prevent the later appearance of de facto first-class matches, especially those played for charitable purposes. A London Counties team, for instance, was drawn up from amateurs past the age of military service, players on leave from the forces, or former greats like 53-year-old Frank Woolley. At Lord's on Saturday 10 August 1940, the Counties XI played a British Empire team for whom Robert Nelson, the young Northants captain now serving with the Royal Marines, scored an even-time 44. His colleague Denis Compton hit a typically brisk 60 and went on to record bowling figures of 6-81 with his unor-thodox left-arm spin. No fewer than 13,865 spectators paid at the gate to see the one-day match, and a collection raised £152 for the Red Cross. The Empire side won by 53 runs.

A week later at Lord's Pelham Warner's XI took on a Club Cricket Conference side again captained by Robert Nelson. This seems to have provided one of those last-gasp one-day finishes more familiar to a later generation of cricket watchers. Nelson's team declared at 269-8, and Warner's men reached their target for the loss of 7 wickets, with four minutes left for play. This time Compton scored 101. Two Saturdays later, on 31 August, a Buccaneers XI led by Surrey's Freddie Brown set their British Empire opponents a stiff task by scoring 268-9 in 47 overs. The Empire response stood at 141-6 when the match was hurriedly called off as a draw owing to the Battle of Britain. Of the season's final match at Lord's, on 7 September, Benny Green notes: 'The war reduced the proceedings to a hopeless chaos, when an air raid warning obliged the cricketers to take cover and not resume until the All-Clear had sounded.'

That the cricketers *did* resume, however – Middlesex beating a Lord's XI by 32 runs – was perhaps another small but telling sign that, as Laetitia Stapleton had remarked at Hove, in the end everything would be 'all right'. A reporter for *The Times* named Tony Gill, who was on the ground to interview Walter Robins, described the maverick ex-Test captain, once bold enough to bring his county's professionals up to change in the amateurs' room, as looking that damp Saturday afternoon 'like a man who had received bad news, but felt the show must go on'. Hedley Verity evoked some of the same spirit when he wrote in the *Cricketer* that the German invasion of Holland in May 1940 was no more than 'an early season setback'. Home Gordon likened playing cricket through the Blitz to Drake finishing his game of bowls before breaking off to deal with the Spanish Armada. Pelham Warner added that Goebbels would have won a significant propaganda victory had he been able to boast that the Luftwaffe had put the English off their summer game. Tony Gill wrote in his diary on 7 September that after the dreary afternoon at Lord's the skies had:

> Suddenly cleared at the close. The drizzle ended, the sun broke through. A mild autumn breeze was blowing and the ground was a picture post-card of green and blue … [Robins] appeared still fresh and trim in a beautifully cut RAF uniform. Like me, he was cheered by the size and mood of the crowd, many flag-waving children among it … His whole vitality seemed to return, as if he had been given a powerful injection.

Happily, too, English cricket still tended to be regularly renewed even in the direst circumstances. The burly young military policeman Alec Bedser played his first match at Lord's on 3 August 1940, recording figures of 4-42 for an RAF side against the London Fire Service. He had narrowly escaped death when being evacuated from Dunkirk just eight weeks earlier. Two hundred miles to the north, 18-year-old Jim Laker was breaking himself in with Saltaire in the Lancashire League. Then considered a batsman who could bowl a bit rather than a specialist off-spinner, Laker finished 1940 with 257 runs at an average of 30 and just 7 wickets at 33 apiece. Alf Burgoyne, the secretary of Saltaire for over fifty years, remarked of a league match in which Laker scored 57 and Len Hutton 52, 'I know which of 'em I would have picked, and it wasn't

Hutton.' Coming up behind them, there was the young Fred Trueman, now already taking wickets on the village green at Stainton in Yorkshire. 'Go and watch Freddie play cricket if you want to know what determination and the right attitude is all about,' he heard a schoolteacher say one summer afternoon in 1940. The Trueman legend probably began at birth; he weighed in at 14lb 1oz and always managed to appear larger than life during the seventy-five years that followed.

The war that changed the world in such drastic fashion need hardly have troubled many cricket-playing Englishmen beyond the obvious shared ordeal of food rationing and blackouts. Had they chosen, they could have taken no direct part in it, either because their age or some other personal circumstances seemed to provide them with a perfectly honourable exemption from the fighting. Yet the minute books of all seventeen county clubs proudly note numerous examples of players who joined the armed services without the least legal or moral obligation to do so. At Kent, for instance, 32-year-old Hopper Levett was both beyond the statutory age for a married man to be called up under the terms of the National Service Act, and as a farmer, furthermore, was in a 'reserved' profession. Even so, Levett was promptly back in uniform, bringing the same essentially light-hearted but conscientious approach to his military duties as he did to his cricket. His county colleague Leslie Todd, also 32, immediately joined the RAF. Their Kent teammate Les Ames was aged 34 and married, as well as suffering from a chronically bad back. Brushing these various handicaps aside, he volunteered for service on New Year's Day 1940 and eventually rose to the rank of squadron leader in the RAF, where he gained a reputation for his no-nonsense training of young pilots. There are literally scores of similar examples of cricketers up and down the country who went to war without any formal summons, or even compelling need, to do so, as well as a much shorter list of those who preferred to take a step backwards, not forwards, when the time came.

Some cricketers were ruined by the war. Of course they weren't alone: the years of fighting and austerity put strain on peoples' marriages, separated fathers from their children, and in some cases brought an authentic Dickensian touch to the streets of Britain. Godfrey Evans recalled going to work in Maidstone one dark winter morning before joining the army in 1940 and seeing 'a gang of ten or twelve young kids sitting or lying on the freezing cold pavement in front of the bakery. One of them, aged about seven, told me they'd been there all night so as not to miss their turn for bread.' Fifty years later, Evans still remembered this small incident more clearly than almost any other single event of the years 1939–45.

To some cricketers the war may simply have intensified or accelerated feelings of depression or despair held over from their civilian lives. Somerset's mercurial batsman Harold Gimblett applied to join the RAF in 1940, but was allocated instead to the fire service, and in time saw duty in badly blitzed towns such as Plymouth and Bristol. His county colleague Frank Lee became an umpire after the war and occasionally stood in matches where a 'very changed' Gimblett appeared. There was a game at Bath in 1947 where:

> Harold looked just like a scarecrow. He must have lost twenty pounds since I'd last seen him … He told me about being on duty in Bristol one night and described a row of houses with a little park in front of them, 'and every time a bomb fell there was a lovely, pink glow and it blew up a piece of someone.'

For all that, Gimblett rarely if ever complained about his own hardships. He played first-class cricket until 1954, if seldom with his old flair. Some of those who knew him believe that he never quite recovered from the experience of what he called the 'infernal firework nights' of 1940–44.

The war also robbed young and old cricketers alike of what might have been either a glorious dawn or a golden sunset to their careers.

Godfrey Evans had to wait until the week of his 26th birthday to make his England Test debut. He was always gracious about the delay – 'I kept telling Hitler to pack it in but the bugger wouldn't listen,' he airily told one interviewer – although in private he sometimes remarked, not without cause, that he should have broken in to the team 'about five years, and 30 Test caps' sooner than he did. At the other end of the scale there was a man like Harold Larwood, the legendary fast bowler who had been his country's shock weapon during the 1932–33 tour of Australia. Larwood was still only in his early 30s, and playing competitive league cricket around Blackpool, on the outbreak of war. He spent much of the next seven years working anonymously as a market gardener. Recognising that he was too old to carry on when cricket eventually resumed, Larwood sent one of his five daughters to retrieve the equipment he had left at the Blackpool ground in September 1939. When she arrived, she found that a new recruit to the team was already out in the middle dressed from head to toe in her father's clothes. If Larwood had had any lingering doubts about his decision to retire, the news that another player was now literally filling his boots on the cricket field seems to have settled the matter.

Born in 1912, Wilf Wooller wryly summed up his early years: 'My childhood was blighted by the first war,' he wrote when he was 58, 'and the second one brought a certain amount of grief to my home life.' In September 1941, Wooller married the 19-year-old debutante Lady Gillian Windsor-Clive, a daughter of the Earl of Plymouth. In the words of *The Times* it was a 'brilliant match' for a talented but unpaid sportsman and middle-manager in a Cardiff coal firm, but the couple had barely settled down together when the artillery regiment Wooller had joined was posted overseas. 'Everything had turned upside down,' he wrote sombrely on his eventual return. His childless marriage to Lady Gillian ended in divorce early in 1947; the couple had been separated for five of their six years together. Perhaps Wooller's combat experience, to which we'll return, had changed him, perhaps one or other of them had had second thoughts, perhaps the war itself swept them in different directions: at all events it was a 'complete restart' for Wooller, as for so many other returning servicemen, cricketers and non-cricketers alike, as they sought to readjust to civilian life. Wooller's second marriage, contracted in 1948 to the former Enid James of Cardiff, lasted until the end of his life nearly fifty years later.

On the sunny bank holiday Monday afternoon of 29 May 1939, the fresh-faced Robert Nelson had toasted the wildly cheering crowd gathered under the players' balcony at the county ground in Northampton. As we've seen, the side he captained had just beaten Leicestershire by an innings, giving them their first championship success in four years, an unenviable record that still stands today. Dressed in his immaculate blue blazer and cravat, Nelson had raised a glass of champagne high in the air and told the spectators massed below him how pleased he was to have put the recent spell of bad luck behind him, before expressing the confident hope that the county would enjoy many more such results in the future. The entire crowd had applauded the sentiment, although, as the *Daily Echo* later wrote, it was perhaps more as a tribute to a popular captain than a unanimous show of faith in their team's prospects. Nelson, still holding his glass aloft, had managed to wave with both hands, nodding to the applause left and right, several times, before disappearing back into the amateurs' dressing room. Although normally not a big drinker, he later admitted that he had been glad of the four-day break in the schedule before the county's next championship match. With just one win to show at the end of the season, Nelson's optimistic prediction could only be deemed a partial success. As the *Echo* wrote, 'Times changed, wars were declared, buried treasures were discovered, revolutions swept foreign lands, but Northamptonshire's dismal record in the county championship race went on forever.'

Just four months after saluting the crowd from the Northampton balcony, Robert Nelson was in uniform as a second lieutenant with the Royal Marines. On the grey Tuesday evening of 29 October 1940, the Italian air corps sent a squadron of Fiat BR.20 bombers, each painted a brilliant green and blue, and flying in perfect wingtip formation, to attack British military installations around the Kent coast. After damaging part of the main London-to-Dover railway line, the planes had circled back over the English Channel by Deal, dropping their remaining bombs, whether deliberately or not, on a row of identical wooden huts separated by a parade ground that marked them out as a barracks. In one of the huts several officers of the Royal Marines Siege Regiment had just sat down to dinner before going out on a planned nighttime training exercise in the hills above Dover.

A local resident noted in his diary:

> The bombs fell in Cornwall Road, Cemetery Rd, and near the railway bridge in Telegraph Rd ... [I] can remember seeing an Italian aircraft flying by after dropping a bomb in front of the officers' mess at the RM depot, Deal, and on the railway line south of Cornwall Rd. There was some damage to the bridge, and houses in Telegraph Rd were badly damaged. The officer killed at the RM depot was Temporary 2nd Lt. R.P. Nelson.

Nelson was 28 at the time of his death, and his parents Robert and Mary, themselves only middle-aged, asked that his gravestone bear the inscription: 'A Lover of Cricket, He maintained in His Life the Spirit of the Game.' Crusoe Robertson-Glasgow later wrote that the young war victim had embodied 'those qualities most hateful and foreign to the arch-enemy: stability, self-control and tolerance'. William Brown, Nelson's predecessor as captain of Northamptonshire and latterly the county secretary, added in a letter to the grieving family: 'He was truly indispensable ... You know, I've been in the position of trying to run the club's affairs for some time, but Robert always made it go.'

Robert Nelson had played his last competitive match as recently as 31 August 1940, when he top-scored with 45 while opening the batting for the British Empire team against the Buccaneers at Lord's.

'No military success thus far compares in its effect on British morale with our keeping the headquarters of cricket open for business,' Robertson-Glasgow wrote. 'Of late I have seen cabinet ministers watching intently from the pavilion, and ladies in almost indecently jolly gowns with parasols at the furl promenading during the tea interval. It is not at all what Dr Goebbels imagines life in these islands must be like.'

Nonetheless, Lord's didn't entirely escape the scars of war. The north part of the ground was damaged by a German air raid on 16 September 1940, and just a month later an incendiary bomb fell on the Nursery End boundary. When the device exploded it shot out a geyser of hot oil, along with a photograph, wrapped in polythene, of a smiling German officer with 'With compliments' written across it.

The young Kent captain Gerry Chalk transferred from the army to the RAF that same month, inspired, he wrote, by the example of 'fliers and aircrews braced to meet the onslaught of the Luftwaffe'. Bill Edrich continued his own operational training on Blenheim bombers at RAF Upwood near Huntingdon. Even for a native son of East Anglia, it was 'bloody cold up here in winter, with not a tree or a hill in sight'. Edrich wrote to his teenaged brother Brian: 'At least when the wind doesn't blow, we are all pretty happy. We just want to get cracking.' Thirty-nine-year-old Bob Wyatt, late of Warwickshire, was also back in the RAF. 'The truth was that [Edrich] was happy under nearly any conditions,' Wyatt later wrote, with just a touch of asperity, after the party-loving Middlesex player had woken him up on his return to the England team hotel in the early hours of a Test match. Wyatt admitted that in war Edrich 'apparently stood inspection, played his part on the drill square. His officers told me he was a model of sobriety, though I personally never saw it.'

The schoolteacher-fast bowler Ken Farnes had also become one of the many cricketers to wear RAF uniform, despite his misgivings about dropping bombs on German civilians. After training in Canada, Farnes was commissioned as a pilot officer on 1 September 1941. It seems curiously poignant that he should have fallen in love quite as heavily as he apparently did just as he went off to war. His final match before signing up was for a British Empire XI against a team raised by the Essex captain John Stephenson at the Victoria ground, Cheltenham. Farnes took 3-59, and then top-scored with an unbeaten 25 out of an Empire total of just 71. The West Indies' bowler Bertie Clarke, now training in London as a doctor, was on the same side. Clarke spoke for many when he wondered about the future of cricket, and wrote of Farnes: 'He is a student of the game, a deep thinker, but not always a commanding figure among men. Ken is a worrier … If cricket survives, will the England team need a professor of philosophy or a red-blooded fast bowler?'

Clarke could hardly have known that in 1959 he himself would join Essex as a 41-year-old on special registration. He took 8 wickets in his first match for the county, later drifted in and out of the side, and retired after the 1960 season. Even then Clarke was still something of a local novelty because of his race. 'The shrewd, dark-hued physician,' wrote the *Havering Post* about their county's 'antique' leg-spinner, 'is a civil, good-natured gentleman with an extremely vital and interesting personality that reflects credit on his native land.'

During the war nine Test cricketers (five English, two South African, one Australian and one New Zealander) perished, together with 112 first-class players. We've seen that many of the domestic game's early recruits served their country in the RAF, galvanised, like Ken Farnes, by reports of the Battle of Britain and of the subsequent night raids on the British homeland. In an attack on London on the moonless night of 9–10 October 1940, there were 385 German bombers, an unprecedented force. 'As I watched those white fires flame up and die down, watched the yellow blazes grow dull and disappear,' announced the dramatic radio voice of Edward R. Murrow, in a broadcast heard on both sides of the Atlantic, 'I thought, what a puny effort is this to burn a great city.' Farnes carried neatly folded in his wallet a copy of Tennyson's 1835 poem 'Locksley Hall' which had predicted aerial combat long before the invention of the aeroplane in its account of 'the nations'

airy navies grappling in the central blue.' A 24-year-old Canadian flier named Teddy Leslie was surprised to learn that the dapper and soft-spoken English recruit sitting alongside him in his training unit later in 1941 was in fact a widely respected and often feared international sportsman whose fast bowling had terrorised opponents on four continents. 'I thought he might just be a fit young vicar,' Leslie recalled years later. Farnes himself frequently quoted the words 'the central blue' when reflecting on their new work environment. It might be a good title for a book, he once told Leslie.

The first of those nine Test players to give his life in the war was also a pilot. We've touched on the career of Geoffrey Legge, who won a total of five England caps between December 1927 and February 1930. Born in Bromley in 1903, he'd gained an early reputation as a forcing batsman for Oxford University and Kent, as well as being a devotee of aeroplanes, fast cars and the casino. In 1929 he married the former Rosemary Frost, with whom he had four children. The family lived in a large home just outside St Merryn on the north coast of Cornwall, a community of about 1,000 souls with a tin mine, five pubs, and the ruins of a medieval chapel.

Unlike many other players, Legge's life had picked up following his retirement from cricket. His position with his family paper firm had allowed him to buy his own plane and certain other luxuries. He was said to have enjoyed roulette and to have had a positive fetish for weekend shooting parties. He was known to take a drink. On the outbreak of war he had volunteered for service with the Fleet Air Arm and been posted to a training unit near Portsmouth. Godfrey Evans's father Arthur, an occasional business colleague, described Legge at the time as 'well nigh unrattled, chipper, the suits smoothly pressed, shoes shined and a spring to his step', although set against these attractive qualities there were also occasional flashes of temper which Evans remembered as 'short-lived, but spectacular while they lasted'.

Legge's obvious enthusiasm made him an effective instructor for the young pilots of 752 Squadron on the Hampshire coast. One of his students described him as 'first up every day at 0530, breakfast at 0545, and then waiting impatiently to take off into a crisp new dawn – [he]

became a familiar sight, striding out to his aircraft, scarf flapping, clapping his hands in encouragement for others to follow him.'

On Friday, 15 November 1940 Legge was officially gazetted as a lieutenant commander in the Fleet Air Arm. He flew himself home to Cornwall that night, returning to his squadron early on Sunday evening. The following Thursday, the 21st, the weather in south-west England was summarised by the Met Office as 'poor … sunshine was deficient and there was considerable excess of rain. Some three inches fell during the day. A lunar halo was observed following nightfall … Wind gusts of 64 mph were recorded at St Mary's, Scilly.' Despite these unfavourable conditions, which grounded all civilian air traffic in the area, Legge and a passenger had taken off late that afternoon in a camouflage-painted Percival Proctor monoplane trainer for their scheduled 100-minute flight back to Cornwall. They never arrived. The plane smashed into a field at Brampford Speke, Devon, about 80 miles short of its destination, killing both men aboard. The accident report noted that they had been 'lost in bad weather'. Slim, dark-haired and debonair, Legge, in the words of his obituary in *The Times*, was 'quiet and undemonstrative, [but] always knew his own mind'. Another paper wrote that 'his beaming grin, when it came, was the kind people warmed to and remembered, as they remembered the temper'. It seems fairly certain that Legge had used his pre-war business trips around Europe to help bring a number of Jewish families out to safety. If he had harboured any regrets or resentment about his relatively modest number of England Test caps, he never let on. Most of Legge's Fleet Air Arm colleagues never even knew he had been a cricketer.

We've followed some of the tribulations of the pre-war Yorkshire and England bowler George Macaulay, who had been heard gently barracking his old county teammate Hedley Verity in a championship match at Bradford early in the 1939 season. Macaulay had immediately volunteered for service on the outbreak of war, by which time he was approaching his 42nd birthday, and eventually been sent as an orderly to a remote RAF base in the Shetland Islands. On 9 December 1940, he was admitted to the camp infirmary, where it was recorded that 'there was an alcoholic history for several years, that he had been drinking heavily during the past ten days, that he retired to his room in a comatose condition and was moved to sick quarters at the request of the O.C. Station'. Macaulay died in his sleep on 13 December, at the age of 43. *Wisden's* obituary paid due credit to this versatile medium and slow bowler, showing him as having fallen 'on active service'. Macaulay's death certificate puts it more starkly: 'Cardiac failure, 3 months, Chronic Alcoholism, 10 years.'

Macaulay's childless widow Edith later took her claim for a war pension to a review tribunal. In time this reached the seemingly paradoxical conclusion that 'we have no doubt whatever that in this case cardiac failure was brought about by a heavy and prolonged bout of drinking', but also that 'we reject, without hesitation, the statement that Mr Macaulay was a chronic alcoholic'. Perhaps they were merely trying to soften the blow for Edith when they refused her application for a pension. She lived for a further forty-eight years, until shortly after her 94th birthday.

In total, George Macaulay took 1,837 first-class wickets at a cost of 17 apiece. He also scored 6,055 runs and held 373 catches. With Macaulay in the side, Yorkshire won the county championship eight times between 1922 and 1935. His simple gravestone notes his name, rank and dates, but makes no mention of any involvement in cricket.

The Nazi era is viewed by posterity as one of darkness, and so of course it was for civilised people. Its effects were felt as much by England's county cricketers and cricket clubs as by any other part of national life. By the end of 1939 the war had already taken a heavy toll on the game in both human and material terms. Recognising that they were in a struggle for survival, the Surrey club sent out a circular to members early the following March which began with the words: 'The Committee are faced with many difficulties and uncertainties in the present Crisis, and rely on the loyal support of the Members, as heavy current expenses have to be met whether cricket is played or not.' This was the exact same phrase that the county had used when appealing for funds under ominously similar circumstances in March 1915.

Being England, there were also numerous examples of dogged perseverance in adversity, and of glorious improvisation amid all the gloom. Reflecting on events in Essex, for instance, *Wisden* reported: 'According to latest advice, the club secretary, Mr B.K. Castor, absent on War Service, has handed over his duties to his wife.' The young Godfrey Evans called in to the St Lawrence ground in Canterbury one dark evening early in that first winter of the war and found his county's secretary Gerald Hough:

> Sitting alone upstairs, with an old-fashioned green eye-shade on, like bookkeepers wear, and he was crouched there, freezing cold, wearing about a dozen sweaters, and he was very, *very* determined that we would all come through all right, just like we had the last time, and play cricket again. And something about this old boy working alone there on a winter's night made you feel more cheerful about the future.

For the time being, however, there was a grim symmetry to the fact that English first-class cricket had lost a total of exactly eleven players by the end of that first winter of the war.

9

ENDGAME

Early in 1941, a brown envelope from Mrs Brian Castor, the acting secretary at Essex, arrived at the modest redbrick home in Enfield shared by 43-year-old Laurie Eastman and his family. Eastman had made his county debut as long ago as 1920 and had scored 13,385 runs and taken 1,006 wickets in the 450 first-class matches that followed. A natural hitter, he used to say that he had batted in every position except number eleven. But despite this boast he had pulled up lame in his own benefit match in August 1939 and been forced to go in last. As we've seen, Essex lost in a tight finish against Middlesex. Eastman never played in the championship again, although a year later he was able to turn out for London Counties against a British Empire XI at Lord's, where he was out for 0 and bowled 10 overs of gentle medium-pace without taking a wicket.

The letter from Mrs Castor discussed the performance of Eastman's benefit fund. She confirmed that the county had raised some £1,030 (£28,000 today) on his behalf, and that this sum had been insured for eight years through the Pluvius Group with a premium of £35. In the normal course of affairs, Eastman could have looked forward to an eventual tax-free sum paid out in 1948 or 1949 of around £1,500, which was then roughly the cost of a three-bedroom semi-detached house in the outer London suburbs, as a reward for his twenty years of service, as both an amateur and a professional, at Essex.

Eastman never collected this nest egg. The account in *Wisden* of his wartime service as an air-raid warden concluded: 'A [bomb] caused him severe shock,' adding that even before this 'he did not enjoy the best of health, otherwise there can be no doubt he would have been seen to much greater advantage on the cricket field.' Eastman had fought in the Great War and could have taken an honourable deferment from civil defence work in 1940 on the grounds of his age and health. But he wouldn't hear of it. 'He wanted to serve,' his younger brother George, also a cricketer, remembered.

Laurie Eastman died in hospital on 17 April 1941. A wounded infantryman called John Daly, who had been hit in the face by a sliver of shrapnel, and then endured a series of botched operations, was on the same ward, and recalled:

> Inhuman nights of men coughing and crying, and [Eastman] himself lying there calm and dignified as he faced the end. One of the last things he told me was 'The new season should be starting about now.' I felt myself choking up. When he died I lost it. The harder I tried to stop the worse it got. I was sickened and revolted to see young boys get hurt and killed day after day, but there was something even worse about this gentle older man slipping away in front of you. That was when it hit me what war was really all about, not just cutting young blokes down in action but destroying ordinary families as well.

Just three days later, Sub-Lt Eric 'Budge' Dixon, RNVR, was lost when flying from HMS *Formidable* off the coast of Libya. His two-seat Fulmar fighter had been one of those deployed to help clear the skies around the main Axis supply port of Tripoli, and it was assumed that he had been shot down while on an early-morning patrol. Dixon was 25 at the time of his death and had been married for just five months. As the captain of the successful Oxford University side in 1939, he had scored 75 invaluable runs in the first innings against Cambridge at Lord's. After coming down, he made 123, exactly half his side's total, in only his second match for Northamptonshire. 'A glittering future beckoned,' the

Cricketer wrote. Now Dixon's father John, who lived alone in Horbury, West Yorkshire, was one of those who looked out of his window to see a messenger arrive on a bicycle with an official telegram that began 'The Secretary of State regrets'; he had lost both his wife and his youngest child in under a year. Eric Dixon's last match, in late August 1939, had been against Somerset. Going in first in the order he scored just 2 and 5, and within a month was training as a navy pilot. Though rarely one to complain, he wrote to an Oxford friend of the rations on *Formidable*: 'We had a dry egg for breakfast, hard cheese and lumps of stale bread for lunch and at night we did not have very much either. They managed slightly better at The Parks.'

Even as the toll of lost or injured cricketers mounted, the game continued in 1940 and 1941. Crusoe Robertson-Glasgow reported in *Wisden*:

> The military crisis having wiped out several matches due to [be] played at Lord's, entertainment was left largely to private enterprise … The London Counties side sparkled with hitters and known fast scorers. Such players as Frank Woolley, Wellard, Jim Smith, Watt, Hulme, Watts and Todd often scored runs at an almost unbelievable pace.

Essex's plans for a full programme of one-day matches were thwarted when the county was declared a defence area, which stopped teams from travelling there. The northern leagues still operated more or less as usual, however. In fact the war could be said to have been the making of some semi-professional players. The occasional county batsman Les Warburton, for instance, played twenty-one times for East Lancashire in 1940, finishing with the impressive average of 122.50. There was another full fixture list of league cricket in 1941, as well as a number of charity matches at Lord's featuring teams that in more normal times might not have enjoyed the chance to grace the game's headquarters: Hornsey v Southgate, for example, or Early Birds v Metropolitan Police 'C' Division. Learie Constantine played for the Yorkshire club Windhill in the Bradford League, at a fee of £25 a match. He had offered his services to the army in 1939 but was instead appointed a Ministry of Labour welfare officer. Constantine's main task was to look after the interests of several thousand West Indians drafted in as munitions workers to help the war effort, a challenge stiffened by the fact that 'Britain was still in the grip of racial prejudice, and this was only aggravated by the eventual arrival of American forces in the country.' One night Constantine was standing with some friends in the ballroom of a Liverpool hotel when 'a US Air Force officer aggressively shouldered the whole length of the hall and shouted "Get out, we don't allow nigs to mix with white people where we are."' When Constantine remonstrated, the officer replied, 'Get out, n★★★★r, before I smash you.'

Constantine also remembered one 'seemingly neverending' rail journey from Manchester to London in the late summer of 1941:

> The train, which was full, frequently stopped and then jerked back into life, with people stumbling over each other in the corridors. We rolled slowly south and finally ground to a halt at Euston. It was the middle of the night. There were no lights. You could hear air-raid sirens. There were explosions and fires in the distance.

When Constantine eventually got to his digs for the night, an unprepossessing establishment tucked away behind the British Museum, he was told that he was free to sleep there but not to take a bath in the morning. On the last occasion a black resident had taken advantage of the facilities in this way, it was explained, the white guests had loudly complained about it and the management had been forced to thoroughly disinfect the tub with bleach before it was deemed fit for general use again.

The young Cambridge University and Hampshire batsman John Blake had a 'moment of startling truth … losing all my more innocent feelings about the war' one day in April 1941 when he called in to collect some letters from the county ground at Southampton. Although it was a sunny spring morning, with no blackout provisions in effect until later in the day, Blake noticed that all the shades were pulled down in the club office:

It was a very gloomy atmosphere, like stepping into an undertaker's, and Mr MacLeod, the secretary, was sitting there at his desk with a single candle burning. He had a black arm-band on. A few days earlier his friend John Butterworth, a good opening bat, had been killed flying for the RAF somewhere in London. I later found out that Butterworth's younger brother had also died in the Dunkirk affair. Now I knew Alister MacLeod. He was a tough old bird who fought in the First War. But he was really broken up on account of that family. And in those early days of the war the way you dealt with something like that was by pulling the curtains shut and sitting there with a solitary candle and a black arm-band. And so every time you went in to talk to him the whole idea of death was brought home to you.

The Hampshire secretary was soon to experience another heavy loss. On the night of 17 June 1941 his county's prolific left-handed batsman and willing part-time wicketkeeper Don Walker was shot down and killed over Best in the Netherlands while on his way with the RAF to bomb a target in Germany. He was just 28 at the time of his death. We've seen that at Taunton, in July 1939, Walker and his batting partner Len Creese had saved the day for Hampshire against Somerset. According to *The Times*: 'Both men for once eschewed attack for a long tenure at the crease, such as might have encouraged the next man in, sitting in the pavilion, to unbuckle his pads and enquire about tea.' A month later, at Portsmouth, Walker hit an imperious century against Surrey. Reporters long remembered how he had drawn slightly away to the on side and cracked the distinctly lively Alf Gover through the covers. In an earlier championship match Walker and his partner Gerry Hill put on 235 for the fifth wicket, which still remains a Hampshire record. Both these players had immediately joined up in September 1939, Hill (despite once being accidentally shot in the leg by a county teammate) living to be 92. Neat and compact, like a jockey, Walker had slicked-down dark hair, thin eyebrows and a dimpled chin – a 'dashing fellow' as the county annual called him, notable for his 'steady gaze' and 'trim, powerful build'. A brilliant fielder and occasional bowler, as well as being 'immediately liked and respected by friend and rival alike', he was widely tipped for future England honours at both cricket and rugby union. Instead, Walker's sporting career, and his life, ended in a fiery crash in a remote Dutch cornfield. 'There was a time when the arrival of a telegram would normally have been a cause of pleasurable excitement,' Alister MacLeod wrote. 'Nowadays the call of the young messenger on his bicycle is to be confronted by the angel of death.'

MacLeod was obliged to put on his black armband several more times before it was finally all over. His family friend Gerald Seeley, who played a single first-class game for Worcestershire while still a teenager and became one of the many cricketers to join the RAF, died when he was shot down over the Belgian coast in July 1941, aged 38. In time the Hampshire players Francis Arkwright and Norman Boswell both fell in action, the latter while a Japanese POW, aged 37 and 39 respectively. *Wisden* had remarked of the county's mixed record in 1939, 'unpalatable as it may be, the truth is that [the players] lacked real fighting spirit'. It is not a judgement that would seem to apply to those same individuals over the six years that followed. Even John Blake, the promising young batsman and part-time schoolteacher who called in to collect his mail at the county ground that sunny spring morning in 1941, later fell while fighting with the Royal Marines in Croatia. The citation for the Military Cross he won shortly before his death read:

> For outstanding gallantry and leadership while serving with the 43rd R.M. commando in the attack which led to the capture of Mt. Ortino, Italy, on 3rd Feb 1944. On reaching the top of the Mount through heavy machine gun fire, without hesitation and heedless of the danger from grenades, he led the forward section of his Troop in a bayonet charge on the enemy and captured 20 prisoners. Later in the day during a strong

enemy counter attack, this gallant officer moved from position to position, encouraging his men and directing their fire.

John Blake was 26 at the time of his death. Blake's younger brother David went on to become a Portsmouth area dentist, playing forty-eight times as an amateur for Hampshire, and died in 2015 at the age of 90.

In early April 1941, as John Blake was standing with Alister MacLeod in the latter's darkened office at Southampton, the 21-year-old club cricketer Kenneth Hewitt left for an extended training exercise with the 1st Battalion of the Green Howards at the garrison town of Omagh in Northern Ireland. 'It was a pleasant and friendly little place,' Hewitt later wrote:

> We took part in a lot of drills throughout the length and breadth of Ulster. Among our company were the celebrated Test cricketers, namely Capt. Hedley Verity and Lt Norman Yardley. There was a very nice pub called the Castle Hotel in the village. I mated up with Archie Coles, a semi-pro footballer, and signed up for London Derry Town whilst we were there. Most matches were played in and around Belfast and I went along with Archie and spent Saturday night at the dances in the YMCA.

The battalion also managed to play a certain amount of cricket in the summer of 1941. In a match at Omagh on 20 September between the Green Howards and a team raised by the local hospital manager Louis Walsh, the two famous Yorkshiremen bowled unchanged throughout the innings: Yardley took 2-51 and Verity took 8-55. Despite these impressive figures, Walsh's XI won the match by 21 runs. According to the local *Tyrone Constitution*, there was 'a small but appreciative crowd of perhaps 80' on hand to witness the proceedings, which took place on the grounds of the municipal lunatic asylum. It was Verity's last game of competitive cricket.

In the bright morning sunlight of Tuesday 12 August 1941, 25-year-old Acting Squadron Leader Bill Edrich was seated at the controls of a twin-engine MK.IV Bristol Blenheim, accompanied by a bombardier and a combined navigator-radio operator, as part of a force of fifty-four aircraft on a mission to attack the German industrial heartland near Cologne. They flew to their target at a cruising speed of around 220mph, and at virtually tree-top altitude. The outward journey took just under two hours, and Edrich later remarked that he had loved every minute of it. 'It was particularly great to see the Dutch farmworkers waving joyously to us as we sped over,' he noted. Something about the wheat glowing in the summer fields immediately below had reminded him of his native Norfolk.

In the words of Edrich's subsequent citation for the Distinguished Flying Cross:

> This officer had the difficult task of bringing his formation in to attack the main power station immediately after the leading box had attacked. This needed fine judgement as it was imperative that the target should be bombed from as low an altitude as possible. He had to delay his attack in order to avoid his formation being destroyed by explosions from the delay action bombs of the previous boxes. By carrying out his orders with the greatest exactitude and determination, he must be given credit for a large part of the success of the attack.

Since fully twelve of the aircraft in Edrich's immediate group failed to return from the mission, perhaps it's not surprising that from then onwards he tended to live each day as though it might be his last, greatly enhancing his reputation as one of life's incurable romantics in the process. Just three weeks later he was back playing services cricket in front of 12,000 spectators at Lord's. The crowd rose to cheer Edrich all the way to the wicket, but he was soon out for just 4, to a brilliant running catch taken in front of the pavilion by Sergeant-Instructor Denis Compton.

Ken Farnes had played his last cricket match on 14 September 1940, as part of the British Empire team which went down to John Stephenson's side at the Victoria ground in Cheltenham. The venue was all a semi-rural English cricket field should be in late summer: flat, brown and tree-lined, with an ancient elm in one corner and an unusually well-stocked beer tent in another. Although perched among the rolling meadows that cut down to where the River Chelt flowed just to the south, the pitch itself was smooth enough to allow keenly competitive games of bowls to be played there on non-match days. All sporting parties agreed it was an idyllic spot. Although the Empire side lost heavily that day, Farnes had acquitted himself well with both bat and ball, and was still there, undefeated on 25 – 'displaying all the skill born of ten years' experience of such encounters,' the *Citizen* wrote – at the end.

As we've seen, Farnes had gone on to train with the RAF in Canada and then be commissioned as a pilot officer on 1 September 1941. He had turned 30 just a few weeks earlier, and had become attached to the pretty, dark-haired Catherine 'Aeron' Narracott, who had recently left her husband – who happened to be the air correspondent of *The Times* – in order to move to the West Country with her young daughter. Rash as it usually is to speculate on such matters, it seems safe to say on this occasion that Farnes and Aeron had fallen deeply in love. He wrote back to his Canadian flying friend Teddy Leslie later in the week he returned to England: 'After lunch I had a never to be forgotten walk with C.N. ... She is perfection.'

On the dark Monday evening of 20 October 1941, Ken Farnes joined eight of his fellow pilots of No. 12 Operational Training Unit in taking off in their twin-engine Vickers Wellingtons from the newly opened RAF Chipping Warden, near Banbury in Oxfordshire. It was Farnes's first unsupervised night training flight, and Aeron was waiting for him in a parked car near the airfield. A cold rain had fallen all day, and the ground was blanketed in a fine mist. Less than five minutes after take-off, Farnes's plane crash-landed near the base's main runway. He and his colleague were both killed instantly. It was thought that they may have become disoriented with so few lights to act as a reference point on the ground. Farnes, who had played fifteen Tests for England and serves as a fast bowling link between Harold Larwood and Fred Trueman, was buried at Brookwood military cemetery in Surrey. His headstone reads: 'He died as he lived, Playing the Game.' In time Aeron moved away with her daughter Diana, who went on to become a distinguished journalist and author, and the wife of the film critic Barry Norman.

On 11 February 1942, the Australian seam bowler Frank Thorn, whose brief playing career had come to an early zenith when, on his Sheffield Shield debut, he dismissed Don Bradman, was shot down during a mission to attack two Japanese ships in Gasmata Harbour, Papua New Guinea. He was 29 at the time of his death and had volunteered for service in the Royal Australian Air Force in the week war was declared. Thorn crashed into a vast expanse of jungle, and it would be another sixty-six years before his bomber was found, buried upside down in the mud.

On the same day Thorn was lost, the West Country club cricketer Joseph Hazel, serving as a lieutenant colonel with the Royal Artillery, began life in the notorious Tandjong Priok POW camp in Batavia, Java. This was among the most brutal outposts of even the Japanese wartime penal system. It is possible to read the wrenching letters Hazel was able to exchange with his wife back in Somerset over the course of the three years, in which she tried to bring him news of their two children growing up in his absence.

Hazel read in July 1942:

Pooh is such a big girl now, and has greatly improved. Your little son is such a pet – how I wish you could see him, you would feel very proud, he is very sturdy, and is going to be his Daddy's build. The Pooh simply adores him. I can only repeat news and hope at least one letter may reach you. If only I could hear from you. It is so long now.

More than two years later, on 20 November 1944, Hazel in turn wrote:

> I am so delighted with your news and the snap, but why none of you?
> How Pooh has grown and how splendid Michael looks … My love and
> thoughts for Christmas to all of you. Ever your loving, Joe.

Among Hazel's other surviving papers is a faded, hand-drawn
programme for a production of *Macbeth* put on in August 1942
by some of the prisoners at Tandjong Priok. It is signed by the
cast members, among them the 29-year-old Welsh rugby cap and
Glamorgan cricketer Wilf Wooller. Wooller entered captivity as a
strapping 6ft 2in, 14-stone all-round athlete and eventually went
home again 60lb lighter and suffering from crippling stomach pains.
He had been physically ill the first time he tried to play rugby on
his return, and rarely did so again. It was reported that in later years
Wooller consistently refused to use Japanese-made calculators due to
his treatment as a POW. He shared some of his time in confinement
with the former Essex batsman-turned-administrator Brian Castor,
who had gone off to war at the age of 50 after pragmatically handing
over his duties as county secretary to his wife. Wooller and Castor
lived to be 84 and 89 respectively.

Also on 11 February 1942, Acting Major E.W. Swanton of the
Bedfordshire Yeomanry, whose 35th birthday it was, arrived with
his unit in Singapore. His first – and only – communication from
Command Headquarters on debarking was a meticulously formal note
from the deputy provost marshal asking him for his particulars, and an
accompanying photograph, prior to the issue of an identity card. The
chit was signed by the ever-efficient Brian Castor. In the event Swanton
was never properly processed while in Singapore, because just three days
later, as he wrote in his book *Sort of A Cricket Person*:

> I was out establishing a new observation post as our ragged line fell back
> towards the perimeter of the city. Lone Jap snipers who had infiltrated
> during darkness were said to be becoming a menace, and as I surveyed

my new zone while my signaller went back for the telephone wire, I spotted something glinting in the sun towards the top of a tree left front … Suddenly, a sub-machine gun started up and I felt a heavy blow on the right elbow. In the first weeks, after the capitulation that followed next day, a lack of food and drugs caused the deaths of many from wounds almost as superficial as mine.

Swanton spent the next three and a half years as a Japanese prisoner. In time he was sent via the Changi camp in Singapore to become one of the labourers on the Burma-Siam railway. This was widely considered a fate as dire as anything the war had to offer. Although systematically starved (he lost 5 of his 15½ stone while in captivity) and subjected to other privations he preferred not to discuss in later years, Swanton was able to make one indelible contribution to Allied morale by helping to establish a camp library. 'The books were the sort that might be expected on the shelves of expatriate Englishmen,' he later wrote. They included 'a good deal of Galsworthy, Priestley, Buchan, Evelyn Waugh, Gunther, and H.V. Morton … Not a POW but by the end had read Arthur Bryant's *English Saga* and Richard Llewellyn's *How Green was my Valley*.'

Swanton's own chief bequest was a tattered 1939 *Wisden*. Rebound several times with gas cape, held together with rice paste, a Japanese stamp indicated that the almanack was considered 'non-subversive'.

Swanton records a daily routine characterised at least at first by boredom and hunger as much as by the psychotic cruelty we tend to associate with the Japanese camp system. 'In the early days, it was quite a common thing to slip out at night to the houses nearby,' he notes:

About three one morning some Jap guards were surprised to hear raucous noises coming from one of these houses, and on entering found a British soldier in fine fettle. Next morning he was brought before the commandant [and] after a long lecture the sentence was pronounced. A board was hung round his neck with the legend: 'I took whisky. This very bad thing.' Then the POW band – an accordion and a trumpet – was called out, and ordered to play the prisoner round the yard.

Despite the relative lenience of the soldier's punishment, life in the camps increasingly became a matter of sheer survival. For the mainly British and Australian inmates, the dying soon began.

Born in 1898, Gilbert Jose may not have had the most statistically illustrious first-class career, with just two appearances for South Australia and a final batting average of 4.50. But even to have achieved that much invests a cricketer with a certain distinction that sets him apart from those of lesser attainment or fortune. Jose, who had sharp blue eyes and neatly parted light brown hair, had gone on to serve with the Australian Army Medical Corps during the war. In February 1942 he was one of those unfortunate enough to be captured and taken to the Changi camp, where his own health soon failed. A fellow Australian POW named Alan Hobbs recorded clinically in his diary:

> Friday March 27: Gilbert Jose (MO Major SX11028) died at 0645 after dysentery lasting only a few days. Extreme toxaemia and delirium for about 3 days, then coma for 2. Buried in AIF Cemetery Changi, on main Singapore road. Total number of dysentery cases: 469.

'Not all of the guards [were] cruel, but the majority of them were stupid and indifferent to our welfare,' Jose wrote shortly before the end. Basic matters of food and sanitation were a common preoccupation for prisoners throughout the worldwide camp system. A Royal Artillery officer named William Bompas was captured early in 1943 and locked up in Oflag 79, which was located in an old German army barracks near Brunswick. His diary is divided into chapters to which he gives titles such as 'A Hungry Officer Writes' and 'Where to Eat in London after the War.' When spring came, Bompas adds:

> Cricket was played on four or five afternoons on the asphalt down the centre, with 6 and more or less out when the ball was hit onto one of the flat roofs. Bill Bowes (Yorkshire), Freddie Brown (Surrey) and John Bowley (MCC) and a lot of club players took part, and the standard was really very good.

Test cricket lost another son in June 1942 when Pilot Officer Ross Gregory of Victoria and Australia died while on air operations near the town of Gaffargaon in present-day Bangladesh. A diminutive but assertive character, he brought a similar directness to his batting. Everything that could be hit, he hit hard and straight. In 1936–37 he played in two tests against England, scoring 23 and a run-out 50 in the first, and then 80 in his only innings in the second, against a visiting side that included Ken Farnes and Hedley Verity in its bowling attack. Earlier in 1942, Gregory had written to his family that in the event of his loss they should 'take a certain amount of comfort from the knowledge that I went down doing my duty'. He was 26 at the time of his death.

In all, more than ten full teams' worth of first-class cricketers were lost during the war. By early 1942 Haddon Whitaker's worst misgivings about the immediate future both of *Wisden* and the game in general had been fulfilled. For each of the next three years, the almanack contained fewer than half the usual number of pages. A large proportion of these consisted of obituaries. They ranged alphabetically from Gunner Sidney Adams, Royal Artillery, who was 'killed, aged 40, with Allied forces – he was a council clerk and leg-spinner who took wickets with his first two balls in cricket [including that of Samuel Beckett], playing for Northamptonshire against Dublin University in 1926', to 'Mr. Denys Witherington, killed while serving as a private in the Loyal Regiment – he captained the Leys School, and showed such capital form as a batsman and wicket-keeper that he played in the Public Schools match at Lord's'. The fast-rolling phrases, so compelling in their simplicity and repetition, could only hint at the individual scenes of horror and sacrifice: 'Died of wounds received … Killed in France … Perished at sea … Fell in fighting in North Africa … Downed on air operations … Previously reported missing, officially stated dead.'

Not every cricketer victim was lost in action, however.

In July 1942, Andrew Ducat of Surrey and England, the holder of six international soccer caps, collapsed at the wicket while batting for the Home Guard in a charity match at Lord's. A few minutes later he was pronounced dead of an apparent heart attack. Play was then abandoned, and Pelham Warner wrote: 'Such an event had never happened here before, and the sudden tragic passing of this very popular cricketer and famous footballer, apparently full of health and vigour, was a severe shock to those present.' Andrew Ducat was 56.

On 31 October 1942, 30-year-old Squadron Leader Roger Winlaw died when the plane he was piloting on a training mission collided with another in mid-air over Caernarfon in North Wales. He was the vicar's son and 'thundering' Winchester, Cambridge University and Surrey batsman of whom Robertson-Glasgow wrote: 'He [saw himself] in a great moral struggle, which he acknowledged quite airily he might not survive.' The pilot of the other plane was 41-year-old Acting Squadron Leader Claude Ashton, a fellow Old Wykehamist who had won a triple blue at Cambridge and gone on to play eighty-one times for Essex. Both men were married with young children. Just three weeks later, the all-rounder Roger Human, of MCC and Worcestershire, fell in action at the age of 33. A soft-spoken history teacher and amateur cricketer, he had once admitted he would be 'honoured and humbled, not to say amazed' in the event he was ever called upon to represent England. After playing just four county matches in 1939, with a top score of 21, and failing to take a wicket or a catch, Human was in fact rather surprisingly chosen for the MCC's winter tour of India. As we've seen, this was cancelled on the outbreak of war. In the end Human did go to India, but as a soldier with the Light Infantry. Having reached the rank of captain, he fell on active service near Bangalore on 21 November 1942. Human left behind a wife, Rosalind, a five-year-old son and an infant daughter.

One Saturday morning in September 1942 a 21-year-old married Sussex builder's mate named Ernest Ridgers opened his post to find that he had been called up by the army. After being 'buggered about' in typical fashion he eventually found himself training with the Royal Engineers in nearby barracks that consisted of 'half-a-dozen perishing cold Nissen Huts surrounded by a very high fence of barb wire … We were short of grub and fags, and most other things as well. It was a ruddy awful life.'

However, there were compensations. 'While in Chichester,' Ridgers later wrote:

My PT Instructor was Denis Compton, the famous cricketer and footballer. After I'd jumped the wooden horse two or three times and run around the field, Sgt Compton called me on one side and said, 'Well done soldier, now go over behind that wall and have a smoke.'

Next day was a Saturday and we had football in the afternoon and I was on the opposite side to Denis and I managed to take the ball off his toe when he was about to score. I won't say what he called me, but after the match he called me over and said 'Doing anything this evening, soldier?' I said 'No', so he said 'I'm going to treat you to the pictures.' Before [that] we went into a pub and he wouldn't let me pay for anything, and while we were there one or two of our chaps came in and one boy was Black and there were two or three Americans in there. Two of the Americans went up to this Black Boy and told him to clear out as they didn't want to drink with Blacks, so Compton said to him, 'Stay put son.' Then two Americans came and walked the black boy outside and the Sarge and our chaps followed and they caught hold of the Americans and whacked them.

While some critics later found fault with Compton's outspoken views on the racial divisions in South Africa, there is no reason to doubt Ridgers's account that in 1942 he was genuinely offended by this treatment of a fellow British serviceman at the hands of some boorish Americans, nor that he waded in to 'whack' them in the soldier's defence.

By now there could be no lingering doubt that the British people were in anything but a struggle for survival. German bombs had not only flattened city centres; the effects of the war had seeped down to every level. Private homes that had been only barely heated in peacetime were often numbingly cold during the successive winters of fuel rationing.

To Denis Compton, there seemed to be an 'awful metallic smell, a sort of sulphur or gas' permanently polluting the air. The taped-up headlights of the army lorry he drove around in gave off a kind of 'soupy glow' that picked out mounds of rubble piled to the right and left of the road. Travel by private car or train had become arduous if not impossible. Even the once well-heeled passenger liner *Athlone Castle*, on which the pre-war MCC tourists had cavorted on their return voyage from South Africa, had been pressed into army service, its once-festive purple superstructure painted over in battleship grey, busy exchanging fresh troops for desperately wounded ones on the coast of Libya.

This still counted as the lap of luxury compared to conditions on board the Japanese freighter *Yoshida Maru* on which Glamorgan's Wilf Wooller and others went into captivity in 1942. A Royal Engineers officer named E.R. Scott later wrote of this ordeal:

> Our party were crowded together so tightly that it was impossible to lie down and those immediately under the hatchways, which were unprovided with tarpaulins, were soaked to the skin every time it rained. No blankets were provided, nor were any medical supplies of any description … The deck latrines, damaged by heavy seas, leaked badly and sprayed infected excreta over everyone.
>
> On arrival all personnel were ordered ashore for a hosedown on the dockside under the supervision of Jap guards. Eventually, after standing in sub-zero temperature, dressed in tropical kit, we were split into one group of 170 and three groups of 169 each and marched [into] camp. A further 17 men died from the effects of the voyage. All suffered from scurvy for several weeks.

Scott also describes a variety of invasive medical treatments for both male and female POWs that could have been carried out for no purpose other than pure sadism. His brother officer Joseph Hazel thought 'the great sportsman Wooller' one of the most resilient among them, and like himself 'quite certain we should be returning to a land fit for heroes'. In fact Wooller came home to find his wife in the throes of divorcing him. Hazel in turn would spend some years in increasingly acrimonious discussion with organisations such as the Inland Revenue and the War Office about relatively small sums of money. The latter body wrote to him on 20 July 1946: 'As you are now released from Army service you are not eligible for the refund of any furniture-removal or transportation expenses under any circumstances.'

Despite – or because of – their daily living conditions, many British and Commonwealth POWs managed to play regular organised cricket while in captivity. 'It was almost schizophrenic going from the horrors of camp life to this wonderful game,' Wooller remembered:

> None of the guards got it. They left us alone. All you heard was the bowler's footsteps, his shoes scuffing the dirt, the swish of the bat, a little click, dead silence. That was a Brahms lullaby compared to the chaos and bedlam that went on the rest of the day.

At Stalag VIII-B, located near the small town of Lamsdorf in Silesia, the inmates managed to stage limited-overs matches most weekends in the summers of 1943 and 1944. After the Other Ranks had easily won the first half-dozen games, something of a social experiment took place, 'with the players swapping themselves around without distinction of rank, and a private aircraftsman who had played in the Leagues solemnly writing out the batting order for the Squadron Leaders and Wing Commanders now under his sway.' It was another small example of how the intensity of war sometimes forges a spirit of mutual comradeship not always available in peacetime.

There were several other notable cases of enterprise shown by imprisoned cricketers. Twenty-eight-year-old William Becher, a former Sussex Second XI captain, was wounded in Libya and was twice captured by the enemy but managed to escape both times. Turning out for Wiltshire after the war in between his administrative duties with both the I-Zingari club and the Board of Boxing Control, he lived to be 84.

In 1940, a 26-year-old Anglo-Irish writer-turned-soldier named Terrence Prittie was captured by the Germans in the retreat from

France. He made six successive attempts to escape from POW camps. As a rule, these places were 'not greatly to [his] taste', he would later note with some restraint. While in captivity, Prittie smuggled out regular essays on cricket, and over the winter of 1942–43 composed an entire waste-paper manuscript called *Mainly Middlesex*, which was published to some acclaim five years later.

In his foreword to the book, Pelham Warner wrote:

> From whatever dungeon he was occupying beyond the Rhine at the time, Prittie managed to send an article to the *Cricketer* on the game as played within the severely limited boundaries of a 30-foot medieval moat. This showed that the old spirit lived and it delighted me. I have since learned that the German cipher experts lost some sleep by assuming his evocations of cricket were all an elaborate code.

The name Freeman Barnardo is largely forgotten by cricket followers today, but in May 1939 this compact, Indian-born batsman was good enough to be chosen by Middlesex while still a fresh-faced Cambridge undergraduate. A month later he was appearing at number four for the MCC at Lord's, for whom he scored 16 in slightly under ten minutes at the crease. Immediately joining the Royal Armoured Corps on the outbreak of war, Lt Barnardo fell in the fighting at El Alamein in October 1942; he was just 24. Others who swapped their whites for soldier's uniform included Ronald Gerrard, who won fourteen England rugby union caps while casually turning out as a middle-order bat for Somerset, 'always looking supremely poised', according to the county annual, if without materially affecting the outcome of too many matches. As a major with the Royal Engineers, Gerrard was killed in action near Tripoli on 22 January 1943, four days short of his 31st birthday. His gravestone reads: 'Gerry, Played, Fought and Died for England.' Lt Peter Blagg of the Welch Fusiliers was also just 24 when he fell in combat in Burma on 18 March 1943. He had been the irrepressible Oxford University wicketkeeper whose final first-class match was the July 1939 victory over Cambridge at Lord's. Blagg was one of the four young cricketers who left the field that sunlit evening after a thrilling finish who would give his life for his country.

Len Hutton had also volunteered in 1939, and like a number of peacetime sportsmen been called up to join the army physical training corps. Fifty years later he remembered that he had wanted to be 'in the heat of it, [but] instead spent most of my time sitting around in barracks with a lot of rather gloomy buggers drinking tea and listening to the war news on the radio'. One day in March 1941 the now unhappy warrior was exercising in an army gym in York when a mat slipped under him and he fell heavily on his left side. X-rays showed a severe fracture just above the wrist. Hutton's active war, such as it was, was over. He underwent three operations before the end of 1941, separated from the army the following summer, and eventually emerged with a left arm almost 2in shorter than the right one.

Hutton played no cricket of any kind in 1942, and the nearest he came to the top level in 1943 was a one-day affair when he somehow represented North Wales against an Empire XI at Colwyn Bay, to be bowled out by the West Indies' Manny Martindale for 22. Occasional high fevers and excruciatingly painful muscle spasms, later diagnosed as fibrositis, underscored the sad truth that England's leading young batsman, with 13 Tests and some 11,000 first-class runs behind him, seemed to many to be finished at the age of 27. Such observers underestimated Hutton's obstinacy and resilience. In time he was back representing first Pudsey, then Yorkshire and finally England, whom he efficiently led to home and away series wins over Australia. Even then, there were those who thought that Hutton's latter-day batting, prolific as it was, never quite recovered the spirit of his youthful brilliance.

As we've seen, Walter Hammond joined the RAF, playing a good deal of cricket, occasionally training new recruits, and gradually resolving a home life that led to the terse Press Association report: 'A decree was granted to Mrs Dorothy Hammond, wife of the England star. Misconduct was alleged with a woman named Harvey.'

It has to be said that Hammond never entirely reconciled himself, either as a man or a cricketer, to the one serious threat to his status as the supreme Test match batsman of the 1930s. He was, however, utterly obsessed by him. Hammond's biographer has written: 'When he assumed the captaincy of England, and even before that, his message, voiced or unspoken, was: "Let's get Bradman out, then we can think about beating the Aussies. He's the obstacle. Bradman … Bradman … Bradman …"' Hammond called his younger rival 'the run-machine', sometimes adding a blunt intensifier before the term. Godfrey Evans saw both players up close when he toured Australia with the MCC side in 1946–47. 'It wasn't enough for Wally to do well,' Evans remembered. 'Don had to fail.'

Born in 1908, Bradman, like Hammond, had what was called in the jargon of the day a 'cushy' war. Initially joining the Royal Australian Air Force before transferring to the army, he was invalided out again early in 1941. Like Len Hutton, Bradman was suffering from as-yet undiagnosed fibrositis, while, to general amazement, a routine army physical revealed that he had 'distinctly sub-par' eyesight. The greatest athlete in Australian history was thus officially declared unfit to serve his country. Later in the war Bradman was further embarrassed when the Adelaide stockbroking firm he represented crashed due to fraud and embezzlement. Although there was no suggestion of any wrongdoing on his part, the scandal left what he called a 'rank smell of impropriety' clinging to him for many years. Before the Tests began in November 1946, Bradman told Hammond that he was just pleased they were both still in the harness and, at 38 and 43 respectively, 'able to assist our countries in the restoration of our great national sport'.

With his habit of turning a conversation into an argument, Hammond took issue with this remark, pointing out that he was there to win back the Ashes, not to 'help your bloody lot feel good about yourselves again'. Relations between the two pre-war icons of Test cricket never quite recovered from this poor start. During the subsequent first Test at Brisbane, Bradman, with his score on 28, edged a ball to Jack Ikin of Lancashire and England, who was standing at second slip. Ikin caught it. The England tourists were then surprised, to use the mildest term possible, to see Bradman still standing at his crease, 'idly looking away over the square-leg boundary', as Hammond put it. Somewhat belatedly, there was an appeal, and the umpire at the bowler's end gave Bradman not out. He went on to score 187. At the end of the over, the England captain strode up to his Australian counterpart and, in one contemporaneous newspaper account, 'remarked that he had grave doubts as to the excellence of the umpire's decision, and also expressed his views on Bradman's own reluctance to quit the crease'. This was a striking paraphrase on the paper's part. What Hammond actually said (as confirmed by Denis Compton, who was standing immediately next to him) was: 'That's a fine fucking way to start a series.'

A player's greatness at cricket was no guarantee of his attaining glory in war, nor of enjoying a relatively comfortable civilian life. Sixty-one-year-old Jack Hobbs of Surrey and England – 'the Master' of the pre-Bradman era – was still running his sports shop in central London. 'I'm glad to hear you are safe and sound,' he wrote to a customer in 1944. 'Life these days is very grim here. My wife stands it very well, but she is alone during the day and it's not nice for her.'

Taken as a whole, the war would prove to be remarkably flexible both in accommodating differing individual circumstances and in providing a rich variety of personal experiences. The fates of English cricketers ranged from those who fell, or were captured, in action, to others whose job was to keep the bureaucratic machinery ticking over rather than to kill Germans. The attacking Sussex and England batsman Hugh Bartlett, at one time Walter Hammond's love rival while on tour of South Africa, was one of those in the forefront of the fight. After being commissioned in the Royal Kents, and later training as a glider pilot, Bartlett served successively at Normandy, Arnhem and in the Rhine crossings. He was never the same strokeplayer again after the war. There were those who volunteered as air-raid wardens, like Laurie Eastman, or as policemen, such as Walter Keeton, the Nottinghamshire and England opener who was named in the 1940 edition of *Wisden* as one of its five players of the year. The seemingly charmed life of Brian Johnston, the debonair Old Etonian whose latter-day cricket commentary dwelt on matters such as the number and variety of cakes to be found in the commentary box, came to an abrupt end in the winter of 1944–45 when his unit took part in the bloody final push into Germany. Along the way he was one of those liberating a concentration camp at Zeven, located on the banks of the Oste river between Bremen and Hamburg. War-hardened British squaddies had been 'physically ill at the sight', he later reported. The essential duality of Johnston's nature surfaced just five days later, when he wrote an urgent letter home to his mother: 'Could you send a parcel sometime? Containing: Wicket-keeping gloves, three cricket shirts, three pairs white socks, cravat … etc.'

Another wartime paradox came in the Indonesian town of Palembang, 300 miles south of Singapore, where the Japanese had established a prison camp in the grounds of the former Mulo School. Here the comparatively healthy inmates worked fourteen-hour days, slept on wooden pallets, and dined off meagre rations of watery soup, rice and fast-decaying meat that was sometimes augmented by boiled rat, one local commodity of which there was no shortage. The sick or injured prisoners were condemned to suffer in fetid cellars, where they were denied access to even basic sanitation, let alone to morphine or other pain-killing drugs. A charge brought against the camp authorities in July 1946 noted that the British servicemen held at Mulo had experienced 'mass beatings by guards, individual beatings using fists, feet, sticks, rifle butt and any weapon at hand … as well as exposure during working hours owing to non-issue of available essential clothing and also in mass parades held at night for long periods without adequate cover'.

In the midst of this horror, a torn scrap of scorecard records that on 6 February 1943 a 'hearty' cricket match was played between two sides of prisoners on the grounds of the Mulo school grounds, with an Australian and an American standing as umpires and an RAF aircraftsman named James Pennock, from Streatham in south London, keeping score. Following stumps, the men would again have been locked in a tin-roofed hut without mattresses, blankets or mosquito nets and with only the most primitive plumbing facilities. The senior surviving British officer in the camp recalled in a post-war courtroom how he had been called in by the camp commandant and told that four prisoners, including two cricketers, were to be summarily executed for attempting to escape. The officer's appeal for clemency was refused, the paper on which he wrote it being torn to pieces, and in short order the four men were led out to be shot. The criminal indictment against the Japanese commandant ends: 'The firing party was inefficient.'

Just eleven days after the ragged but indomitable inmates at the Mulo school had managed to play cricket, 32-year-old Flt Lt Gerry Chalk, the pre-war captain of Kent, took off with his fellow Spitfire pilots of 124 Squadron to provide cover for an Allied bombing raid on German shipping at Dunkirk. A high wind blew up as they approached their target, causing some of the planes to become separated from the main force. A group of thirty or so Luftwaffe Focke-Wulf 190 fighters then appeared in the skies above Ardres, a few miles south of Calais, where a British Wellington had just mistakenly dropped its load of bombs. As shells began exploding all around, a local farmer named Guy Haultcoeur hurriedly glanced up as he ran for cover. He remembered being both 'thrilled and appalled' to see 'the long red and white trails spinning and looping and rolling, in a colourful and macabre dance' that ended only when the numerically superior Germans broke off and circled back to Dunkirk. Four British aircraft were lost in the action. In time Gerry Chalk was officially listed as missing, presumed dead. After joining the army in 1939, he had transferred to the RAF as a rear gunner and won the DFC in June 1941 when 'by his cool and accurate fire [he] undoubtedly saved his aircraft, and probably destroyed its attacker' during a daylight raid on Hanover. Chalk, who left behind his widow Rosemary, was widely mourned by his former teammates. The Kent secretary Gerald Hough wrote in *Wisden* that his county captain would be 'greatly missed by his many cricket friends', while the young wicket-keeper Godfrey Evans – generally fatalistic when it came to accepting life's losses – remembered fifty years later that he had broken down and wept at the news.

The attempt in March 1943 by the British eighth army under General Bernard Montgomery to break the German defences at Mareth in Tunisia had ended badly, as even the *Daily Express* admitted: "'Monty', a great cricket man, was left to remark that he had been caught on "a bad wicket", and that, despite some initially strong "biffing" of the enemy "our chaps [had] been forced onto the back foot."' If so, this would seem to be a notable euphemism for an operation that cost the British over 4,000 casualties, and which was saved from total disaster only by a simultaneous hooking manoeuvre by a New Zealand army unit. Among those to fall in the dust and heat at Mareth was Geoffrey Fletcher, the rising young Charterhouse and Oxford batsman who had played his first and only county match, representing Somerset against Northamptonshire, in late July 1939. Fletcher was 23 at the time of his death.

In 1943 cricketers fell in action, piled in clumps awaiting burial in the arid plains of North Africa, or lying pulverised somewhere in the mud of France, irrespective of rank or nationality. Lt Frederick Boult, of the Grenadier Guards, who was killed in Tunisia, aged 22, was the fifth former Oxford captain to die in the war. In the same month, 20-year-old John Cowley fell in action with the King's Rifles; just four years earlier, he had been the youngest boy on the field when taking 5 wickets for Harrow in their long-awaited win over Eton at Lord's. South Africa's leg-spin bowler Richard Evans, 28, was lost at sea, also in May 1943. Robin Whetherly, of Oxford and MCC, died in service with the Special Operations Executive in Yugoslavia while saving a fellow soldier from a bomb during a German raid. Major Whetherly was 27, and with his 'wavy black hair falling down over the right eyebrow' and 'slightly cruel mouth' – and, more pertinently, his friendship with the young Ian Fleming – he has a primary claim to be the inspiration for James Bond. A less exotic soldier, but an equal sacrifice, was the Australian all-rounder Glen Baker, who made the last of his twenty-nine appearances for Queensland in a Sheffield Shield match against New South Wales in December 1941, hitting one Ray Lindwall bouncer with an overhead smash back into the Brisbane pavilion. Baker died while serving as an officer in the Australian army in New Guinea in December 1943, at the age of 28.

These losses, appalling enough in themselves, were far from the only blows cricket would suffer in the year that began with the German defeat at Stalingrad and ended with the arrival of US General Dwight D. Eisenhower in London to begin planning for the invasion of Europe.

In October 1941, 36-year-old Hedley Verity left the relative tranquillity of his Irish training camp with orders to report to the War Office in London prior to being shipped overseas with his fellow Green Howards. There followed a strange, twilight waiting period which he was able to share together with his infirm wife Kathleen before his unit's embarkation. Verity's sister recalled:

> Kathleen was with Hedley in London. She knew that it wouldn't be long. He had been issued with his tropical kit but he didn't say anything about his impending departure.
>
> One night he said: 'Kathleen, I'm going now.' He put his arms round her and repeated: 'This is it, I'm going. I must go tonight.' And he went. It was a frosty night and she could hear his footsteps right away down the garden path until they died away in the distance.

In March 1942, the first battalion of the Green Howards set up a camp among the rolling red hills and vast sandstone forts of Ranchi, in the modern Indian state of Jharkhand, where Verity suffered terribly from dysentery. In time there was even talk of his being invalided out of the army. 'Hedley was getting a bit old,' his fellow Green Howard and county cricket colleague Norman Yardley remarked unsentimentally. 'He was struggling a bit. And he wasn't 100 per cent fit ... He [should have] been sent home so he would have been safe and able to play for Yorkshire again after the war.' However, Verity remained. In March 1943, the battalion was deployed to the Suez Canal zone for further training, and then to Qatana in Syria. Later in the spring they began to prepare for their role in Operation Husky, as the Allied invasion of Sicily was known. A week or two into their exercises, the Green Howards received a visit from a cigar-chewing US General George S. Patton. He commended the men under Verity's command and reminded them that the German was a breed of rabid dog and that there should be no compunction on their part when it came to exterminating him.

In the early hours of 20 July 1943, 'B' Company of the Green Howards began their assault on the heavily defended plains of Catania, a normally placid Sicilian resort overlooking the Ionian Sea. There were chaotic scenes as the soldiers struggled uphill in the moonlight under attack from both German artillery and small-arms fire.

'We were more or less surrounded by the enemy,' one of the enlisted men reported. 'They were in front and on either side of us.' As a result, it was 'thunderously loud', and 'star-shells regularly burst overhead', momentarily turning the scene from night to day. The strobe-like flashes of light allowed the German defenders to open up at point-blank range, some of the British soldiers mown down as they advanced in columns, falling side by side, their uniforms cut to shreds. Attempting to secure the position, Captain Verity was hit in the chest by shrapnel and had to be left behind as his company withdrew. The last order he gave to his men was 'Keep going.'

Although Verity was well enough treated by his German captors, his medical care was primitive. There was an initial operation carried out in a Sicilian field hospital which stank of 'gore and sweat and human excretions'. The prisoner was then taken by slow boat across the Strait of Messina, and by train to a German military infirmary near Naples. There were some 1,500 casualties piled up in two rooms there, including men who had lost their arms or legs, and others whose stomachs were ripped open and who lay begging for death. Another hot train journey followed the next morning, when Verity was sent on to an Italian hospital at Caserta. A surgeon there operated on the victim's chest, removing part of his rib. Only a local anaesthetic was used. A 23-year-old fellow British inmate and club cricketer named James Blackburn later wrote that nothing much had shaken him in the war up until then, but when 'somebody said that Verity, the bowler, had been injured – he was very well known – that hit home'. Corporal Henty, another wounded

Yorkshireman at Caserta, leaned across to the heavily bandaged figure lying on the next bed. 'I asked him his name,' said Henty, 'and when he gave it I remarked, "Are you the cricketer?" He replied, "Yes, that's me."'

Verity lived for three more days following his operation. Although in increasingly terrible pain, he remained calm and alert, talking about his plans to return to Yorkshire and showing off photographs of his wife and young sons. 'It was very touching, and he was clearly proud of them,' Henty later wrote. On the Friday night of 30 July, Verity weakly signed a form presented to him by the Italian authorities in order to conform to Red Cross regulations. 'I am all right, I have only been slightly hurt,' it read, over the printed message *Saluti affettuosi*, or 'Affectionate greetings'.

That night Verity suffered the first of three successive haemorrhages. Some of his fellow British patients desperately looted the hospital kitchen and brought back ice cubes to try and staunch the bleeding. Their efforts were in vain. Verity died later in the afternoon of 31 July. He was just 38 and was buried in Caserta with full military honours. A hundred and fifty miles to the north, Bill Bowes of Yorkshire and England was then embarking on his second year as a prisoner of war in a camp at Chieti on the Adriatic coast. One morning early in August he was chatting idly to two Canadian airmen who had been shot down over Naples and brought up by train after a night spent in the hospital at Caserta. 'And say,' one of the Canadians remarked lightly, 'there was some cricketer guy down there.' He puzzled over the name for a moment, then added: 'Yeah, that's right. Verity …'

The news reached England only on 1 September 1943, which happened to be the fourth anniversary of the day on which Verity took 7 Sussex wickets for 9 runs in what proved to be his final appearance for Yorkshire. Crusoe Robertson-Glasgow wrote of him in *Wisden*:

> Judged by any standard, Verity was a great bowler. Merely to watch him was to know that. The balance of the run-up, the high ease of the left-handed action, the scrupulous length, the pensive variety, all proclaimed the master. He combined nature with art to a degree not equalled by any

other English bowler of our time. He was the ever-learning professor, justly proud yet utterly humble.

Some people believed that Robertson-Glasgow's own dark moods grew worse after he heard the news of Verity's death. Even in the first years of the war, Crusoe had generally managed to put up a good front; people were accustomed to his infectious laugh, his impish smile and the gleam in his eye. But from the autumn of 1943 onwards he was seemingly less confident, writing poignantly: 'I sometimes think of those we have lost in two wars. It adds up.'

'The ghastly toll will certainly continue,' Robertson-Glasgow wrote elsewhere, and in 1944 it duly did. The Argentinian-born Peter McRae, who showed what *Wisden* called 'bright batting' during his twenty-fourth and final match for Somerset, which had ended at Taunton on the evening Hitler invaded Poland, died on 25 February at the age of 28 when HMS *Mahratta*, which he served as surgeon lieutenant, was torpedoed in the Barents Sea. The author Noel Simon wrote of this incident: 'Having managed to climb onto one of the few Carley floats to have come through the sinking, [McRae] set about hauling the others aboard. The float soon became overcrowded. Remarking almost casually, "There's not enough room for us all," the doctor slipped over the side and was never seen again.'

We've noted the death the following June of 26-year-old John Blake in the ghastly infantry charge through the German minefields at Brač in Yugoslavia. Less than a month later, Charles Packe of Leicestershire and the Royal Fusiliers fell, aged 35, in the action that followed the Normandy landings. His wife Margaret gave birth to their daughter two weeks after his death.

On the night of 4–5 August 1944, some 400 officers and men of the 1st Battalion, Welsh Guards, advanced on the small French village of Montchamp, about 40 miles inland, to block the key crossroads for German supply columns following the Allied invasion. With daylight there was fierce house-to-house fighting, and some of the men became pinned down at the end of a narrow lane shrouded in a drifting, waist-high mist. With a hail of intense fire directed at them, they could only burrow deeper into the rubble. 'Resistance never let up,' wrote one of the Welsh officers, 'and we were soon up against a counter-attack by a line of Panzers grinding towards us.' When the moment came for the British forces to break cover, a sniper's bullet instantly struck down 38-year-old Major Maurice Turnbull. In civilian life he was the wavy-haired, blue-eyed, quintessentially British all-round sportsman who had captained Glamorgan from 1930 to 1939. A short time later Sgt Fred Llewellyn was able to recover Turnbull's body and carry it away from the front line. He found a photograph of the officer's wife and three young children in his wallet and made sure it was returned to the family.

Wisden wrote:

> The news of [Turnbull's] death came through while Glamorgan were fulfilling one of their war-time fixtures at Cardiff Arms Park, the scene of his first century and many subsequent triumphs. And, as the crowd stood in respectful silence, perhaps the more imaginative or sentimental among them may have pictured for a fleeting instant the well-known figure out there on the field, and derived some small measure of comfort. For Glamorgan were carrying on: and he would have wished that.

Just over a month later, the Cardiff-born Sir Julien Cahn died while seated at his desk one morning at Stanford Hall, the stately home he had partly turned over for use as a military hospital. He was 61. One obituary remarked that Cahn had 'tried hard to establish himself as a landed English gentleman – he had the money but not quite the style'. His estate's private theatre survives today, although the lido with its coral walls holding fountains and artificial caves where the likes of Bill Edrich once unwound after a day's cricket has been reduced to a sombre, weed-filled grotto, and Cahn's performing sea lions have also long since gone.

Amid the fear and deprivations of the Second World War, many experienced a kind of liberation from the comparative drudgery of civilian life. Some cricketers, like Edrich himself, were clearly shaped and toughened by the events of 1939–45. Others fought a relatively comfortable war more characterised by what Godfrey Evans called 'being ballsed around' than by any direct physical jeopardy. But even Evans had his moments. On 29 July 1944 he was appearing for the Army against the RAF at Lord's when a German V-1 rocket cut out immediately overhead. 'There was a long silence, followed by a whistle,' Evans remembered.

> We could hear it coming closer. The players and umpires threw themselves flat on the ground. People in the stands were hiding under their seats, although I can still see one old boy in a straw hat sitting bolt upright in front of the gate, glass in hand, looking for all the world as if it was just an ordinary day out for him.

In the event the bomb fell about 200 yards short. 'We felt the place shake,' said Evans, 'and after that a loud cheer went up round the ground. Everyone picked themselves up again and Jack Robertson hooked the next ball he faced for six, straight into the grandstand.'

Sidney Adams, the Northampton town clerk who went to war, was probably the last first-class cricketer to die in action, when he fell on 24 March 1945, at the age of 40, while serving with the Royal Artillery in Germany. Many others later succumbed to the long-term effects of combat-related illness or injury. One of these was the young Middlesex seamer Paul Brooks, who in 1938 became a teenaged celebrity by bowling Don Bradman in the nets at Lord's, and many thought had a golden future in the game. Brooks was wounded in the spine while serving with the Coldstream Guards in April 1945 and died of his injuries in hospital nine months later, still aged just 24.

That same spring, the surviving inmates of the worldwide POW camp system were variously liberated by advancing Allied troops or herded out by their captors and lined up for an exodus that often proved to be a death-march. Thirty-four-year-old Freddie Brown was among those freed by American forces. He had lost roughly a third of his body weight while in captivity, despite which he went on to resume his cricket career and to captain England on their 1950–51 tour of Australia. Wilf Wooller was one of 5,000 or so prisoners – starved, sick, poorly clothed – shoved out of their camp gate before the Americans could reach them. The guards harried the men through the wire early one morning in a drenching rainstorm, and those who couldn't keep up were shot and left in the mud. In later years, Bill Bowes rarely referred to his own ordeal as a guest of successively the Italians and Germans, although he admitted that he had come to dislike the sound of whistling. 'Everyone did this in camp and it [brought] back painful memories,' he explained.

E. W. Swanton had to wait until August 1945 for his own release and maintained a robust attitude towards the Japanese race for the remaining fifty-five years of his life, during which he found religion, married, and gradually came to wield as much influence on the game as any cricket writer before or since him. Perhaps only a thundering W.G. Grace in his prime carried as much clout at Lord's as Swanton did in the second half of the twentieth century. In general he wasn't a man given to excessive self-doubt. Writing of his liberation, for instance, Swanton noted:

> The allied invasions [of Japan] were planned for early September, so our expectation of life was roughly a month when the atom bombs fell on Nagasaki and Hiroshima. Any [delay] must have cost many more thousand allied lives, including in all probability our own. So in the arguments on the moral issue of dropping the bomb some of us find objectivity difficult.

When Swanton returned from the war, his father walked past him at the station, failing to recognise his own son.

General, later Field Marshal, Montgomery, born in a house immediately opposite the Oval, and a gifted enough cricketer in his own right to be mentioned in the 1906 edition of *Wisden*, led the eighth army to victory in Libya with the famous injunction to his troops: 'Hit Rommel for six right out of Africa.' It in no way detracts from his undoubted organisational genius and dedication to the cause of total Allied victory to say that in later years 'Monty' enjoyed a somewhat equivocal reputation when it came to his dealings with young men. There was an odd and rather touching instance of this when, on 30 June 1945, the 57-year-old commander-in-chief of the British Liberation Army, fresh from taking the surrender of over a million German troops in northern Europe, found time to attend the annual schools' cricket match between Eton and Winchester. After the game, Monty treated the 18-year-old Winchester captain, Hubert Webb, to a week as his personal guest at Ostenwalde Schloss, the Lower Saxony estate the British commander had requisitioned as his headquarters. Webb later remembered being picked up in his host's Rolls-Royce, eating long meals together, and going sailing at Kiel ('idyllic, but for the bodies floating in the water') before being escorted around the ruins of Berlin. Monty wrote to Webb after the teenager had returned to his family in England: 'Now we have made friends we must not lose touch; and I may possibly be able to help you in times of difficulty: which do occasionally occur in life.'

Webb went on to play cricket for Oxford University and, on a single occasion, Hampshire. In later years he became a distinguished professor of neurology and was still at work at St Thomas's Hospital in London up until the time of his death in November 2010, at the age of 83.

A Test-strength England under Walter Hammond had meanwhile played a series of five 'victory' matches against an Australian Services XI led by Lindsay Hassett. Thirty-four-year-old Graham Williams of South Australia opened the visitors' bowling. He had been freed from a German POW camp only six weeks before going out to play in the first match at Lord's on 19 May and had to drink glucose and water between overs to keep his strength up. The series was drawn 2-all. Some 400,000 spectators attended one or more of the fifteen days of cricket.

Hammond himself played on for another season, leading England on a hastily arranged (and, on purely competitive grounds, disastrous) goodwill tour of Australia before going on to remarry, lose most of his money and eventually emigrate to South Africa. In February 1965 the England team was playing a Test at Port Elizabeth and happily agreed to pass round the hat in order to take their old skipper out to dinner. In recent years Hammond had both lost his job and been involved in a serious car crash, events that perhaps served to further darken a personality already prone to the choleric.

The England wicketkeeper John Murray remembered:

> We got to the hotel and there was Wally waiting for us. Everyone said a cheery hello and told him we had to nip in to another room to shake some hands, but that we'd be right out again and then on our way to dinner. When we got back fifteen minutes later, Wally was gone. He left a note behind. It said he'd never been so insulted in all his life by our behaviour in making him wait for us. 'I am a former captain of England and you buggers have dishonoured the office' was the gist of it. He died just a few months later. All very sad.

Norman Yardley and Freddie Brown, both former prisoners of war, successively captained England following Hammond's retirement, having beaten a third POW, Wilf Wooller, to the job. The collective memory of army life remained strong in those years, and when Godfrey Evans broke in to the Test side in 1946–47 he remembered that some of the players had addressed each other without irony as 'Major, or Corporal, or Sergeant, etc. – and [that] the team was still run exactly as if you were in uniform'. Len Hutton eventually emerged to become England's first professional captain of the twentieth century. Despite his maimed arm, he continued to score runs at a near-industrial rate of efficiency and quantity, while at the same time never bothering to affect any particular 'people' skills with his teammates, nor for that matter ever enjoying the full confidence of certain England selectors who still preferred their captains to be drawn from the ranks of the nation's ancient universities. 'My face never fitted,' Hutton once confided.

While serving in India later in the war, Denis Compton had written home: 'I am afraid [the] wise men of cricket are wrong if they think we will all care to go back to the tired life of bowing and scraping to our so-called superiors.' Yet in many ways the domestic game picked up in 1946 exactly where it had left off in 1939: Wally Hammond topped the first-class averages for the eighth time in succession, as well as steering England to a 1-0 home series win; it rained during much of the summer; and in early September Yorkshire were vying at the top of the championship table with Middlesex and Lancashire. The author Derek Birley writes of this season:

> The old regime was back in force, reactionary as ever … [MCC secretary] Col Rait Kerr, restored to civilian life, brought military precision to a painstaking and prolonged revision of the laws, which were buttressed by all manner of ancillary regulations and rendered even less penetrable to the unschooled mind by copious explanatory notes. The deckchairs on the *Titanic* were now arranged in a manner befitting a great institution.

Those, like Compton, who had fondly hoped that the 'tired life' might be improved by the mutual comradeship and shared horrors of the recent war would have to wait another sixteen years before the authorities ended the distinction between 'gentlemen' and 'players' and referred simply to 'cricketers'. It's true that over time certain first-class counties took such bold initiatives as allowing their professionals and amateurs to eat lunch at the same table, or even on occasion to share a common dressing room, but in general the *ancien régime* proved as tenacious in the era of socialised medicine and the hydrogen bomb as it had in that of exquisitely well-bred young rakes whose essentially Edwardian air of languor had tended to exceed any technical playing merit, or even aptitude, on their part. The master-servant composition of most English county clubs was still strong enough for Compton, in 1955, to be rebuked by the Middlesex secretary for the impossibly tasteless offence of having strolled down the pavilion stairs at Lord's following stumps one evening without having first troubled to put on a jacket and tie, and then for the equally hideous lapse of keeping his hands in his pockets throughout the subsequent lecture. Compton, who likened the experience to 'a schoolkid being bollocked by the headmaster', was then approaching his 40th birthday.

While English cricket lost some of its most illustrious players on the battlefields of 1939–45, others were simply part of that unlucky generation to forfeit six years of their already brief sporting careers to the war. Yorkshire's opening batsman and sometime wicketkeeper Paul Gibb had played 98 first-class matches as an amateur between 1934 and 1939, including the timeless Test at Durban in which he eked out a second innings score of 120 in nearly eight hours. Gibb served with distinction as an RAF flying-boat pilot during the war. When cricket resumed he was 33 years old and Godfrey Evans was waiting impatiently for his chance as England's stumper. Gibb played just three more Tests and eventually moved south to become a professional at Essex. He was the first Cambridge blue ever to become a paid cricketer, and as a consequence he was forced to resign his membership of MCC. In time Gibb became a bus driver in Guildford, where he suffered a heart attack when about to begin his shift one morning in December 1977 and passed away at the age of 64.

Peter Smith of Essex, the man on the receiving end of the pre-war England call-up hoax, similarly remembered coming home from his army service in January 1946 'feeling about twenty years older' than when he signed up in September 1939. In 1947 Smith hit 163 batting at number eleven for Essex against Derbyshire at Chesterfield, still a record score for that position, and belatedly played four actual Tests for England while in his late 30s. A different fate awaited Kent's Norman Harding, who had been one of the fastest bowlers anywhere on the county circuit in 1939 – Godfrey Evans remembered having to soak his hands in iced water after keeping to him one hot day at Dover – but who contracted polio shortly after returning to civilian life and died of the disease in September 1947, aged 31.

Perhaps the final lesson for those who returned to cricket after the war was simply to make the best possible use of the time available to them. 'To be alive, to be able to see, to walk, to have food, drink, sport, women – it's all a miracle,' Bill Edrich later observed, though it's not sure if he listed these enthusiasms in any particular order of precedence. As well as his achievement in scoring 36,965 runs and taking 479 wickets in an interrupted twenty-four-year first-class career, Edrich also proved quite prolific in his off-the-field activities. Impressively polygynous even before he went off to join the RAF, he eventually married five times. 'Bride or groom?' the Middlesex and England bowler John Warr was asked at Edrich's penultimate wedding. 'Season ticket,' he returned. Another Middlesex colleague assured me that he'd watched, with some anxiety, from the pavilion balcony as Edrich went out to toss before the start of play one day at Lord's, and that 'Bill was so tight he had to lean on the other team's captain just to make it out to the middle and back'. In 1947 Edrich and his Test and county teammate Denis Compton famously signalled a return to an altogether happier and saner post-war life when they scored 3,539 and 3,816 first-class runs respectively. Neville Cardus wrote of going to Lord's one summer's day to sit among 'a pale-faced crowd, existing on rations, the rocket-bomb still in the ears of most, and see[ing] the strain of anxiety and affliction passed from all hearts' as England went on to beat South Africa in, for once, blazing sunshine.

Edrich would surely have played far more than his 39 Tests but for his faux pas in disturbing the sleep of the chairman of selectors during his late-night return to the England hotel in 1950. Crawford White, writing in the *News Chronicle*, considered the Middlesex player, 'while unpopular in certain quarters', to have been the man best qualified to captain his country at that particular time. Edrich died as a result of falling down a flight of stairs late on the night of St George's Day 1986, aged 70. Compton followed him exactly eleven years later, at the age of 78. Godfrey Evans was another of the same fraternity to adopt Peter Pan's 'second star to the right and straight on till morning' as his dominant motto in life, in his case going on to become arguably

England's greatest ever wicketkeeper, if never quite allaying the fears Gerald Hough had had in July 1939 when the Kent secretary wrote, 'One just prays he will keep his feet on the ground.' Keith Miller of Victoria, New South Wales, Australia, and the Royal Australian Air Force perhaps expressed this credo best when he said: 'Pressure is a Messerschmitt up your arse. Playing cricket is not.'

The new European political order that emerged from the ashes of war was accompanied by an equally important social development which, in Britain, came to fruition at least in part due to the efforts of the great West Indian cricketer Learie Constantine. In early August 1943, the 41-year-old all-rounder was chosen to play for the Dominions against an England XI at Lord's. As a result he had booked a room for himself, his wife and their teenaged daughter at the Imperial Hotel in London's Russell Square for four nights. When Constantine arrived on 30 July he was told that he and his 'lot' could stay for only one night because their presence might offend the large number of US service-men billeted at the hotel who were more comfortable with their native tradition of racial segregation. When one of Constantine's colleagues tried to intervene, he was told by the Imperial's manageress: 'We will not have n*****s in the hotel because of the Americans,' and that, should the family attempt to prolong their stay, 'their luggage will be put out tomorrow and the doors locked.'

Constantine accepted the decision, noting merely that he was sur-prised to find such an equivocal welcome awaiting him when he was in London to play cricket for a team representing the British Empire and Commonwealth, and that the hotel would hear further in the matter. In the subsequent lawsuit, the High Court ruled that 'although the plaintiff is a man of colour, no ground exists on which the defendants were enti-tled to refuse to receive and lodge him on the premises.' While the law limited the award of damages to 5 guineas, the case was widely seen as a turning-point in the long campaign for British racial equality. In 1969

Constantine became the first black man to sit in the House of Lords but died just two years later at the age of 69.

Constantine's experience at the hands of the Imperial Hotel also proved to be a significant milestone down the road to the eventual passage of the Race Relations Act of 1965. The new legislation was first debated in parliament on 4 March of that year, when heavy snow covered much of the English south-east. At his home in the Berkshire countryside, 63-year-old Raymond 'Crusoe' Robertson-Glasgow, the perennial saucy schoolboy of cricket writing, spent much of that Thursday morning laboriously clearing a pathway in front of his house. It was quite possible, he had written on an earlier occasion, 'that I become not quite normal' when feeling as 'horribly caged' as he apparently did now. At some stage Crusoe went back indoors and his wife Elizabeth, the former nurse, went out with a shovel to finish the job. By the time she returned a few minutes later, her husband's life was already ebbing away. He had taken a massive overdose. Depression, for all his long struggle to deny it, had had the last bitter laugh.

Thirteen years later, Harold Gimblett of Somerset and England committed suicide by taking an overdose of prescription drugs. He had been in poor health and left behind a wife and a son. Gimblett had played his 368th and final first-class match only in May 1954, when, after scoring 0 and 5, he abruptly packed his bags and walked out of the Taunton ground forever. In its way it was as dramatic a farewell to county cricket as his arrival on the scene had been nineteen years earlier. Gimblett later remarked that he 'wished [Somerset] had shown more concern about my problems, more love even', but this was not the dominant characteristic of the relationship between the typical English cricket club and its professional employees of the 1950s. Harold Gimblett was also 63 at the time of his death.

Early one morning in April 1989 a farmer working on his field just south of Calais came upon the wreckage of a long-buried

British aircraft. The authorities were called, and in time the plane was identified as the RAF Spitfire that Flt Lt Gerry Chalk, the dashing pre-war captain of Kent, had taken up on the day he went missing in February 1943. Word of the find reached the ground at Canterbury, and an honour party including Godfrey Evans, Les Ames and Hopper Levett assembled to pay its final respects. On the crossing to France the former cricketers reminisced about an era now archaically distant. Fifty years earlier, it was Chalk who had had the imagination to devise and carry off a plan that had allowed the three once and future England wicketkeepers to happily coexist in the same county team. 'He was the most human of all the skippers I ever played under,' Evans told me, fondly remembering the days when 'Mr C' would saunter up, put a woolly arm round a tired bowler's shoulder, and confidently tell him, 'They're on the ropes now, Jack' – or Les, or Tom, or Doug – 'just keep it up', even though the score at that particular point might have been 200-1, with half an hour still to go before tea on the first day. Now, after the simple French funeral ceremony, the three old stumpers convened to a local pub and drank a toast to their fallen captain's memory. Despite the solemnity of the occasion, the mood was essentially light-hearted. 'After all,' said Evans, 'that's the way we played it.'

SOURCES AND CHAPTER NOTES

The following pages show at least the formal interviews, published works, and/or primary archive material used in the preparation of this book. Although it necessarily lacks the direct input of all but a very few sportsmen-combatants of the Second World War, I was lucky enough to know a number of such individuals, notably Godfrey Evans of Kent and England, in earlier years. Several relatives or other interested parties also kindly put their ancestors' diaries or other material at my disposal. A warm thanks to all the individuals and clubs listed, who should find their names in the acknowledgements at the front of the book.

CHAPTER 1

Godfrey Evans, whom I interviewed on numerous occasions while writing his biography in 1989–90, provided much of the material about the day-to-day workings of Kent CCC, and the club's distinguished secretary Gerald de Lisle Hough, in the 1939 season. I was also fortunate enough at around that same time to meet and ask questions of the inimitable E.W. Swanton. Swanton, while never one to exude millions of volts of synthetic charm, was extraordinarily kind and patient with me.

Evans also provided an introduction to, among others, Leslie Ames, Alec Bedser, Denis Compton, Reg Hayter, Len Hutton, Howard 'Hopper' Levett, Keith Miller and Doug Wright; it was perhaps the greatest pleasure of an already lucky life to able to loiter with some of the above in the downstairs dining room of the old Cricketers Club in Blandford Street, London. I am eternally grateful to Godfrey for the privilege. A good social overview of the English summer of 1939 can be found in Martin Pugh's book *We Danced All Night* (London: Bodley Head, 2008) and Marion Yass's *The Home Front* (London: Wayland Publishers, 1971), as well as in the back pages of *The Times* and other newspapers. I also consulted the records of the various MCC meetings of the period held in the MCC Library at Lord's; my thanks to both Neil Robinson and Robert Curphey for their generous help.

E. W. Swanton's quote about the broadcasting of the 1939 Tests being the result of a 'rash promise made by the Governor of the BBC …' appears in Swanton's book *Sort of a Cricket Person* (London: The Pavilion Library, 1989), p. 281.

CHAPTER 2

The quote by Walter Hammond protesting, 'But Dot, you know what it's like at these affairs …' appears on p. 194 of David Foot's excellent *Wally Hammond: The Reasons Why* (London: Robson Books, 1996). My friend the late Tom Graveney kindly helped me with his reminiscences of Gloucestershire's Tom Goddard, and of other county players who survived the war. The minutes of the UK cabinet meeting of 8 November 1938, and of other cabinet meetings, are held by the UK National Archives (PREM files). Adolf Hitler's quote about German 'living space' appears in Ian Kershaw's *Hitler: 1936–1945: Nemesis* (New York: W. W. Norton, 2000), p. 168. E. W. Swanton's comments on social conditions in South Africa appear on p. 138 of his book *Follow On* (Glasgow: William Collins, 1977). Swanton's memory of Hugh Bartlett as a 'magnificent player and very attractive chap' is quoted in Foot, p. 120.

I am also grateful to the Peter Edwards Museum and Library at Essex CCC, and more especially to David Pracy, for kindly providing access to certain material by or relating to the great Essex and England fast bowler Ken Farnes.

E. W. Swanton's description of 'Lord Ebbisham, father of the present peer' and of certain other well-heeled cricketers, appears on p. 114 of Swanton's *Follow On*, as previously cited. Neville Cardus's portrait of Herbert Sutcliffe appears in his book *Cardus in the Covers* (London: Souvenir Press, 1978), p. 91. Learie Constantine's reflection, 'I was dissatisfied …' is quoted on p. 65 of Peter Mason's fine *Learie Constantine* (London: Stanley Paul, 1954). I also reread Ronald Mason's book *Sing All a Green Willow* (London: Epworth Press, 1967), and am delighted to have the opportunity of expressing my thanks to this particular author, whose cricket writing was the treat of an otherwise healthily austere childhood.

Other material in this chapter was made available by the staff or friends of Hampshire CCC (my thanks to Dave Allen), Lancashire CCC, Surrey CCC and, again, the MCC. I also of course consulted the pages of the 1940 edition of *Wisden Cricketers' Almanack* (London: John Wisden, 1940).

My thanks, too, to the UK Family Records Centre, and the FBI – Freedom of Information Division.

CHAPTER 3

The tribute to Gerry Chalk, the captain of Kent in the 1939 season, is quoted on p. 282 of Benny Green, ed., *The Lord's Companion* (London: Pavilion Books, 1987). The peerless cricket writer David Frith describes Chalk's counterpart at Yorkshire, Brian Sellers, as 'a disciplinarian with a fruity sense of humour.' The excerpted lines beginning 'Cahn also arranged and paid for winter tours …' appear in Duncan Hamilton's fine biography *Harold Larwood* (London: Quercus, 2009), p. 191.

Other material in this chapter was provided by Alex Legge, who very kindly supplied me with photographs and other material concerning his grandfather Geoffrey Legge; and by David Robertson, David Pracy, Rob Boddie and Phil Britt, respectively of Kent CCC, Essex CCC, Sussex CCC and Warwickshire CCC; I am warmly grateful to all of those listed. Among newspapers I consulted were: *The Cambridge Evening News*, the *Daily Express, Jamaica Gleaner, Kent Messenger, Northampton Daily Echo, Sutton Post, The Times*, the *Western Evening Herald* and the *Yorkshire Post*.

E.W. Swanton kindly put his memories of the Aigburth Ground, Liverpool, at my disposal. Cambridge University Cricket Club provided access to their archives. The UK Ministry of Defence was able to provide a service record and other material relating to the great George Macaulay of Yorkshire and England.

Other printed sources included Michael Manley's *A History of West Indies Cricket*, Laetitia Stapleton's *A Sussex Cricket Odyssey*, Pelham Warner's *Cricket Between Two Wars* (London: Chatto & Windus, 1942); and, again, the indispensable *Wisden Cricketers' Almanack* for 1940.

I should also acknowledge Peter Wynne-Thomas's *The History of Hampshire County Cricket Club* (Bromley: Christopher Helm, 1988), a title for authorship of which my own hat was briefly in the ring. The better man won.

CHAPTER 4

It's a pleasure to again acknowledge both *Wisden* and other published sources including Neville Cardus's *Autobiography* (London: Collins, 1947), Gerald Howat's *Len Hutton* (London: Heinemann, 1988), Laetitia Stapleton's *A Sussex Cricket Odyssey* (Havant: Ian Harrap, 1979), and E.W. Swanton's *Follow On*. I should also particularly acknowledge the help, resources and kindness of David Pracy at Essex CCC, Dave Allen at Hampshire CCC, David Robertson at Kent CCC, Rob Boddie at Sussex CCC, and Andrew Hignell for his peerless knowledge of English and more particularly Welsh cricket of the period. The principal newspapers consulted were the *Daily Telegraph, Liverpool Echo, Northampton Echo*, the *Observer, Sporting Life, The Times* and the *Worthing Herald*.

The quote beginning 'Basil, that Wally Hammond of yours ...' appears in David Foot, *Wally Hammond: The Reasons Why*, p. 101. The quote beginning 'I knew Wally Hammond from 1937-45 ...' appears in Foot, p. 183. The account beginning 'A solemn schoolmaster ...' appears in E. W. Swanton, *Follow On*, p. 180. Raymond Robertson-Glasgow's lines 'How I loathed them, and loathe them still ...' appear in his book *46 Not Out* (London: Hollis & Carter, 1948). E. W. Swanton's memory, 'We had no transport to speak of ...' appears on p. 119 of his book *Sort of a Cricket Person*, as previously cited. Adolf Hitler's statement, 'England is our enemy ...' is quoted on p. 192 of Ian Kershaw's *Hitler: 1936– 1945: Nemesis*, as previously cited. Learie Constantine's reflection, 'I was roundly condemned as old-fashioned ...' is quoted on p. 67 of Peter Mason's *Learie Constantine*, as previously cited.

Some of the material in this chapter comes from The Papers of Lt Col E.J. Hazel (Document 3750); The Papers of Kenneth Hewitt (Document 17354); The Papers of William Bompas (Document 3468); and The Papers of Ernest Ridgers (Document 7942), all held in the Imperial War Museum, London; I'm again grateful to Jane Rosen for making them, and other material, available to me. I should also thank the staff at the archives of both the Cambridge University and British Libraries, and those at the Harry Ransom Center, the University of Texas at Austin. Unlikely as it seems to connect the US National Security Archives with a book touching on historical English cricket, that institution also very kindly put diaries and letters covering the years 1939–45 at my disposal.

Other source material came from the London Library, CricInfo, the Cricket Archive site, the Public Record Office and the National Army Museum in London.

I was fortunate enough to know Leslie Ames, Alex Bannister, Denis Compton, Godfrey Evans, Tony Pawson and E. W. Swanton, and each of these individuals helped in various ways with their reminiscences of the 1939 season. Harold Pinter spoke to me fondly and at length about Arthur Wellard at the time I interviewed Pinter in November 1999.

CHAPTER 5

The quote by Hedley Verity beginning 'This is no chuffing garden party …' appears in Alan Hill, *Hedley Verity* (Tadworth: Kingswood Press, 1986), p. 123. James Barrie's letter to Cynthia Asquith of 10 July 1920 is quoted in Benny Green, ed., *The Lord's Companion* (London: Pavilion Books, 1987), p. 207. E. W. Swanton's line beginning, '"Buffer" does not in any way fit the eccentric personality …' appears in Swanton's book *Follow On*, as previously cited, and also closely follows an oral description Swanton gave me of the same subject. The minutes of the MCC meeting which begin 'The Secretary disclosed that while the material damage …' can be found in the archive of the MCC Library at Lord's. Len Hutton's remark beginning 'Only when the boundary shot hit the fence …' is quoted on p. 46 of Gerald Howat, *Len Hutton*, as previously cited. The minutes of the MCC meeting which begin 'The Secretary reported that with the approval of the news reel companies …' are from the archive of the MCC Library. The note beginning 'Smith has again asked to be paid …' is similarly from the MCC Library. J.M. Kilburn's observation ruing that '… witticism became vulgar banality, loyalties became myopic and the huge crowd became an empty and echoing shell' was published in *The Cricketer* of August 1973. The description of the climax of the match between Worcestershire and Yorkshire at Stourbridge is taken in part from the account included on p. 116 of J.M. Kilburn's *A History of Yorkshire Cricket*, as previously cited.

As well as the above, I again consulted the files of the Imperial War Museum, which contain journals and scrapbooks of sportsman-combatants in the war; the Cabinet Papers (PREM 11) of the UK National Archives; and the correspondence files of 1939–45 of the National Archives and Record Service, Washington DC. It's a great pleasure to again acknowledge the help given by the secretaries or staff of Essex CCC, Hampshire CCC, Kent CCC, Lancashire CCC, Northamptonshire CCC, Surrey CCC, Sussex CCC, Warwickshire CCC and Worcestershire CCC. It was a particular thrill to again visit the County Ground, Hove (my thanks to Jon Filby and Rob Boddie), where I first watched county cricket while incarcerated at a local prep school fifty-odd years ago.

Other published material came from the archives of the *Cambridge Evening News*, the *Daily Express*, the *Manchester Evening News*, *Oxford Times*, *Sporting Life* and *The Times*.

Denis Compton, Bill Edrich, Godfrey Evans, Len Hutton, Jim Parks (son of the 1939 Sussex player of the same name), John Pocock and Doug Wright all put their memories of the 1939 season at my disposal. I also remember a dinner with the elderly Gubby Allen in June 1989 which thrillingly evoked the cricket world of fifty years earlier. As well as the above, I also consulted the service records of the Ministry of Defence, the British Newspaper Library, CricInfo, the Cricket Archive site and the Public Record Office.

CHAPTER 6

E.W. Swanton's memory that 'By then, the frivolities were all but over: the west-end lights were soon to give way to the long blackout …' appears on p. 105 of his book *Sort of a Cricket Person*, as previously cited. That author's line remembering that 'premonitions of war led many …' appears on p. 103 of the same book. The account of the scene at Eastbourne on the Saturday afternoon of 19 August 1939 is on p. 51 of Laetitia Stapleton's book *A Sussex Cricket Odyssey*, as cited. J.M. Kilburn's description of Yorkshire as one of the 'best rounded cricket teams' appears on p. 115 of Kilburn's book *A History of Yorkshire Cricket*, as cited. For Neville Chamberlain's comment, 'I can announce that the Polish Ambassador to Germany, M. Lipski …', see the minutes of the cabinet meeting (CAB/23/100) of 24 August 1939, held by the UK National Archives. The line of Adolf Hitler insisting that war would be all Britain's fault, since it was 'determined to destroy and exterminate Germany' is quoted on p. 212 of Ian Kershaw, *Hitler: 1936–1945: Nemesis*, also as cited.

Newspapers consulted in this chapter included the *Daily Telegraph*, *Daily Worker*, *Frankfurter Zeitung*, the *London Evening News*, *The Times* and the *Worksopian*. Newspaper archives included *Collier's Weekly*, *Essex Times*, the *Globe*, the *Morning Post*, the *New York Times*, *Sporting Life*, *The Sportsman* and *Weekly Sun*. I would like to again acknowledge the help and encouragement of the various English county cricket clubs listed above, as well as that of Neil Robinson at the MCC Library and Jane Rosen at the Imperial War Museum. My friend Peter Perchard, former benevolent tsar of *The Cricketer International*, very kindly put a number of contacts at my disposal, as did my childhood hero and latter-day friend the late John Murray. Generally reliable accounts of scores, if not necessarily of the individual players involved, can be found both in *Wisden Cricketers' Almanack* and on the Cricket Archive website. I'm again grateful for archive material, including unpublished diaries, letters and scrapbooks, to the Cambridge University Library, as cited, and also for the service records supplied by the UK Ministry of Defence.

Harold Pinter gave me an oral history of his own youthful exploits during the 1939 English cricket season. Godfrey Evans provided what he admitted were the 'spotty' memories of his 19th birthday party that August.

Other secondary sources included the back pages of *Cricket* magazine, the records of Surrey County Council (which currently include much of their county cricket club's archive material) and the photograph collection at the National Army Museum in London. Fred Trueman's book *As It Was* (London: Macmillan, 2004) gives a gripping account of that player's early cricket prowess, if not one that labours under any false modesty. I should also particularly acknowledge Denis Compton's memoir *End of an Innings* (London: Oldbourne, 1958), as cited, as well as Compton himself, an indefatigable fund of jokes and stories about the county and Test cricket scene in the months immediately before the war. He is much missed.

CHAPTER 7

E. W. Swanton's memories of standing with George Mann of Middlesex on the Lord's pavilion balcony appear on p. 103 of Swanton's book *Sort of a Cricket Person*, as previously cited. The comments of Roy Peskett on the same occasion are quoted in Benny Green, ed., *The Lord's Companion*, p. 288. Neville Cardus's remarks on attending Lord's at around that same time (which suggest that Cardus may have been confused by the fast-breaking events of that week) similarly appear in *The Lord's Companion*, p. 290. The minutes of the Hampshire CCC special meeting of 26 August 1939 are held by the Hampshire Record Office; I am grateful to their archivist Adam Jones. Records of the cabinet meeting of 30 August are courtesy of the UK National Archives. Bill Bowes's remarks beginning 'As early as 1937 he was certain …' appear on p. 122 of Alan Hill's book *Hedley Verity*.

The remarks attributed to Lt General Halder ('France and England will not march …') are quoted in John Toland, *Adolf Hitler* (New York: Anchor Books, 1992), p. 568. The quote by Oliver Locker-Lampson describing the supposed appearance of Adolf Hitler on a Great War battlefield cricket pitch first appeared in an article by Locker-Lampson called 'Hitler As I Knew Him'. Originally published in the *Daily Mirror* of July 1930, it was revisited by the *Daily Mail* of 19 March 2010.

Brian Sellers's remarks beginning 'We are public entertainers …' appear in Alan Hill's *Hedley Verity*, p. 117. E. W. Swanton's reminiscences of Liverpool cricket in 1939 are included in Swanton's book *Follow On*, as previously cited, p. 183. The quote by Bill Edrich beginning 'Flattened low on the water …' appears on p. 78 of Alan Hill's definitive biography *Bill Edrich* (London: Andre Deutsch, 1994). The account by the author Storm Jameson of the evacuation of London schoolchildren was first published in *The Atlantic*, October–November 1939. The minutes of the emergency MCC meeting of 11 September 1939 are held in the MCC Library at Lord's; I'm grateful both to Neil Robinson and Robert Curphey for allowing me to read them.

Newspapers or periodicals consulted included the *Birmingham Gazette*, *Cricket,* the *Globe*, the *Daily Telegraph*, *Hampshire Chronicle*, the *Melbourne Herald*, the *Morning Post*, *The Times* and the *Yorkshire Post*.

I'm grateful for the opportunity to have interviewed Les Ames, David Blake, Godfrey Evans, Howard 'Hopper' Levett, Barry Norman, Jim

Parks, Harold Pinter, John Pocock and Doug Wright, all of whom put their memories of the years 1939–45 at my disposal.

I should also particularly thank David Pracy at Essex CCC, David Robertson at Kent CCC and Rob Boddie at Sussex CCC for their support and help in locating archive material at their respective clubs.

CHAPTER 8

Raymond Robertson-Glasgow's remarks beginning 'The idea of having anything remotely resembling the ordinary county championship …' appear in his Notes included in the 1940 *Wisden Cricketers' Almanack*. The minutes of the MCC emergency meeting of 13 November 1939 are held in the MCC Library, as previously cited. E.W. Swanton's memory of *The Cricketer* beginning 'When war came Plum went to his duty …' appears on p. 214 of Swanton's book *Follow On*, as previously cited. The insight into Neville Cardus's domestic arrangements while living in Australia appears on pages 169-171 of Christopher Brookes's *His Own Man* (London: Methuen, 1985). Raymond Robertson-Glasgow's account beginning 'Success at games demands total freedom from care …' appears in his book *All in the Game* (London: Dennis Dobson, 1952).

The memory of Laetitia Stapleton at Hove beginning 'The pilot swooped right above us …' appears on p. 57 of her book *A Sussex Cricket Odyssey*, as previously cited. The reflection 'At all times officers in uniform in the British and Allied forces were allowed …' appears on p. 302 of Benny Green, ed., *The Lord's Companion*, as previously cited. The remarks beginning 'The war reduced the proceedings to a hopeless chaos …' similarly appear in *The Lord's Companion*, p. 291. The comment by Alf Burgoyne of Saltaire CC reflecting on the respective merits of Jim Laker and Len Hutton insisting 'I know which of 'em I would have picked …' is quoted on p. 42 of Don Mosey, *Laker: Portrait of a Legend* (London: Queen Anne Press, 1989).

Primary source material in this chapter was kindly provided by the Peter Edwards Museum and Library at Essex CCC, where I'm grateful to David Pracy; the UK Ministry of Defence, which supplied service details for George Macaulay; and the Imperial War Museum, London, which gave me access to the already cited material, as well as to The Papers of James Pennock (Document 7850), The Papers of Hugh Webb (Document 19653) and the Sound Recording by James Blackburn (Catalogue No. 27065); I'm extremely grateful to the IWM's Jane Rosen for her help in the matter.

I should also particularly acknowledge the help and support of Alex Legge with material relating to his grandfather Geoffrey Legge of Oxford University, Kent and England.

I also consulted the back pages or archives of *The Cricketer*, *The Daily Telegraph*, *Der Angriff*, *Essex Times*, the *Northampton Daily Echo*, *Sporting Life*, *The Sportsman*, *The Times*, the *Weekly Sun*, and, of course, *Wisden*. News reports or other material were provided by the UK National Archives, the Clydesdale Cricket Club Papers, the Mitchell Library of Glasgow, and the National Archives and Record Service, Washington DC.

Godfrey Evans very kindly put his memories of army life at Ossett in West Yorkshire, and much else besides, at my disposal.

CHAPTER 9

The account of Learie Constantine's reception at the wartime Liverpool hotel that includes the line 'Get out, we don't allow nigs to mix with white people ...' appears on p. 80 of Peter Mason's *Learie Constantine*. The remarks by Kenneth Hewitt beginning 'It was a pleasant and friendly little place ...' are included in The Papers of Kenneth Hewitt held in the Imperial War Museum, London, as previously cited. The quoted letter beginning 'Pooh is such a big girl now ...' is similarly part of The Papers of Lt Col E.J. Hazel at the IWM, as cited. E.W. Swanton's memory of his capture in Singapore, beginning 'I was establishing a new observation post ...' appears on pp. 22–3 of his book *Sort of a Cricket Person*, also as cited. Swanton's remarks beginning 'In the early days, it was quite a common thing ...' similarly appear in *Sort of a Cricket Person*, p. 130.

The diary notes by Major Alan Hobbs concerning prisoners' treatment at the notorious Changi camp ('Friday March 27: Gilbert Jose died …') are included on the website *Prisoners of War of the Japanese 1942–1945* under the heading 'Diary of Hobbs, Alan Frank, Major, 2/4 Casualty Clearing Station'.

The memory of prison life beginning 'Cricket was played on four or five afternoons …' is included in The Papers of William Bompas held at the Imperial War Museum. The diary account of Sapper Ernest Ridgers of his induction into the Royal Engineers and his encounters there with Denis Compton is similarly found in The Papers of Ernest Ridgers, Late of 665 Artisan Company, R.E., held at the IWM, London. The account of the British servicemen's lives while en route to captivity is included in the 'Report on Conditions on board SS *Yoshida Maru*' by Lt Col E.R. Scott, R.E.M.E., also held at the IWM London. The comment on Walter Hammond beginning 'When he assumed the captaincy of England …' appears on p. 143 of David Foot's book *Wally Hammond: The Reasons Why*, as previously cited. The letter written by Jack Hobbs admitting 'Life these days is very grim …' forms part of Document 8575 also held by the IWM London. The scorecard of the match played on the grounds of the Mulo school in February 1943 is also held by the IWM London under the title 'Report of Game at Chung HWA of 6 February 1943.'

The quote by Brian Johnston enquiring 'Could you send a parcel sometime … ?' appears on p. 116 of Barry Johnston, *Johnners: The Life of Brian* (London: Coronet Books 2003). The obituary of the Kent captain Gerry Chalk appeared in *Wisden Cricketers' Almanack* 1945. The passage beginning 'Kathleen was with Hedley in London …' is quoted on p. 129 of Alan Hill's *Hedley Verity*, as previously cited. The memory of Hedley Verity's last hours while in the hospital at Caserta is included in The Sound Recording by James Blackburn (Catalogue No. 27065) held by the IWM London. E. W. Swanton's remark beginning, 'The allied invasions were planned for early September …' appears on pp. 135-36 of Swanton's *Sort of a Cricket Person*, as previously cited. The memoir of Hubert Webb and his adventures with General Montgomery form part of The Papers of Hugh [*sic*] Webb (Document 19653) also held at the IWM London; Webb went on to play fifteen first-class matches, including a single appearance for Hampshire. The remarks by Derek Birley beginning 'The old regime was back in force …' appear on p. 270 of his magisterial book *A Social History of English Cricket* (London: Aurum Press, 1999).

I should also particularly acknowledge the help of David Pracy in making available his then-unpublished article on Ken Farnes of Essex and England included in the Newsletter of the Peter Edwards Museum and Library; and also the warm support of Rob Boddie, the indefatigable curator of Sussex CCC at Hove.

Periodicals consulted included *Cricket*, *Cricket Lore*, *Essex Times*, the *Globe*, *London Mercury*, the *Melbourne Herald*, *The Times*, the *Tyrone Constitution*, the *Yorkshire Post* and *The Weekly*.

As before, I interviewed Les Ames, David Blake, Godfrey Evans, Barry Norman, Harold Pinter, John Pocock and Doug Wright.

I can never repay the debt to my old teacher Malcolm Robinson, to whom the book is dedicated.

SELECT BIBLIOGRAPHY

Birley, Derek, *A Social History of English Cricket* (London: Aurum Press, 1999)

Cardus, Neville, *Autobiography* (London: Collins, 1947)

Compton, Denis, *End of an Innings* (London: Oldbourne, 1958)

Constantine, Learie, *Colour Bar* (London: Stanley Paul, 1954)

Edrich, W.J., *Cricket Heritage* (London: Stanley Paul, 1948)

Foot, David, *Wally Hammond: The Reasons Why* (London: Robson Books, 1996)

Fry, C.B., *Life Worth Living* (London: Eyre & Spottiswood, 1939)

Green, Benny, ed., *The Lord's Companion* (London: Pavilion Books, 1987)

Hill, Alan, *Bill Edrich* (London: Andre Deutsch, 1994)

————, *Hedley Verity* (Tadworth: Kingswood Press, 1986)

Howat, Gerald, *Len Hutton* (London: Heinemann, 1988)

Kilburn, J.M., *A History of Yorkshire Cricket* (London: Stanley Paul, 1970)

Larwood, Harold, *The Larwood Story* (London: W.H. Allen, 1965)

McCrery, Nigel, *The Coming Storm* (Barnsley: Pen & Sword Books, 2017)

Manley, Michael, *A History of West Indies Cricket* (London: Andre Deutsch, 1995)

Mason, Peter, *Learie Constantine* (Oxford: Signal Books, 2008)

Press Association, *100 Years of Cricket* (Lewes: Ammonite Press, 2008)

Prittie, T.C.F., *Cricket North and South* (London: Sportsman's Book Club, 1955)

Rayvern Allen David, ed., *Cricket's Silver Lining* (London: Willow Books, 1987)

Robertson-Glasgow, R.C., *46 Not Out* (London: Hollis & Carter, 1948)

Sandford, Christopher, *Godfrey Evans* (London: Simon & Schuster, 1990)

Stapleton, Laetitia, *A Sussex Cricket Odyssey* (Havant: Ian Harrap, 1979)

Streeton, Richard, *P.G.H. Fender* (London: Michael Joseph, 1981)

Swanton, E.W., *Follow On* (Glasgow: William Collins, 1977)

Trueman, Fred, *As It Was* (London: Macmillan, 2004)

Warner, Pelham, *Cricket Between Two Wars* (London: Chatto & Windus, 1942)

Whitaker, Haddon, ed., *Wisden Cricketers' Almanack 1940* (London: John Wisden, 1940)

Wynne-Thomas, Peter, *The History of Lancashire County Cricket Club* (Bromley: Christopher Helm, 1988)

INDEX

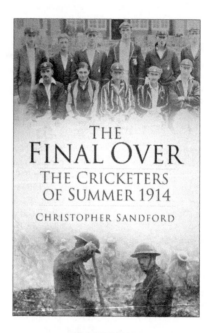

978 0 7509 6298 8

The Final Over is the very personal story of how some of the greatest characters ever known in English cricket performed some of their greatest feats against the ticking clock of the First World War.

Shortlisted for the 2015 Cricket Society and MCC Book of the Year Award

You may also enjoy …

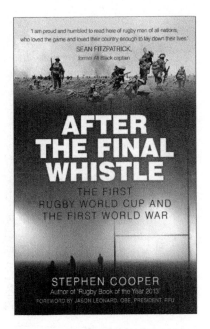

978 0 7509 6999 4

When Britain's went to war in 1914, rugby players were the first to volunteer: they led from the front and paid a disproportionate price. When the Armistice came after four long years, their war game was over; even as the last echo of the guns of November faded, it was time to play rugby again.

Shortlisted for the 2016 Cross Sports Book of the Year award

You may also enjoy …

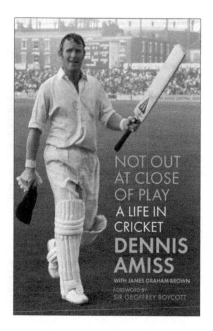

978 0 7509 9245 9

Not Out at Close of Play explores how
Dennis Amiss' passionate quest for
success led a Birmingham boy from
humble origins to achieve sporting
stardom. At the heart of the' story,
however, lies the paradox nature of
a quietly spoken and apparently conventional man who rebelled against
the establishment.